Strategic Consulting

Philippe Chereau • Pierre-Xavier Meschi

Strategic Consulting

Tools and methods for successful
strategy missions

palgrave
macmillan

Philippe Chereau
SKEMA Business School
Lille, France

Pierre-Xavier Meschi
IAE Aix-en-Provence
Aix-en-Provence, France

ISBN 978-3-319-64421-9   ISBN 978-3-319-64422-6   (eBook)
DOI 10.1007/978-3-319-64422-6

Library of Congress Control Number: 2017955040

Cover illustration: SireAnko/DigitalVision Vectors/Getty

Printed on acid-free paper

This Palgrave Macmillan imprint is published by Springer Nature
The registered company is Springer International Publishing AG
The registered company address is: Gewerbestrasse 11, 6330 Cham, Switzerland

Foreword: What Strategy for Strategy Consulting?

My dear fellow strategy consultants, you are in the greatest job on earth. Each of you can truly make the world better. Don't you work with all the levels critical to corporate success, ranging from the CEO to the most operational roles, for companies that consume resources (more or less sustainably), provide products and services (more or less valuable for customers) and employ people (in more or less enjoyable and rewarding activities)? Working every day with your clients, each of you makes a difference in whether the coin falls in a way that makes the world better or worse.

But your job also guarantees one of the bumpiest rides of all. Few professions are as widely criticized as consulting. Consultants are said to be in the business of borrowing (or stealing, or charging for) someone's watch to tell them the time. Blaming the consultant is one of the most effective ways to reach a corporate consensus. What about strategy itself? In the business world, what can be heard most often: people praising the company's strategy, or people criticizing it? As a *consultant* in *strategy* you are really looking for trouble.

That is why this book is important: it is a companion that will help overcome many of the hurdles that stand in the way of the great cause you serve. The book lets you into the dialogue between theory and practice, giving you the scientific underpinning you need to carry out successful strategy-consulting assignments. This dialogue is more necessary now than ever, since strategy, even in management literature, has become increasingly controversial: Is strategy about long range planning or diagnostic? Should we go for the position-based view, or the resource-based view? Each approach gives rise to new debates and dichotomies. The number of strategy frameworks has increased tenfold over the last 40 years.[1] Which approach should be used and when? The underpinning theories in the book provide practical help for navigating different strategy tools and client issues.

The ride is getting even bumpier as the very nature and usefulness of strategy are challenged by the volatility, uncertainty, complexity, and ambiguity of the business landscape (VUCA). According to the Complexity Index—developed with my teams at The Boston Consulting Group Institute for Organization—business complexity has multiplied six-fold since 1955.[2] Organizations respond to this external complexity by becoming more complicated, piling on structures, processes, scorecards, committees, and systems. According to our measurements, organizations have become over 35 times more complicated over the same period, choking productivity and disengaging people. Business complexity can only keep growing, since it arises from the multiple requirements companies must meet to create value for a growing number of stakeholders. These include customers, shareholders, and employees as well as many political, regulatory, and compliance authorities. Each of these groups has its own requirements, and companies cannot afford to satisfy one group at the expense of the others. These requirements have become more numerous, are changing faster, and are often mutually conflicting. In 1955, companies typically had to meet between 4 and 7 performance imperatives. Now they need to satisfy between 25 and 40—of which almost half may be contradictory. This was certainly not the case back in 1955. In order to attract customers, keep customers and build competitive advantage, companies now need greater speed and reliability, innovation and efficiency, global consistency and local responsiveness, lower cost and higher quality. Companies also face greater uncertainty. They need to be able to detect, interpret and act upon weak signals; my teams and I have also measured the decline in the signal-to-noise ratio companies can rely on.[3] My colleagues at The Boston Consulting Group's Henderson Institute have measured the evolution of volatility by counting the number of changes in the ranking of companies; for instance, for sales or market capitalization. Today's volatility is much greater than during the 1950–1959 period. The predictability of higher profitability based on market share leadership has been divided by 5. VUCA is a proven fact, not a buzzword.

Do organizations even need strategy, let alone strategy consultants, when what happens is so unpredictable, complex and fast changing? I must admit that, after more than 30 years in this business, I came close to saying that they don't. But I remembered the joke about strategy consultants stealing their clients' watches. I realized that saying there was no point in strategy would have been like saying, "What's the point in having a watch since the time changes all the time?" Like many catchy paradoxes this one does not stand up to scrutiny. What makes it useful to know the time is not *the* time, it is that we all share the same time all the time. This enables us to synchronize, live and coordinate with one another. What matters with strategy is not *the* strategy itself, but the collective energy and intelligence that its development and achievement enable—including through disruptive moves that prove smart in the end because the whole organization is engaged and succeeds. This collective engagement is precisely what helps organization deal with greater business complexity.[4] The more complex and turbulent the business world, the less we can rely on standard or predefined criteria for making important decisions. Is it speed to market, market share, growth, profitability, competitive pressure, an *ad hoc* combination of these, or something else? Only a conversation—with all relevant roles and levels in the organization—will help build the pertinent criteria and give the answer. What I call "conversation," however, is not a cozy chat: this conversation must be led, structured, factual and grounded. Frameworks, like those provided in this book, help to guide and structure the argument. They help identify the data necessary to engage in factual discussion, a world beyond opinions or gut feeling. The underpinning theories described in the book provide grounding by helping to explain the often-implicit assumptions made when using one framework or another. Enabling a strategy conversation that is structured, factual and grounded makes this book particularly valuable in today's business landscape.

As for consulting itself, there will be a market as long as 50% of companies are below the median, which will hold true in the foreseeable future.

No doubt then, strategy consulting remains a useful business. But what is the sustainable competitive advantage of strategy consultants in this business? On what bases do they build advantage? Do we consultants know the client's company better than the client or other consultants do? For sure we may discover something the client had not realized. However, the client's company is constantly evolving: things happen that we are not always aware of. Do we know their industry better than their clients do? Not really—there is always somebody in the client company or its competitors who knows something about the industry that we don't. Do we know our frameworks better than the client does? Yes, hopefully. But clients also know the frameworks of other consultants. Or is it that we have longer days than clients, or other consultants? I doubt it—I have seen many clients stay late at night and have long meetings on weekends. Some have more than 50 hours of meetings per week, and then there is the real work and homework. Of course, we can skip sleeping; many of us have done this, sometimes for days…but unfortunately, there are only 24 hours in a day. What about education, hiring MBAs? This is exactly what clients do, and they also hire competent graduates in many other specialized areas. Perhaps we should rely on being uniquely clever then? That would be a risky bet since, as Descartes wrote in his tongue-in-cheek opening of *Discourse on the Method,* "Of all things, good sense is the most fairly distributed." So what exactly is our sustainable competitive advantage? The answer is very simple: it is work, a way of working which uniquely matches the essence of our profession. The crux of our profession is producing insights to resolve business problems. These range from strategy formulation to strategy execution, from transformation to corporate development, from capability-building to post-merger integration. We need to work in a way that systematically produces more insights and that proves more useful in solving business problems. Our way of setting targets and evaluating work must encourage creativity. Beyond individual creativity, we need to make sure the team is organized in a way that allows for insights. Some ways of organizing a team into "modules" can be sterile, while others are fertile. Having a module for product analysis and another for competition analysis is likely to be much less insightful than having a module to understand the full customer path for each segment. The sequence of assignments also drives insight generation: it must allow for opening up at the beginning and convergence towards the end. Sustainable competitive advantage in strategy consulting requires the business and its operating models to enable the production of superior insights.

For large consulting firms, the business model is likely to become a constellation of interconnected and very specialized units that share an umbrella brand. How can a consultant remain a generalist, a man of all trades in strategy, when clients have access to all consultants in the world? Adam Smith's theorem in the *Wealth of Nations*—specialization is limited by the extent of the market—also holds true for strategy consulting. Specialization is not an option when the market is global. All of us must become part of the handful of world champions in one area.

Given the rapid changes in the business landscape, the operating model must enable innovation in approaching and solving client problems. Otherwise, solutions will fail to ensure advantage for the client company and frustrate its customers. These solutions must be practical and based on proven results. If not, your client will not be reassured and engaged. The operating model must also ensure that consultants learn and grow throughout assignments. This is what matters to them; otherwise, they will go elsewhere. And, of course, the model must also foster productivity among the consulting teams. Without sufficient productivity, it will be impossible to get the necessary surplus to invest and prepare for the future. However, all these requirements are contradictory. Innovative approaches are hardly proven, practical and battle-tested solutions. Consultants will learn and grow only if they do things they have never done before. After 5 market segmentation assignments, a consultant needs to work on a merger to learn about corporate development; even if he or she never becomes an expert in this, it is part of the expected common knowledge, a prerequisite to moving into a more senior role at some point. Nevertheless, this consultant will be much less productive in this assignment than another colleague who has already worked on 5 mergers. So what should you do in this case? This is the complexity faced every day in strategy consulting. When you manage to reconcile productivity, learning, innovation and practicality, you break compromises. Breaking these compromises unleashes new value for all stakeholders. This new value fuels sustainable growth… and you will have even more opportunities to make the world better.

Yves Morieux is a senior partner and managing director in the Washington, D.C. office of The Boston Consulting Group (BCG). He leads the BCG Institute for Organization and is a BCG Fellow. He divides his time between conducting research and working with the CEOs and leadership teams of the most prominent companies around the world.

Yves Morieux

Notes

1. Ghemawat Pankaj, "Competition and Business Strategy in Historical Perspective", *Business History Review*, vol. 76, no 1, 2002, p. 37–74. Freedman Lawrence, *Strategy: A History*, Oxford University Press, New York, 2013. Research by the Boston Consulting Group Strategy Institute. Quoted by Reeves Martin, Haanaes Knut and Sinha Janmejaya, *Your Strategy Needs a Strategy*, Harvard Business Review Press, Boston, 2015.
2. Morieux Yves, "Smart Rules: Six Ways to Get People to Solve Problems Without You", *Harvard Business Review*, vol. 89, no 9, 2011, p. 78–86.
3. Morieux Yves, Blaxil Mark and Boutenko Vladislav, "Generative Interactions: The New Source of Competitive Advantage", in Cool Karel O., Henderson James E. and Abate René (eds), *Restructuring Strategy: New Networks and Industry Challenges*, Blackwell, Oxford, 2005, p. 86–110.
4. Morieux Yves and Tollman Peter, *Six Simple Rules: How to Manage Complexity without Getting Complicated*, Harvard Business Review Press, Boston, 2014.

Acknowledgments

The authors wish to acknowledge the contribution of Gillian Rosner for her very accurate translation and copyediting work as well as her enthusiasm for this project. We also take this opportunity to thank Professor Ludovic Dibiaggio, Head of KTO research center at SKEMA Business School, for his continuous support to our dedication to bridging the gap between theory and practice. These thanks are extended to Professor Philippe Very from EDHEC Business School for his precious help in accessing company and industry databases.

Contents

List of Figures

List of Tables

1

Introduction

"*There is nothing so practical as a good theory.*" It was during the 1940s that Kurt Lewin, the founder of social psychology research, pronounced these words that were to become so well-known to students and scholars in the social sciences. In 2012, another psychologist, Anthony G. Greenwald, professor at Washington University, reversed the quotation, declaring, "*there is nothing so theoretical as a good method*".[1] Beyond their stylistic effect, these two quotations represent an effort to draw together theory, methods and practices.

This dual perspective has guided us in writing this book. For too long, those who produce theories in strategy and those who devise and implement strategy inside companies have either ignored or misunderstood one another. However, in the early days when company strategy emerged on the academic stage, nothing could have foreseen the slow but sure drifting apart of theory from practice.

This drift arose in the theoretical camp with the development of strategy as a specialised field in teaching and research. The quest for academic legitimacy led scholars to strive to build up a specific theoretical corpus for this field, borrowing freely from industrial organisation economics, the sociology of organisations and behavioural psychology. As a consequence, strategy gained in legitimacy, scientific rigor and academic influence. However, at the same time, it also drifted away from its original roots and ambition, which viewed strategy from a general approach that synthesized and encompassed the other management disciplines, and was directly linked to companies and their top managers. The fundamentals of strategy were incarnated by scholars who divided their time between teaching, publishing and consulting. This was the context that presided over the inception of strategy as an academic discipline

© The Author(s) 2018
P. Chereau, P.-X. Meschi, *Strategic Consulting*, DOI 10.1007/978-3-319-64422-6_1

in American business schools in the 1960s. This new discipline, described at the time as *business policy*, was supported notably by H. Igor Ansoff at Carnegie Mellon University and Edmund P. Learned, C. Roland Christensen, Kenneth R. Andrews and William D. Guth at Harvard Business School. Since then, the structure of teaching and research in strategy has been defined according to the dichotomy between strategic analysis (Learned, Christensen, Andrews and Guth) and strategic management (Ansoff). In this business policy context of teaching and research, the strategy professor and the strategy consultant might well be one and the same person.

The theory-practice drift mentioned above was also observed for strategy practitioners. Indeed, CEOs, corporate executives in charge of strategy and strategy consultants all developed their own tools, without feeling the need to attach these to the theoretical corpus in vogue. In fact, the theory-practice drift occurred as a consequence of certain constraints weighing on strategy practitioners. First, these practitioners face short timeframes. They often have to renew their tools, adapting them to ever more complex company environments and following fashion effects that also impact on strategy. This short timeframe also explains the difficulty of simplifying ever more specialised and compartmentalised academic production to make it accessible to companies and managers. Second, practitioners rarely possess the codes that would allow them to demonstrate the practical value of academic research by transforming it into tools and methodologies directly applicable to the company context. Third, consultants have made a point of differentiating themselves through a certain form of opacity and agility in developing and using their tools and methodologies. Clayton M. Christensen, Dina Wang and Derek Van Bever, in their article published in 2013 in the *Harvard Business Review*,[2] underline this situation as something that is inherent to big strategy consulting firms. These authors show that solutions and recommendations for client companies are produced inside the "*black box of the consulting room*" (p. 108), without clients being able to access the process that leads to the production of solutions and recommendations. Thus, client companies are unable to easily appropriate the consulting deliverables because they lack a shared theoretical framework, if indeed one exists. Christensen, Wang and Van Bever then highlight consultants' propensity to shift too easily from one "*big idea*" to another. This form of hyper-agility, imposed by the need to follow novel trends in strategy, prevents them from investigating the theoretical frameworks underlying emerging strategy tools. Finally, these consultants are obliged to propose in-house tools that ensure the legitimacy of their brand and secure their relationship with client companies, resulting in a plethora of tools for dealing with similar strategic phenomena and issues but using different analysis criteria. Thus, McKinsey,

Arthur D. Little and the 1960 Boston Consulting Group matrices all assess the competitive position and attractiveness of the company's strategic business units but use different perspectives and measures. Similarly, A. T. Kearney's and the Boston Consulting Group's profitable growth matrices analyse the company's growth strategies but with different growth and profitability measures.

This book comes at a time when new business models are emerging in strategy consulting. The traditional consultant's *"solution shop"* business model is no longer the only one available (see the article by Christensen, Wang and Van Bever for more details). This business model, which accounts for the success of large consulting firms such as Bain & Company, McKinsey or the Boston Consulting Group, was built on general strategy consulting that resembled a Swiss Army knife: it covered a wide range of strategy missions, relying on the renowned expertise of their consultants, obligation of means and high consulting fees. This *"solution shop"* business model was often implemented on one hand, by consulting firms specialised in devising and proposing strategy for client companies, and on the other, those specialised in accompanying and leading the strategic change.[3]

Three new business models have emerged recently. The *"knowledge builder"* business model charges client companies to access a network including market and competitor databases, industry experts, strategic intelligence technicians, and big data specialists. The added value of this service is found in the interfacing between the client and the different players producing the knowledge bases. Emblematic players of this new business model for strategy consulting are Gartner in technology (with GartnerG2 and Gartner Dataquest databases), IDC in strategic intelligence and IMS Health in pharmaceuticals. The *"temporary expert agency"* business model has developed as an extreme form of implementing and accompanying strategic recommendations. Here, consultants offer an ultra-customised, high-end service that usually spans an extended timeframe (from 6 months to 2 years). In practical terms, this business model generally places one or several senior consultants at the client company's exclusive disposal. Missions have a strong operational emphasis with consultants fully embedded with the client company and its teams. In the simplest form of this business model, the consulting firm transfers a consultant who then takes on the role of transition manager to conduct post-acquisition integration, restructure a division or oversee the implementation of a joint venture. This consultant has a very specific profile: he/she is highly specialised in transition missions and has already successfully managed several similar operations in the past. For a client company that lacks such specialists inside its organisation, or which is embarking on restructuring, refocusing or external growth operations for the first time, the transition consultant-manager has high added value. In a more complex form of the "*temporary expert agency*" business model, the consulting firm can provide an entire multi-specialised management team and transfer it to the client company to staff its main operational and support functions. This temporary management team, or task force, is entrusted with full autonomy to explore and create a new business or rapidly launch a start-up for the client. All such ventures entail strategic opportunities and high growth and profit potential, but their implementation, future evolution and market and competitive context are highly uncertain. As George Stalk Jr. and Ashish Lyer, consultants at the Boston Consulting Group, have shown, the client company can use consultants to create a "*temporary organisation*" that is run as a "*strategic option*".[4] If the venture realises its full potential, the temporary organisation gives way to a permanent managerial structure and the client company can recruit permanent employees. If the venture turns out to be a failure, the temporary organisation can quickly be dissolved without engaging heavy bankruptcy procedures and avoiding high restructuring and layoff costs. Even if the consulting fees are high (costing from two to four times more than a permanent senior manager in the client company), the advantages in terms of flexibility, reversibility and uncertainty control, not to mention experiential learning and the appropriation of new capabilities, are incomparable for the client company.

Another business model has recently emerged as the consequence of strong pressure to reduce consulting fees. Described as a "*consultant network*," this business model relies on freelance senior consultants specialised in one activity of the consulting value chain. These consultants are recruited occasionally by consulting firms or broker consultants in contact with the client company. The distinctive capability of broker consultants in this business model is made up of their network of independent, specialised consultants and their precise knowledge of each network consultant's expertise; this means they can group them together intelligently whenever a new consulting mission is signed. These ephemeral and highly flexible consulting firms have greatly reduced fixed and administrative expenses, allowing them to charge lower fees on certain missions, extend their client base and specifically, reach small and medium enterprises (SMEs), which until now could not afford the services of large strategy consulting firms.

This book aims to rebuild bridges between the theoretical and practical fields of strategy. More specifically, our objective is to root the tools of strategic consulting into the corresponding theoretical corpus; we incorporate these tools into incremental sequences of analysis to produce value-added consulting methodologies. In this book, we present six consulting missions that correspond to strategic analysis, repositioning and growth issues that all CEOs and top managers face at one stage or another during their company's lifecycle: Assessing the environment, defining a strategic positioning, choosing a growth strategy, expanding internationally, combining strategy and innovation or (re)designing the business model. Each type of mission corresponds to a chapter and each chapter is organised as follows:

- The consulting mission and its content;
- The theoretical background;
- The methodology and tools for the mission.

The six different consulting missions were chosen on the basis of our own experience in both strategic management consultancy and executive education programmes with senior executives from various companies and industries. Building on this experience, we have sought to present the best tools and methodologies from the most famous strategy consulting firms, while systematically underlining the theoretical background, appropriate context, mode of use, and potential limitations. To our knowledge, this book is the first to highlight the theoretical background to the methodologies and tools of strategic consulting, putting them into context. In this way, we hope to bring the theoretical corpus of strategy closer to its practical application inside companies.

The volume has two key intentions, one professional, the other pedagogical. On the professional level, it is aimed at company CEOs and top managers who seek a methodological guide to assessing, rethinking and redesigning their company strategy; it is also of use to consultants who wish to take on a complete methodology for the main strategic consulting missions and appropriate the theoretical background to better explain and justify their recommendations and deliverables. On the pedagogical level, this book is intended for students at the MBA, Masters or graduate levels who wish to acquire strategy consulting methodology to seek employment as consultants or want to use this methodology in their future managerial position. This pedagogical dimension is also relevant to consultants who today, besides their role as experts, have also become "knowledge disseminators" among their peers and clients. It is also of interest to CEOs and top executives who will find relevant contextual support to help them self-train in strategy. With this in mind, each chapter concludes with suggestions for further reading. These references have been carefully selected from the academic literature in strategy and provide a link between theory and practice. The book makes lavish use of the most recent articles published in the *Harvard Business Review* and the *MIT Sloan Management Review*. We hope you enjoy reading it!

Notes

1. Greenwald Anthony G., "There is Nothing so Theoretical as a Good Method", *Perspectives on Psychological Science*, vol. 7, no 2, 2012, p. 99–108.
2. Christensen Clayton M., Wang Dina and Van Bever Derek, "Consulting on the Cusp of Disruption", *Harvard Business Review*, vol. 91, no 10, 2013, p. 106–114.
3. Schmidt Sascha L., Vogt Patrick and Richter Ansgar, "Good News and Bad News: The Strategy Consulting Value Chain is Breaking Up", *Consulting to Management*, vol. 16, no 1, 2005, p. 39–44.
4. Stalk Jr. George and Iyer Ashish, "How to Hedge your Strategic Bets", *Harvard Business Review*, vol. 94, no 5, 2016, p. 80–86.

2

Assessing the Environment

2.1 The Consulting Mission

The environment is a generic term in strategy. It does not have today's some-what ecological connotation. In its strategic understanding, the environment refers to an ecosystem where a set of distinct players interact individually and collectively with the company. Thus, all companies operating in a specific industry are embedded within the associated ecosystem.

The players in the ecosystem have various levels of interaction with the company. A first circle of players interacts with it intensely and regularly. This immediate environment is made up of the company's clients, suppliers, service providers and competitors. These players each have their own immediate environment, also made up of their clients, suppliers and service providers. These second- or third-tier players are distant from the company and its immediate environment, even though they are connected to it indirectly. They can also join the company's first circle as new entrants if they manage to overcome the entry barriers.

Moreover, certain specific environments such as digital platforms (for example, Airbnb for short-term lodging and hospitality services or Steam for using and distributing computer video-games), otherwise known as *"platform environments,"*[1] are intrinsically integrative and open to ever more client-users, application suppliers and service providers. Indeed, the success and value of a digital platform come from the number, frequency and variety of interactions among its ecosystem players.

Other players are also present in the company's environment, but their interactions are less regular and their position in the ecosystem is more

© The Author(s) 2018
P. Chereau, P.-X. Meschi, *Strategic Consulting*, DOI 10.1007/978-3-319-64422-6_2

peripheral. However, depending on the times and circumstances, some of these players may draw closer to the company's immediate environment. This may be observed for banks and financial partners, investment funds, public and socio-political institutions and lobbying groups.

All the ecosystem players can be analysed with regard to their history, evolution, number, structure and possibly their strategy. However, above all they should be considered with regard to their influence on the company's strategy, growth and profitability. This influence is measured according to different scales that can be combined: weak or strong, cyclical or structural, favourable or unfavourable, direct or indirect, current or future. The assessment of the many facets of the influence of the different ecosystem players ultimately determines the value (and attractiveness) of the company's environment. So, at one extreme, the company's environment may be subject to numerous pressures and forces, making it highly dependent on the ecosystem players, constraining its strategic choices and locking it into an unfavourable profitability cycle that eventually may threaten its survival. At the other extreme, the company is able to exert pressures over its environment, thereby broadening the company's strategic choices, multiplying its opportunities and benefiting from accelerated growth and profit.

This assessment of the environment is one of the most classic missions for a consulting firm. However, the consultant should not lose sight of the fact that the conclusions of this mission are crucial for the client company. Indeed, the environment's value and attractiveness directly impact the company's growth and profitability.

Many different consulting missions relate to assessing the environment. Evaluating the value of the company's environment may be the main reason for initiating a consulting mission, but today this is rather rare; it is more often the first step in a broader mission whose objective is to help the company CEO to formalise, validate and make a strategic choice.

A first series of consulting missions consists of helping CEOs and top managers clarify the boundaries and challenges of their company's current or future environment. This involves updating their data and formalising their observations and intuitions related to assessing the value of the company's environment. These missions are often linked to an internal analysis of the company's competences and resources (human, technological, financial…). For the company seeking to achieve strategic fit, this internal analysis has to be aligned with the external analysis of the environment's opportunities and threats. On this basis, the consultant can check whether the client company is able to respond to the environment's opportunities and threats and thus build a solid competitive advantage. In other words, such consulting missions mean answering the following key questions of CEOs and top managers:

Which characteristics and opportunities of the market could be exploited by my company? Which market segments allow me (or could allow me) to get the most value from the company's current competences and resources and create a solid competitive advantage?

A second series of missions seeks (i) to identify and evaluate the key players of an environment (in terms of threat, competences and resources, profitability and value capture), (ii) to monitor the behaviour and strategy of these key players, and (iii) to suggest strategic responses and scenarios, including direct competition or collaboration with these players. Here, the key questions asked by CEOs and top managers are:

What is the strategy of my direct competitors? What are their respective practices and behaviours in the market? Which positioning should my company adopt to maintain or create competitive advantage?

A third series of missions occurs when the company intends to grow into new geographical markets, new client segments and/or new businesses. The assessment of the associated environment is necessary before any decision to expand is made. This assessment is unavoidable and is a prerequisite to international expansion, product/service range extension to new client segments, or diversification. By determining the value of a new geographical market, client segment or business, the company can formalise and refine its growth strategy. The conclusions of this type of mission are often useful in helping CEOs to convince their boards, main shareholders and the company's employees of the pertinence of initiating a growth strategy. Here, the key questions are:

Which markets would be receptive to my company's current offer? Do these target markets possess many and high entry barriers or do they operate in an open and integrative format such as a platform environment? How should my company adapt its offer in this respect? Which new markets will allow my company to deploy my company's competences and resources and develop a new offer?

Consistent with the company's intention to grow, a fourth series of missions seeks to analyse the environment to detect new markets and client segments and facilitate their emergence. Here, analysing the environment serves to identify new competitive spaces, or "*blue oceans*" as defined by W. Chan Kim and Renée Mauborgne. In this case, consultants need to adopt a "*reconstructionist approach*" whose objective is to "*help companies systematically reconstruct their industries and reverse the* [environment] *structure-strategy sequence in their favor*"[2] (p. 74). Building on a scenario-based or future anticipation approach, consultants help CEOs and top managers to define the boundaries of these new high potential markets and segments. To this end, they must also formalise the strategic actions required to give form and reality to these new competitive spaces. Here, the key questions are:

> *Are there competitive spaces that are favourable and unexploited within my environment? If so, how should my company proceed to make them emerge and benefit from a first mover advantage? Should my company invest in innovations that will rejuvenate and renew the lifecycle of certain markets and segments in my environment? Or should my company re-segment its market and seek to highlight new or unexploited competitive spaces?*

A fifth and final series of missions relates to business refocusing and divestment decisions. For a diversified company, regular assessment of the environment (of each geographical market, product/client segment and business) allows a review of the company's different (products, activities, competences, alliances…) portfolios and to restructure them if needed. The evaluation of the relative value and attractiveness of these different environments is one of the steps within the process that can lead a CEO to sell off a business, divest a foreign subsidiary or stop producing and selling a product range. Here, the key questions are:

> *How are the markets of my company evolving? What are the company's perspectives for growth in those markets? Can my company sustain a solid competitive position in the current configuration of the company?*

2.2 Theory, Methodology and the Tools for the Mission

2.2.1 Theoretical Background

Missions aiming to assess the environment are based on solid theoretical frameworks that have empirically proved their added value. Most come from industrial economics. These consulting missions are based on the assumption that the value and attractiveness of the company's environment determine its profitability and survival. This theory was initially postulated by Joe S. Bain, professor of economics at Berkeley, in his *Industrial Organization*, published in 1959. In 1970, Frederic M. Scherer, professor of economics at Harvard's Kennedy School of Government, took Bain's research further in *Industrial*

Market Structure and Economic Performance. Scherer advocates structuring the relationship between the company's environment and its performance using the "*SCP*" ("*Structure-Conduct-Performance*") paradigm.

Without going as far as "environmental selection" of companies in a sort of organisational Darwinism (see on this subject the theory of organisational ecology), the SCP paradigm is nevertheless based on industry determinism. Scherer shows that the market structure, the behaviour of companies operating in this market and their performance follow a causal sequence. At the top end of this sequence is the market structure, which is analysed with the following criteria: height and number of entry barriers, degree of competitive concentration and cost structure of competitors, and market growth rate. From this viewpoint, analysing the market structure is similar to assessing the intensity of competition within the market in question. This assessment of the intensity of competition allows a determination of the value and attractiveness of a market: the higher the intensity of competition among companies, the lower the value and attractiveness of their environment, with the converse also true. At an intermediary level in the SCP's causal sequence is company behaviour. This constitutes the company's strategic response (in terms of pricing, R&D, communication and collaborative/competitive behaviour) towards a particular market structure. At the other end of this sequence, we find company performance that results from strategic choices. In other words, the high or low level of performance for companies competing in a market is a direct outcome of the favourable or unfavourable structure of that market.

The SCP paradigm benefited from a major advance thanks to the research of Michael E. Porter, professor of strategy at Harvard Business School. First, in his book *Competitive Strategy* published in 1980, he deepened and extended the analysis of market structure and company strategy—the two keystones of the SCP paradigm. He then proposed his own framework of the market structure known as the "*structuralist approach.*" This went well beyond Scherer's assessment of competition structure. In fact, Porter proposed assessing the structure and value of a market from a model that combined not just one (competition), but a whole set of competitive forces. A thorough assessment of a market structure requires the inclusion of other players adjacent to the competition: suppliers, clients, new entrants and substitutes. In fact, within Porter's model, the intensity of competition is only one competitive force among others, and it is this influence combined with other competitive forces that determines successively the value and attractiveness of an environment, the strategy of companies and their performance.

There are five of these competitive forces in the structuralist approach and they constitute as many threats for the value and attractiveness of an

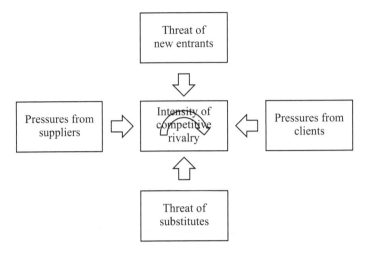

Fig. 2.1 Porter's model of competitive forces
Source: Porter Michael E., *op. cit.*, 1980

Table 2.1 Evaluation criteria of competitive forces

Competitive force	New entrants	Substitutes	Suppliers/clients	Competitors
Evaluation criteria	Entry barriers Expected retaliation from existing competitors Deterring entry price	Existence or risk of products or services offering the same customer function but using different technologies or business models	Relative concentration Related quality and differentiation of products (or services) Switching costs Risk of forward/ backward integration	Market growth Level of fixed costs Product/service differentiation Diversity of competitors Exit barriers

Source: Porter Michael E., *op. cit.*, 1980

environment. As shown in Fig. 2.1 and Table 2.1, only a thorough evaluation of each of these forces, using *ad hoc* criteria, will allow a determination of the reality and intensity of the threat they pose to an environment's value.

By teaching his model to multiple cohorts of MBA students at Harvard Business School in the 1980s and 1990s, Porter largely contributed to the dissemination of the SCP paradigm within SMEs, multinationals and large strategy consulting firms.[3] By isolating the opportunities and threats resulting from the evaluation of competitive forces, he also complemented one of the first tools for strategic analysis, the "*SWOT*" ("*Strengths, Weaknesses, Opportunities, Threats*") method, which has been in use since the 1970s. The SWOT analysis, still widely used, is too often implemented over simplistically: firstly, the SWOT analysis is usually limited to a macro-analysis of the environment, whereas the evaluation of competitive forces makes it possible to really describe the environment's opportunities and threats. Secondly, merely determining the client company's strengths and weaknesses often neglects the necessary investigation of the company's real capacity to respond to the key success factors of the markets and segments on which it intends to expand.

It is with the definition of the PIMS principles that the SCP paradigm received the blessing of empirical support and with that, its strong reputation. In 1987, Robert D. Buzzell and Bradley T. Gale published *The PIMS Principles: Linking Strategy to Performance*. This book presented the results and conclusions of an empirical study carried out since the early 1970s using a unique database of 450 European and American firms of all sizes, involving 3000 industries and segments. This empirical study was initiated by General Electric. It was intended to highlight the main drivers of company profitability. To this end, a large survey was conducted as part of a research project named *Profit Impact of Market Strategy* (or PIMS). Its main objective was to test, on a vast scale, a performance model including a set of variables considered potentially critical to company performance. The PIMS model can be summarised as follows:

$$\text{performance} = f\left(\text{market structure and company's internal variables}\right)$$

Company performance was measured using the profit-to-assets ratio or the profit-to-cumulated investments ratio, also known as return on investment (ROI). The market structure corresponds to external/environment variables and is measured using Porter's competitive forces. Internal/company variables refer to the company's different capabilities and resources. These allow the company to differentiate itself from the competition at different levels: management and organisation (internal organisation, routines, management style, reputation…), products and services (quality, price, cost structure…), processes, operations and technologies (patents, R&D, production) and financial resources.

The outcomes and conclusions of the model's empirical tests are known as the PIMS principles. They are summarised in a work by Buzzell and Gale, who emphasise the necessity for companies to pick attractive markets and segments. Building on the significant statistical results obtained with several thousand companies, industries and segments, these authors put forward guidelines for a winning strategy: *"to pick the 'right' markets or industries in which to participate. Some kinds of competitive arenas have high inherent profit potential, while in others even the most diligent competitors earn only modest rates of return"* (p. 52).

These PIMS principles constitute the final step of the theoretical SCP approach. They empirically define, formalise and support the assumption that the value and attractiveness of the environment, whether pipeline or platform, determines a company's strategy and profitability. This is roughly equivalent to stating that companies are positioned either (i) in 'good' environments, with few threats and pressures from new entrants, substitute products or services, suppliers, clients and competitors, and where the market is growing; or (ii) in 'bad' environments, which have reached maturity or are, even worse, declining, and are greatly destabilized by strong threats and pressures from new entrants, substitute products or services, suppliers, clients and competition. Growth, profitability and the survival of companies are determined by their capacity to detect the very nature of their own environment, monitor that environment and its (favourable or unfavourable) evolution over time, and direct their investments towards "*right*" markets and segments environments.

Best Consulting Practices in Brief

The consultant who is familiar with the SCP paradigm and Porter's competitive forces will be able to recommend to his/her client company to conduct an assessment of the environment. It is often easy for consultants to link the strategic problems and challenges of any company to this theoretical framework and convince the client company's CEO by demonstrating this framework's causal mechanism, which is intellectually very attractive. When negotiating with the client company, consultants can usefully refer to the PIMS principles and propose some significant examples of "right" and "wrong" markets and the relationship to the profitability for companies operating in these markets.

2.2.2   Methodology and Tools for the Mission

The strategy literature abounds in tools for strategic analysis, namely, tools intended to assess the value and attractiveness of an environment. Strategic analysis is by far the dimension of strategy that has produced the most tools for consultants. However, when a consultant is hired by a company to assess its environment, he/she may wonder not so much which tool to use but rather which methodology to deploy. Indeed, a methodology suited to this kind of mission should propose a few tools in a step-by-step approach. Each step corresponds to a specific tool and each tool produces information, analyses and knowledge, which should allow the consultant to obtain the most refined and thorough assessment of the environment while remaining coherent with the client company's frame of reference.

Best Consulting Practices in Brief

When assessing the environment and using strategic analysis tools, more does not mean better. It is not by piling up tools that such a consulting mission will gain in value. Accumulating tools only multiplies information, data and results. It is not the tool itself that is key, but rather the consultant's ability to articulate the various tools coherently to propose a logical progression in the strategic analysis process.

The following step-by-step process is the basic architecture of the environment assessment mission. It is certainly not exhaustive. For some steps, we suggest going deeper by using other strategic analysis tools. We have chosen to present this process rather than another because, to our knowledge, it is the one that offers the best coherence and the most thorough and pertinent outcomes.

This strategic analysis process is organised around five steps. These are summarised in Fig. 2.2. Each step corresponds to the implementation of a specific tool. These steps follow a logical progression, which means that the results obtained in one step are often a prerequisite for embarking on the next.

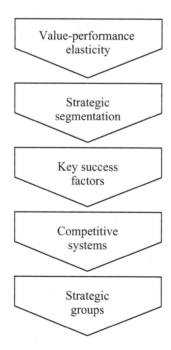

Fig. 2.2 The five steps of strategic analysis
Source: Authors

2.2.2.1 The Value/Performance Elasticity Test

The first step in the strategic analysis consists of defining the strategic nature of the environment. This may be done by examining the strength of the relationship between the value and attractiveness of a market and the performance of companies operating in this market (otherwise known as value/performance elasticity). An environment will be highly strategic if this relationship is strong. In this event, the influence of the environment's characteristics on company performance is determinant and we find ourselves in a perspective which is fully consistent with the PIMS principles. In other words, here, the environment turns out to be strategic for the company due to the presence of environment-performance causality. On the other hand, an environment loses its strategic nature if its value/performance elasticity is weak. This type of environment configuration is found in industries and segments where, despite their weak (strong) value, certain companies prosper (decline). Nevertheless, in such an event, the client company may maintain the mission of assessing its environment. However, for the consultant, this mission will mean shifting from an SCP (or structuralist approach) paradigm to a reconstructionist approach to the environment. In the event of a weak value environment, the mission will then aim to seek one or several niches within an unfavourable environment. In the event of a strong value environment, the consulting objective will be to concentrate on highlighting the reasons for the company's under-performance and the misalignment between the company's competences and resources and the environment's characteristics.

Best Consulting Practices in Brief

The initial step of value/performance elasticity may be viewed as a "make or break" test for the consultant. Indeed, the elasticity test is not only the first step in the strategic analysis process, it also examines the pertinence of taking this process further or not. If the elasticity is strong, the question is not relevant: the whole strategic analysis process must be rolled out. On the other hand, if the elasticity is weak, the question of whether to continue the mission has to be discussed with the client company. This test can easily be carried out during the negotiation and framing phase of the consulting mission and the client company should be warned of these preliminary results. On this basis, the client company will be able to make an informed decision about whether to take the analysis further.

This first step, known as the value/performance elasticity test (or PIMS test), is generally carried out using a simple direct measure of a company's environment and performance. As regards the assessment of environment value, an immediately applicable and easily accessible measure is market growth rate. This is an essential measure of value as it occupies a central position in both Scherer's SCP, Porter's competitive forces and PIMS models. Some strategy tools have also used market growth rate to measure the value of an environment. This is notably the case of the Boston Consulting Group's matrix, which assesses the value and competitive position of the company's strategic business units. As regards the assessment of the company's performance, using the ROI ratio (profit-to-assets ratio) presents the advantage of being consistent with the PIMS model and avoids the inconclusive debate on selecting an appropriate measure for performance.

From Theory to Practice

The two environments (pharmaceuticals and paper/pulp) analysed below constitute a good illustration of the PIMS test and shed light on strong value/performance elasticity. For these two markets, the measure of value gives very different results.

The pharmaceutical industry has been growing strongly for many years. IMS Health (www.imshealth.com) regularly produces prospective reports on the world pharmaceutical market. One of its latest reports (*Global Medicines Use in 2020*, published in 2015), presents this market's growth rate between 2015 and 2020. For the 2011–2016 period, the growth rate was over 35% and from 2015 to 2020, it is expected to be between 29% and 32%. This report highlights the strong drivers of growth in the pharmaceutical environment: growing demand from emerging economies (two thirds of the world pharmaceutical market), the upsurge of the generic medicine segment and the steep price increases expected in the North American market (consistent with large innovation efforts and market launching of new blockbuster pharmaceuticals). For this last growth driver, the IMS health report foresees a growth hovering around 35% over the 2015–2020 period! In contrast, the paper/pulp market has the opposite configuration with a constantly decreasing market in developed countries over several years. This decline is the direct outcome of the upswing in the digital press, online books and the increasing trend to recycle paper. In sum, the analysis of the current and future growth rates of these two markets shows two opposite situations regarding the assessment of environment value: high value for the pharmaceutical market while the paper/pulp market has low value.

Figure 2.3a and b summarise the performance analysis of the main companies operating within these two environments. In both environments, we can observe a high elasticity between the environment value and the company's resulting performance: in the fast growing pharmaceutical market, companies are located in favourable ROI zones ranging from 0% to 25%; on the other hand, in the mature paper/pulp market, companies are in ROI zones that are negative or near zero.

As shown in the two examples above, the value/performance elasticity test is easy for a consultant to carry out. The required information (current and future market growth rate and company's ROI) are publicly available. The conclusions that can be drawn using the PIMS principles go well beyond a simple description

(continued)

(continued)

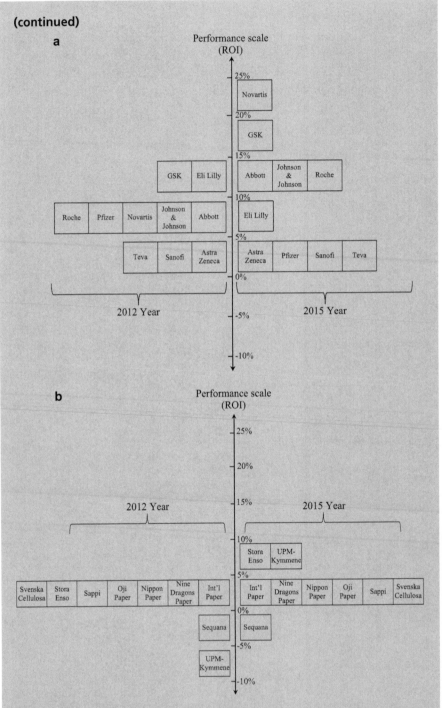

Fig. 2.3 (a) The ROI scale for the pharmaceutical market (2012 and 2015).
(b) The ROI scale for the paper/pulp market (2012 and 2015)
Source: Authors

(continued)

Table 2.2 Largest shareholdings of NBIM (2016)

Company	Country of origin	Industry	Shareholding amount (in € million)
Nestlé	Switzerland	Agrifood	5631
Royal Dutch Shell	Great Britain	Oil	5097
Apple	United States	Consumer electronics	4966
Alphabet (Google)	United States	Internet services	4038
Microsoft	United States	Software	3828
Roche	Switzerland	Pharmaceutical	3633
Novartis	Switzerland	Pharmaceutical	3572

Source: www.nbim.no

of an environment. They can easily lead to initial recommendations concerning possible investment choices. Therefore, by focusing on the pharmaceutical market and integrating an analysis of the shareholdings and targeted industries by the large investment funds, the consultant can turn the environment description into expert recommendations. To take this to its logical conclusion, it is worth considering the main shareholdings in 2016 by the Norwegian sovereign wealth fund NBIM (Norges Bank Investment Management), whose main objective is to manage the financial surplus derived from the exploitation of oil and gas in the North Sea. With total financial assets worth over €850 million, NBIM is the largest sovereign wealth fund in the world, ahead of the Chinese CIC (China Investment Corporation), Emirati ADIA (Abu Dhabi Investment Authority), Kuwaiti KIA (Kuwait Investment Authority) and Saudi SAMA (Saudi Arabian Monetary Agency). It is hardly surprising therefore, when looking at Table 2.2, that the pharmaceutical industry is high in the short list of NBIM's largest shareholdings.

2.2.2.2 Strategic Segmentation

With strategic segmentation, the consultant steps right into the process of the strategic analysis of the environment. This second step in the strategic analysis consists of mapping out the company's market. Strategic segmentation only concerns one aspect of the company's environment: its market. A company's market can be seen as a competitive space that is often not uniform and whose boundaries are more or less blurred.

An initial approach to strategic segmentation should result in a structured presentation of a market, its boundaries and associated market sub-sets. It is a description seeking to identify the company's critical market, *i.e.*, one or several market sub-sets in which the company operates. Indeed, it is rare for a company and its product portfolio to occupy the whole of a competitive space or achieve equivalent performance over all of the market sub-sets. This first approach to strategic segmentation therefore tries to organise a market into homogenous sub-sets and restrict the company's competitive space to some of these. In a second, less descriptive approach, segmentation becomes more strategic by offering the company's CEO and top managers a map of the positions and moves that the company could adopt within the different sub-sets in its market. By taking this dynamic approach to segmentation, the market sub-sets appear as both spaces of growth and opportunities for the company to expand businesses sharing similar expenses and resources. From this view, segmentation lies at the intersection between the environment assessment and strategic decision making. This implies that segmentation should not be undertaken by the consultant alone or by the consultant interacting with various departments (especially marketing). In all its phases, segmentation must result from discussions and interactions involving the consultant and the client company's CEO and top managers.

In the first phase, the consultant must ask about the pertinence of embarking onto segmenting the company's market. He/she must know whether the market in question is heterogeneous or not. The assessment of the level of market heterogeneity will trigger (or not) the segmentation process. At this level and based on the method proposed by Derek F. Abell (professor of strategy at IMD Lausanne) in *Managing with Dual Strategies* (published in 1993), three criteria are usually mobilised to define the level of market heterogeneity (see Fig. 2.4).

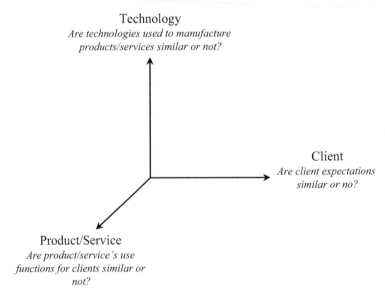

Fig. 2.4 Market heterogeneity and strategic segmentation criteria
Source: Authors

- Product: this criterion refers to the characteristics of the product(s), service(s) or solution(s) sold in the market. Beyond a product's physical characteristics, it is important to identify its use function. A first level of market heterogeneity related to this criterion can be assessed with the following question: do the products, services or solutions sold within this market have similar use functions for clients or not?

- Client: this criterion describes the different groups of customers in the market. Highlighting these customer groups can be done using marketing segmentation. However, this results in a great number of client groups divided by geographical, socio-demographic (age, social, education, occupational, gender…), key accounts and lifestyle dimensions. By identifying so many potentially overlapping customer groups, the resulting segmentation may be more fine-grained but it will be less easy to work with. Practically speaking, the best way to describe customer groups in a market is to identify their main expectations regarding products, services and solutions sold in the market. Therefore, a second level of market heterogeneity associated with this criterion can be assessed with the following question: do the clients in this market have similar expectations or not?

- Technology: for Abell, this criterion refers to "*alternative ways of fulfilling a particular customer function*" (p. 57). If, for example, we take the customer function of using public transport, planes, trains or buses are several ways of fulfilling this function; in the same vein, traditional "brick and mortar" and digital "click and order" technologies are associated with the food distribution function. From this example, we see that the customer function is strongly related to the technologies used for manufacturing products. To identify and analyse these technologies, consultants are recommended to not adopt an overly technical view but to stay at the level of customers' perception. A third and final level of market heterogeneity related to this criterion can be assessed with the following question: are the technologies associated with the products, services or solutions similar or not?

If there is a positive response to the above three questions, we can conclude that the market in question is highly homogenous with regard to the product, client and technology criteria. This homogeneity is only observed in rare environments, such as primary resources (raw materials extraction, mining and commodities) and emergent high technology markets (life sciences, DNA research, hybrid batteries, 3D printers, biotechnologies…). In these environments, the product has a single customer function, customers have similar and basic expectations and the technologies are the same. But this situation is not frequent and the vast majority of markets show one or several forms of market heterogeneity. In these markets, segmentation is necessary. The role of strategic segmentation is to turn a heterogenous market into a set of homogenous (market sub-sets) segments with regard to the product, client and technology criteria.

Best Consulting Practices in Brief

When the consultant is asked to carry out a strategic segmentation of a platform environment such as video games online distribution or professional social networks, he/she has to adapt Abell's three traditional criteria (product, client, technology) to the specific characteristics of these industries. The technology criterion is not relevant here as all these industries use the same digital technology, even though the operating systems and devices may vary (smartphones, tablets…) from one platform to another. On the other hand, the product and client criteria must find equivalents in platform environments. The product criterion is not very important in these environments because unlike traditional pipeline environments, the company's value creation is built on other drivers such as the number, frequency and variety of interactions between the application providers and platform users. For platform industries, a first level of market heterogeneity can therefore be evaluated with the following question: are the platform provider-user interactions associated with similar use functions or not? The client criterion is also not very relevant as in these industries, the frontier between client, user and application provider is blurred; clients can successively be any of these in a platform. In platform industries, a key criterion is the platform community. Community, which has a more open and inclusive dimension than the client, is a more meaningful criterion to assess the heterogeneity level of platform environments. Therefore a second level of market heterogeneity of platform markets can be evaluated with the following question: do the communities within these platforms have similar expectations or not?

After validating the pertinence of strategic segmentation, a second phase begins. This aims to identify and formalise homogenous segments. Segmentation should be guided by the response to the three previous questions. More specifically, the effort of segmentation should be based on the criterion or criteria for which a form of market heterogeneity appeared. If only one criterion of market heterogeneity is validated, segmentation should be carried out using that criterion. If there are two it should be carried out according to these two, and so on. As shown in Fig. 2.5, the approach must be progressive: it begins with an analysis of the product criterion; if this is pertinent, the segments corresponding to this criterion must be identified as product segments. Next, we consider the client criterion. If this is significant, a second dimension of segmentation must be introduced and client segments combined with product segments. Segmentation ends with the technology criterion. If this is significant, a third and final dimension is added. In this case, the client segments, product segments and technology segments must be articulated to get the final strategic segmentation.

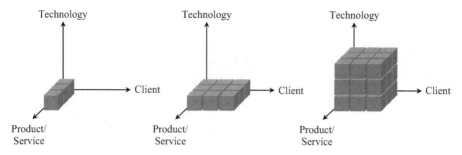

Fig. 2.5   Strategic segmentation criteria and process
Source: Authors

Best Consulting Practices in Brief

The strategic segmentation step is crucial as it determines the quality of the following strategic analysis process. Indeed, the next steps use the outcome of the strategic segmentation as their starting point. This means that consultants must be particularly careful when identifying and formalising the different market segments. Strategic segmentation results in a snapshot of the company's market. Like any snapshot, the focus has to be adjusted by the consultant: do you want a fine-grained segmentation based on a detailed analysis of the three criteria, highlighting a large number of segments, or on the contrary, do you expect something less refined, focused on one or two criteria that will produce a smaller number of segments? This question must also be answered by the client company in line with the objectives that it assigned to the environment assessment mission. Consultants must bear in mind that several segmentations are possible for the same market. It is therefore recommended to produce several variants corresponding to different levels of aggregation and focus, and discuss these with the client company so that a working segmentation can be chosen.

From Theory to Practice

Strategic segmentation must always be fitted to the consulting mission. Many missions concern evaluating the pertinence for a company to enter into a new geographical market. In this event, two possibilities arise: first, the targeted foreign market has identical characteristics to those of other geographical markets. In this situation, the segments are globalised and the segmentation will be valid across all geographical markets. A second possibility is that the foreign market has unique features that distinguish it from other geographical markets. Here, a specific segmentation must then be produced.

The tyre market in India corresponds to the second case and needs specific segmentation.[4] Indeed, several features distinguish this market from the global tyre market: a two-digit growth rate, a large number of competitors (39 in 2012), a large proportion of OEM (car, motor bike and rickshaw makers) sales relative to replacement sales, and finally, the persistence of diagonal or cross-ply technology (which has been replaced in the rest of the world by radial technology).

(continued)

(continued)

More specifically, the Indian tyre market is highly heterogeneous. First, there are several distinct product categories. These relate to three main product segments: car tyres, commercial vehicle tyres and two-/three-wheeler tyres. Other product segments exist (for example, agricultural vehicle tyres) but their size makes them more like niche products. Secondly, there are two categories of clients for companies competing in this market: car makers (OEM) and garages/tyre dealers (replacement). Finally, two technologies are available: diagonal and radial. The combination of the three product segments, the two client segments and the two technology segments results in twelve segments (see Fig. 2.8). These are reduced to eight because (i) the two segments combining car tyres/diagonal technology with OEM and replacement have almost disappeared from the Indian market; (ii) two- and three-wheeler tyres hardly use radial technology (for the sake of simplicity, the segments of two- and three-wheeler tyres using radial technology have been removed).

Finally, these eight segments are homogenous with regard to the product, client and technology criteria.

2.2.2.3   Key Success Factors

The third step in the strategic analysis process consists of identifying the key success factors of each segment. Key success factors correspond to the specific purchasing criteria used by clients in each segment. In other words, key success factors are the criteria that spur clients to acquire the products or services that companies sell in a market or a segment. For example, key success factors may include criteria such as price, intrinsic product quality, product range, level of customisation, associated services and/or brand image. Key success factors are always defined with regard to the market or segment to which they belong. They are unique to a segment.

Even if key success factors are intrinsically related to products and services sold in a segment, they have nevertheless to be distinguished from the customer function of these products and the benefits or value that clients obtain from consuming them. Indeed, the customer and value functions of a product are defined with regard to the satisfaction of one or several specific client needs; however, key success factors refer to the conditions (price, quality, range…) in which the customer and value functions are fulfilled and made available to clients.

Key success factors have a direct consequence on the ability of companies in this segment to build a solid competitive advantage. Competition within a segment is organised and competitive pressures are exerted around these key success factors. The company's ability to "control" key success factors, *i.e.*, to identify and respond to them effectively, will help it build a solid competitive advantage. An effective response to key success factors means that the company has to develop and deploy internally the capabilities and resources that allow it to position itself as the best offer on one or several purchasing criteria.

Best Consulting Practices in Brief

The key success factors step contributes a supplementary view of the pertinence of strategic segmentation covered in the previous step. Indeed, the combination of key success factors, or at least their ranking by order of importance, should differ from one segment to another. If this combination is identical for two segments, the validity of the segmentation should be questioned: it is highly likely that the two segments are in reality, only one!

Identifying and analysing key success factors, just like the initial value/performance elasticity test, contributes a useful view of the value of a market's segments. Therefore, the number and nature of a segment's key success factors are indicative of its value. A segment with very few key success factors, mostly linked to price, is often characterised by strong competition. Indeed, in such a segment configuration, companies have no strategic alternatives but head-on competition and price wars. As a consequence, the segment has low value. In a different configuration, a segment with a large number of key success factors often shows a low level of competition. Here, companies may concentrate their efforts on responding to some, but not all key success factors. Through this specialisation, competition is fragmented, niches are formed and eventually, competitive intensity decreases. In sum, key success factors should be seen as sources of differentiation and competition avoidance: the greater the number of key success factors, the lower the competitive intensity and the higher the segment value, and conversely.

From Theory to Practice

To complete the strategic segmentation of the Indian tyre market, we need to shed light on the key success factors for each of the previously identified market segments (eight in total). This means identifying who are the clients in each segment and what are their purchasing criteria. Table 2.3 summarises these features.

(continued)

(continued)

Table 2.3 Key success factors of market segments in the Indian tyre market

	Segment 1	Segment 2	Segment 3	Segment 4	Segment 5	Segment 6	Segment 7	Segment 8
Product	Car tyres	Car tyres	Commercial vehicle tyres	Commercial vehicle tyres	Commercial vehicle tyres	Commercial vehicle tyres	Two- and three-wheeler tyres	Two- and three-wheeler tyres
Client	Car makers	Specialised distribution	Car makers	Specialised distribution	Car makers	Specialised distribution	Car makers	Specialised distribution
Technology	Radial	Radial	Diagonal	Diagonal	Radial	Radial	Diagonal	Diagonal
Key success factors	1. Price 2. Tyre performance (speed and road adhesion)	1. Price 2. Brand image 3. Tyre performance (speed and road adhesion) 4. Product range	Price	1. Price 2. Lifetime 3. Load capacity 4. Product range	1. Price 2. Fuel consumption 3. Tyre performance (speed and road adhesion)	1. Price 2. Fuel consumption 3. Tyre performance (speed and road adhesion) 4. Brand image 5. Product range	Price	1. Price 2. Product range

Source: Adapted from Chitnis Ameya and Meschi Pierre-Xavier, op. cit., 2007 (updated in 2014)

2.2.2.4 Competitive Systems

The competitive systems step goes beyond describing segments based on their specific combination of key success factors. This step complements the previous key success factors step by going further in the environment value assessment and recommending which strategy should be conducted in each segment. This is where the main benefit of the competitive systems analysis lies: determining the rules of the game in the different types of environment in which a company might operate.

The competitive systems were initially developed by the Boston Consulting Group in 1980, which explains why it is also known as BCG 80. They take the form of a four-quadrant matrix, which is easily accessible and whose implications for the strategic analysis are relevant and straightforward for companies to implement; this is why it has been so successful. Each matrix quadrant represents a particular type of environment, which, according to the BCG, is defined as a competitive system. The basic idea of the competitive systems matrix is that any segment or market can be positioned in one of these four competitive systems.

The competitive systems matrix is organised with two axes (see Fig. 2.6). The first axis, solidity of competitive position, is split in two categories of segments: in the first category, we can find strong segments, where companies can build a solid competitive position. In the second category, we can find non-solid or

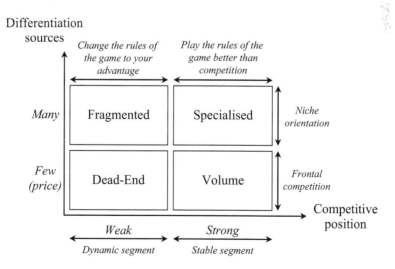

Fig. 2.6 The competitive systems matrix
Source: Adapted from BCG 80

weak segments, where it is very difficult to build a solid competitive position. The distinction between stable and dynamic environments, proposed in 2011 by Christopher B. Bingham, Kathleen M. Eisenhardt and Nathan R. Furr,[5] echoes the solid (strong) and non-solid (weak) segment categorisation. Belonging to one or the other of these categories depends on how a solid competitive position is defined and assessed. Two conditions are usually required to conclude that a company enjoys a solid competitive position:

- First, the competitive position must be durable, *i.e.*, it must last over several years. More specifically, this means that at least one company within the segment effectively responds to the main key success factors over the long term. This enduring response to the key success factors is not observed systematically. In some environments, responding to key success factors is easy but remains temporary. In this situation, the company's competitive position is not durable as it is destabilised by certain factors, the most common of which being the lack of entry barriers, frequent technological changes, short product (service or solution) lifecycle, pressure from fashionable trends, and easy imitation of products, technologies, or the entire business model. Indeed, these destabilising factors, alone or in combination, contribute to weaken a company's competitive position and frequently renew the competitive hierarchy within the segment.
- Second, the competitive position must be significant, *i.e.*, it must be accompanied by a profitability gap that can be observed among the segment's competitors. Therefore, segments with a clearly observable profitability gap where some companies stand out from the competition, are associated with a significant competitive position. On the contrary, segments where competitors are not, or hardly, differentiated for their profitability (which is often low), correspond to a non-significant competitive position.

The second axis, differentiation sources, distinguishes segments according to the number and nature of their key success factors. On one side, there are segments with many key success factors that are also sources of differentiation for companies. Here competition is not head on and many niches can be exploited by companies. On the other side are segments with few key success factors, mostly price-based. Here, the sources of differentiation are reduced to the minimum, there are no possibilities for exploiting niches and the resulting competition is fierce and head on.

Four competitive systems (volume, specialised, fragmented and dead-end) result from the combination of these two axes. The main characteristics of these competitive systems are presented in Table 2.4.

Table 2.4 The characteristics of competitive systems

	Volume	Specialised	Fragmented	Dead-end
Definition	Segments where price is the main key success factor and where some companies have managed to build a solid competitive position based on price and cost leadership	Segments where there are numerous sources of differentiation and where some companies have managed to build a solid competitive position based on providing unique products, services and solutions	Segments where there are numerous key success factors but these are always evolving. Companies in these segments cannot build a solid competitive position as a consequence of these destabilising factors	Price-based segments that are mature or declining, where companies cannot build a solid competitive position
Examples	Low cost industries (hard discount retail, air travel...), generic pharmaceuticals, mass market products and commodities	Luxury segments (cosmetics, perfumes, jewellery, leather goods...), defense, biotechnology, aeronautics and strategy consulting	Garment, restauration, fashion products and electronic commerce	Landline telephone, paper/pulp, glass, agro-chemicals, pesticides and postal services
Performance indicator	Market share	Unit margin	Product renewal	Cash flow
Strategic objective	Reducing cost and price	Providing clients with products, services or solutions perceived as unique	Increasing organisational flexibility (reducing time-to-market)	Surviving, gaining time and/or divesting the business
Strategy	Cost reduction strategy relying on economies of scale and variety, process innovation, accelerated internationalisation, outsourcing and delocalisation	Differentiation strategy relying on niches, unique marketing expertise, unique technological know-how and vertical integration	Flexibility and focus strategy relying on product innovation, imitation, product range increase, market and competitive surveillance, project-based and flat organisation	Divestment strategy, diversification or market rejuvenation strategy (with high investments in radical innovation and relaunching lifecycle)
Core competences and resources	Finance, manufacturing, supply chain, cost management and process-oriented R&D	Human resources, manufacturing, creativity, innovation, product-oriented R&D, distribution, branding and marketing	Leadership, reputation, marketing, product-oriented innovation and strategic intelligence	Finance, human resources, social, innovation and cost management

Source: Authors

Best Consulting Practices in Brief

Linking a segment or a market to a specific competitive system is always a subject for discussion. To support their competitive systems analysis and conclusion, consultants are advised to position the main companies in the studied segment or market in a profitability/size graph. To elaborate this graph, turnover and ROI (profit-to-assets ratio) may be used to measure the company size and profitability, respectively. The observed distribution pattern makes it easy to define the segment or market with regard to one of the four competitive systems (see Fig. 2.7). This graph can be used prior to conducting the competitive systems analysis or afterwards to support its conclusion.

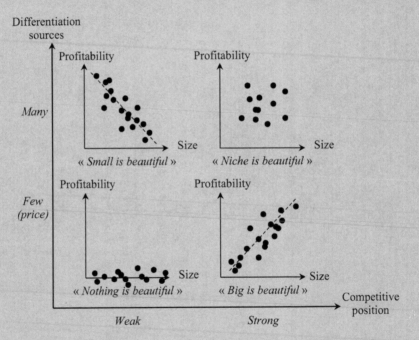

Fig. 2.7 The profitability/size relationship and the competitive systems matrix
Source: Authors

The competitive systems matrix should be analysed using a dynamic approach, since by definition, a competitive system is not fixed in time. Indeed, it is highly likely that segments positioned at one time in this matrix will occupy a different position a few years later. The dynamic approach to competitive systems matrix closely follows the evolution of segments within their respective lifecycle:

- At birth, a segment often starts as a fragmented system. During this first phase of the lifecycle, few companies or first movers are active within the segment. As a consequence, the intensity of competition is weak. With the first business developments in the segment, we see the emergence of key success factors that may multiply and change rapidly over time.
- When the segment enters the growth phase, we see a stabilisation in the (low or large) number of key success factors, the building of a solid competitive position by some companies and the subsequent emergence of entry barriers and/or niches. As a consequence, the segment may approach either a volume system (few key success factors) or a specialised one (several key success factors).
- When the segment reaches maturity, this leads simultaneously to a tightening up of key success factors around pricing and the destabilisation of the solid competitive positions built over the previous phases. The segment may then move in two directions: either it slowly declines and finally disappears, or it completely renews itself through the rejuvenation effect of radical innovations. In the latter case, the segment transforms itself and gives rise to another segment that positions itself in a fragmented system, thereby relaunching the dynamic of the competitive systems matrix.

From Theory to Practice

After the steps of strategic segmentation and key success factors, the example of the Indian tyre market ends up by positioning its segments in the competitive systems matrix. For the horizontal axis, the eight segments are associated with a strong competitive position, even though there are competitive nuances from one segment to the other. The two- and three-wheeler tyres segment has the strongest competitive position solidity, with two companies in a dominant position (two local companies, MRF and TVS Srichakra, control over 50% of the market share). On the two other segment categories, we find an uncontested leader: MRF for car tyres and Apollo Tyres for commercial vehicle tyres. The positioning on the vertical axis is derived from the previous key success factors' analysis for the eight segments. Figure 2.8 shows that the Indian tyre market as a whole belongs to a volume system. The gradual decline of diagonal technology giving way to the radial tyre for commercial vehicles draws these segments (3 and 4) closer to a dead-end system.

(continued)

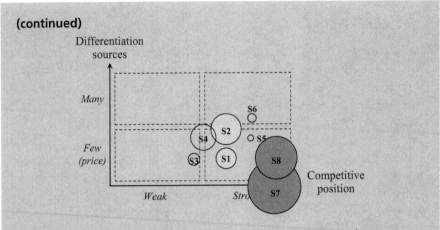

(continued)

Fig. 2.8 Segments and competitive systems in the Indian tyre market
Source: Adapted from Chitnis Ameya and Meschi Pierre-Xavier, *op. cit.*, 2007 (updated in 2014)

2.2.2.5 Strategic Groups

Strategic groups constitute the final step in the strategic analysis process. This step focuses on a key force in the environment: competition. This step relies on mapping the competition for a segment or a market and as such its purpose remains mainly descriptive. The mapping procedure is straightforward: competitors are first positioned on a two-dimensional map and then companies presenting similar or identical dimensions are grouped together. These groups of companies are called strategic groups. At this level, the issue is to choose the two dimensions that will serve to draw up the map and position the companies. When choosing these dimensions, the following conditions must be kept in mind: they must not be correlated, they must differentiate competitors clearly, and they must allow the competitors to be observed both by their volume (or resulting cost advantage) and differentiation orientations. Companies' market share and turnover are generally used to measure volume or induced cost advantage, whereas product or service range, R&D or marketing budget are used to observe company differentiation.

Best Consulting Practices in Brief

If the consultant has the available information, it is advisable to draw the strategic groups map on the scale of the segment level because the resulting analysis will be more accurate. If this is not possible, the map can also be drawn for the whole market by aggregating the competition of the different market segments.

(continued)

(continued)

This loss of focus can be compensated, on the client company's demand, by a broader analysis of the other competitive forces in the environment (see Porter's competitive forces model): suppliers, clients, substitution products, services or solutions, and new entrants.

The strategic groups map can be exploited first with a descriptive purpose. Identifying the different strategic groups is a way of structuring the competition in a market. More specifically for the client company, this structure allows it to identify its own strategic group and the associated competitors. This descriptive analysis gives a clear view of the client company's competitive space. Indeed, the companies within the same strategic group constitute the client company's direct competitors. It is worthwhile for the client company to highlight its direct competitors as they have made similar strategic choices. It is also worth monitoring these direct competitors closely, checking their evolution over time and regularly benchmarking their performance, strengths and weaknesses, and capabilities and resources.

Second, after examining the client company's own strategic group, it is fruitful to study the other strategic groups. This helps to formulate scenarios on the competition's future developments. Producing such a map of the competition should also serve the consultant as a basis for discussion with the client company: do the strategic groups reflect different strategies from one group to another? Will these strategic groups remain stable over time? Are there zones in the map with strategic groups being significantly more (less) profitable? If so, what are the best practices of the most profitable companies? Do they own specific competences and resources? Will some companies reposition themselves in other strategic groups? Are there any unexploited zones on the map? Could we use these zones to bring out new competitive spaces or "*blue oceans*" in the sense of Kim and Mauborgne? If so, is it worth pioneering in this zone? The answers to these questions can help the consultant and the client company to generate new ideas and recommendations.

From Theory to Practice

Figure 2.9 shows the strategic groups map of the olive oil market in France[6]. The vertical axis corresponds to a volume indicator based on company turnover. The horizontal axis refers to the degree of product differentiation based on average retail prices. Three strategic groups can be highlighted in this map: leader brands, organic, fair trade and specialised brands, and regional and "terroir" brands.

(*continued*)

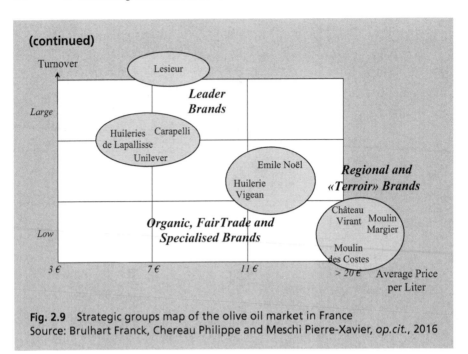

Fig. 2.9 Strategic groups map of the olive oil market in France
Source: Brulhart Franck, Chereau Philippe and Meschi Pierre-Xavier, *op.cit.*, 2016

2.3 Conclusion

The strategic analysis process should result in a series of recommendations for the client company. Indeed, the information, analyses and knowledge produced at each step of this process have not just a descriptive, but above all a prescriptive outcome. Based on the most fine-grained and thorough assessment of the company's environment, the consultant will be able to work with the client company to establish scenarios and strategic choices. Here we arrive at the point where strategic analysis becomes strategic decision-making. Exploiting the strategic analysis to produce scenarios and strategic choices depends on the consultant's analytical perspective. If the consultant adopts a structuralist approach, the resulting scenarios and strategic choices will above all aim to improve the existing situation (in terms of competitive position, market share, product positioning, and response to key success factors…). To do so, the client company will seek to play the rules of the environment better than the competition. On the other hand, if the consultant uses a reconstructionist approach to strategic analysis, the scenarios and strategic choices will tend towards seeking and exploiting "*blue oceans.*" It will then be a matter of modifying the rules of the environment or creating new ones.

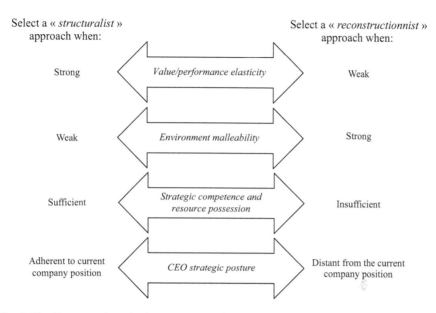

Fig. 2.10 How to select the best approach for the strategic analysis?
Source: Adapted from Kim W. Chan and Mauborgne Renée, *op. cit.*, 2009, and Reeves Martin, Love Claire and Tillmanns Philipp, *op. cit.*, 2012

Figure 2.10 is directly inspired from the research of Kim and Mauborgne (2009). It shows the external (market) and internal (company) conditions that help select either approaches. The consultant can take practical inspiration from this graph to decide on the best orientation to be taken for the strategic analysis process. Two external conditions must be assessed in particular: the first is the elasticity condition, based on the value/performance elasticity test, which is the first step of the strategic analysis process. The second, the malleability condition, was proposed and defined in 2012 by three consultants from the Boston Consulting Group (Martin Reeves, Claire Love and Philipp Tillmanns). For these authors, an environment is malleable if the companies operating it can influence the demand, competitive dynamics and key success factors of this environment. To specify the degree of an environment's malleability, Reeves, Love and Tillmanns recommend assessing *"industry youthfulness, concentration, growth rate, innovation rate, and rate of technology change—all of which increase malleability"*[7] (p. 82). For internal conditions, it is recommended to use the extent to which the client company possesses strategic competences and resources (*i.e.*, allowing it to build a solid competitive position in the environment in question) and the strategic posture of CEO and top managers (*i.e.*, their frame of reference).

Notes

1. These new platform environments are distinguished from traditional environments known as *"pipelines"* (or *"pipeline environments"*). These are organised into vertical supply chains including procurement, production and distribution of products and services. Their overall value is ensured by barriers that protect the different existing players (competitors, clients, suppliers and service providers) against potential new entrants. Van Alstyne Marshall W., Parker Geoffrey G. and Choudary Krishna, "Pipelines, Platforms, and the New Rules of Strategy", *Harvard Business Review*, vol. 94, no 4, 2016, p. 54–62.
2. Kim W. Chan and Mauborgne Renée, "How Strategy Shapes Structure", *Harvard Business Review*, vol. 87, no 9, 2009, p. 73–80.
3. There are about 76000 Harvard Business School alumni who are alive (of whom 33% work outside the U.S.), the largest business school alumni network in the world. McDonald Duff, *The Golden Passport: Harvard Business School, the Limits of Capitalism, and the Moral Failure of the MBA Elite*, HarperCollins Publishers, New York, 2017.
4. The information illustrating the different steps of strategic segmentation, key success factors and competitive systems are taken from the case study *Michelin in the Land of the Maharajahs (A): Note on the Tire Industry in India*, Ivey Publishing, Ivey Business School, 9B07M030. This case study was written and published by Ameya Chitnis and Pierre-Xavier Meschi in 2007 (updated in 2014).
5. Bingham Christopher B., Eisenhardt Kathleen M. and Furr Nathan R., "Which Strategy When?", *MIT Sloan Management Review*, vol. 53, no 1, 2011, p. 70–78.
6. The information used to illustrate the strategic groups step comes from the case study *A Terroir Olive Oil Mill Against Agri-Food Multinationals*, Ivey Publishing, Ivey Business School, 9B16M030. This case study was written and published by Franck Brulhart, Philippe Chereau and Pierre-Xavier Meschi in 2016.
7. Reeves Martin, Love Claire and Tillmanns Philipp, "Your Strategy Needs a Strategy", *Harvard Business Review*, vol. 90, no 9, 2012, p. 76–82.

Further Reading

On the Distinction Between *"Platform"* and *"Pipeline"* and Its Implications for Strategic Analysis

Van Alstyne Marshall W., Parker Geoffrey G. and Choudary Krishna, "Pipelines, Platforms, and the New Rules of Strategy", *Harvard Business Review*, vol. 94, no 4, 2016, p. 54–62.

Ryall Michael D., "The New Dynamics of Competition", *Harvard Business Review*, vol. 91, no 6, 2013, p. 80–87.

On the SCP Paradigm or the *"Structuralist Approach"* to Strategic Analysis

Bain Joe S., *Industrial Organization*, John Wiley & Sons, New York, 1959.

Scherer Frederic M., *Industrial Market Structure and Economic Performance*, Rand McNally & Co., Chicago, 1970.

On the *"Reconstructionist Approach"* to Strategic Analysis

Kim W. Chan and Mauborgne Renée, "How Strategy Shapes Structure", *Harvard Business Review*, vol. 87, no 9, 2009, p. 73–80.

On Strategic Analysis

Bingham Christopher B., Eisenhardt Kathleen M. and Furr Nathan R., "Which Strategy When?", *MIT Sloan Management Review*, vol. 53, no 1, 2011, p. 70–78.

Porter Michael E., *Competitive Strategy: Techniques for Analyzing Industries and Competitors*, Free Press, New York, 1980.

On the PIMS, Its Origin, Its Database, Results and Current Developments

Buzzell Robert D. and Gale Bradley T., *The PIMS Principles: Linking Strategy to Performance*, Free Press, New York, 1987.

The following website can also be consulted: http://pimsonline.com.

On the Process of Strategic Segmentation

Abell Derek F., *Managing with Dual Strategies*, Free Press, New York, 1993.

On Identifying Key Success Factors and Value Functions

Almquist Eric, Senior John and Bloch Nicolas, "The Elements of Value", *Harvard Business Review*, vol. 94, no 9, 2016, p. 47–53.

On Using Strategic Groups to Create New Competitive Spaces and *"Blue Oceans"*

Kim W. Chan and Mauborgne Renée, "Creating New Market Space", *Harvard Business Review*, vol. 77, no 1, 1999, p. 83–93.

3

Defining Strategic Positioning

3.1 The Mission

Defining a company's strategic positioning as part of a consulting mission usually means establishing its positioning with regard to the competition. This means defining its strengths and weaknesses compared to competitors in the same strategic group, for each of its strategic segments in terms of their value (or attractiveness). This process should provide the company with factual information as to the intrinsic value of each of its strategic business units (SBUs)—sometimes called product/market domains—and suggest development choices relative to this value.

Understanding the company's environment and thereby assessing its value is key for building a company strategy. This external/internal approach to competitive advantage, embodied by Michael E. Porter, was long-favoured by strategy researchers and consultants; however, its limitations are evident in highly competitive contexts where numerous external influences are likely to weigh heavily on the company's adaptive capabilities. According to Rita Gunther McGrath[1] this hypercompetitive situation renders competitive advantage *"transient"* so the company needs to possess a portfolio of ever-renewing advantages to pass from one position to another more quickly than the competition. Learning to do this depends on two prerequisites: first, the company needs, more than ever, to pursue a long-term vision, for it has to decide on its competitive space and how it intends to pass from one competitive advantage to another; second, it requires the capability to possess and develop company-specific resources and competences—true strategic capabilities—likely to generate, exploit and renew this portfolio of transient advantages.

© The Author(s) 2018
P. Chereau, P.-X. Meschi, *Strategic Consulting*, DOI 10.1007/978-3-319-64422-6_3

This view of strategy moves the company towards a strategic intent, completing the value assessment of the competitive environment and opening up a range of possible positionings; it thus combines the external/internal approach with an internal/external approach to competitive advantage.

In fact, evaluating the environment to identify strategic segments, (*i.e.*, those likely to enhance the value of the company's product portfolio), and identifying its strategic groups, leads the company to choose from three different strategic models of value creation: overall cost leadership, differentiation and focus.

These generic strategy models are built around notions of congruence, alignment or fit between the company's strategic choices and the resources, structure and organisational processes that make these choices feasible.

Generic strategies are thus configurations of the company; they comprise characteristic postures of strategic groups based on the idea of a double fit of strategic choices: an external fit between the environment and the strategy and an internal fit between the strategy and the company's strategic capabilities.

The notion of fit is central to working out the company's strategic positioning. Indeed, generic strategies are mutually exclusive. This means, for example, that strategic positioning choice A cannot be implemented with organisational configuration B. Similarly, organisational configuration A would not allow the company to influence its environment effectively if strategic positioning B is chosen. Choosing the wrong alignment is a frequent cause of company failure and raises the vital matter of how to formulate a strategy and subsequently, how to actually implement it. This brings up several important questions:

- Do the CEO and top managers have detailed knowledge of the "winning" alignments of strategic positioning and organisational configuration?
- If so, do the company's strategic capabilities really draw maximum benefit from the competitive environment or could they even modify this?
- Given the chosen configuration—the strategic posture—and the company's strategic capabilities, what are the options for company development?

From these questions arise various consulting missions that focus on analysing the company's internal strengths and weaknesses, assets and constraints. This analysis completes the environment analysis described in Chap. 2. For example, in a first type of mission, the consultant tries to assess the level of fit or deviance from fit between the CEO and top managers' strategic choices and the appropriate company configuration, with reference to the targeted generic strategy.

More traditionally, the consultant tries to assess the company's competences and resources and their relevance for managing the key success factors of the targeted market segments. This will show the company's ability to develop or maintain a competitive advantage based specifically on these strategic capabilities. In this type of mission, the company's CEO and top managers need to answer the following key questions:

What capacities does my company have in terms of resources, competences and know-how that will allow me to develop on my chosen markets? Are these capabilities advantages vis-a-vis my competitors?

In another type of mission known as strategic positioning, consultants first highlight the intrinsic value (*i.e.*, the attractiveness) of chosen market segments and second, the company's capability (*i.e.*, its assets) to manage the key success factors of these segments better than its competitors. From the correlation between these two, the consultant can suggest different go/no go options for development, thus responding to the following key questions:

What are the different development options given the current and future market segments and the company's assets on each of these? How far will these options allow us to implement the chosen generic strategy?

Finally, the consultant can complete the strategic diagnostic by formulating diagnosed options for development. This means imagining scenarios, assessing their feasibility and formalising tools to plan and evaluate/monitor the strategy. In this process, undertaken jointly with the company's management, the consultant must base recommendations on the prospective analysis of the strategic segments and a thorough examination of the company's strategic capabilities to respond to the following essential questions:

What are the possible development choices given the company's resources and competences? Which are the most worth considering? How should we go about actually implementing them?

3.2   Theory, Methodology and the Tools for the Mission

3.2.1   The Theoretical Background

3.2.1.1   Strategic Positioning: A Key Stage in Strategic Planning

Most strategic management consulting missions are rooted in a global process of company strategic planning. H. Igor Ansoff,[2] professor of management at Carnegie Mellon University, in his work *Corporate Strategy*, published in 1965, defined strategic planning as a logical, continuous process over a number of sequential steps that allow the company to reach its objectives. These steps are: defining the company's mission and long-term objectives, analysing the environment, formulating and evaluating various possible strategies, implementing these and finally, assessing the results. Strategic planning, thus described as a rational undertaking, supposes three dimensions frequently mentioned in the literature and considered as integral parts of the deliverables of a strategic management mission: Formalisation, exhaustiveness and strategic control/assessment.

- *Formalisation* supposes that the strategic planning process is organised by rules (methods) procedures (tools) and written records.
- *Exhaustiveness* implies that the company disposes of all the information relative to its environment and that all aspects of its internal organisation are taken into account when formulating the strategy.
- *Strategic control* defines measurement criteria regarding the performance expected from the chosen strategy; it also monitors the development and effective deployment of that strategy.

After long being considered the basis of strategic management, strategic planning has now been called into question. Its detractors accuse it of emphasising the expansion of existing activities to the detriment of exploiting new opportunities; they accuse it of being built on the postulate of a stable environment, of fossilising strategic thinking by turning it into a process of administrative control and finally, of measuring the efficiency of company activity solely by the "truth in numbers." In this line, Henry Mintzberg and Joseph Lampel[3] separate strategy formulation and planning from its actual implementation. They postulate that rather than being designed, strategies emerge and change in a process of adaptive strategic management, influenced by environmental changes and how the company uses its resources to reconfigure itself as a result of these (see Fig. 3.1).

However, recent studies have shown that even in a changing environment, in a context of uncertainty, strategic planning increases companies' financial and non-financial performance because it triggers a systematic process of collecting relevant information to maintain the alignment of the company with its environment. Consequently, far from fossilising the strategy, strategic planning keeps the ball of strategic thinking rolling in an iterative process that is in fact, adaptive.

The analysis of the company's strategic positioning is the keystone of the strategic planning process. Strategic positioning has to do with the impact of the company's competitive environment, of its intrinsic capabilities, of its vision and mission on the company's strategy. By completing the diagnostic of the environment with an internal diagnostic, strategic positioning identifies the company's assets and constraints that will in turn determine the range of development options for reaching its strategic objectives.

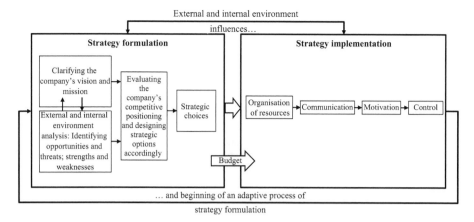

Fig. 3.1 The strategic management process
Source: Adapted from Nasi Juha and Aunola Manu 2003

3.2.1.2   Strategic Capabilities

The internal analysis of the company gradually developed alongside theories proposing that competitive advantage should be based on each company's own competences and resources. From this viewpoint, rather than analysing the company's boundary in terms of the fit of its offer to its competitive environment, in other words in terms of its product/market domains, strategic analysis consists of determining the competitive potential of the competences and resources that the company possesses or controls that led to formulating its strategy. Robert M. Grant,[4] professor of management at Georgetown University, suggests five stages for this strategic formulation focused on resources (see Fig. 3.2).

Resource-based theory (RBT) and knowledge-based theory (KBT) take up ideas that have been seen before, developed notably by Edith Penrose[5] and Birger Wernerfelt.[6] These authors demonstrate the capacity to create competitive advantage based on efficiency and capture of opportunities grounded in company's experience of how to use its resources.

Following the analysis of Wernerfelt, Jay Barney,[7] professor of strategy at Fisher College, Ohio State University, described a company's resources as the combination of tangible and intangible assets (employees, equipment, installations, capital, processes, information, patents, reputation, etc.) that, when well-exploited, contribute to designing and implementing strategies that increase the company's effectiveness and efficiency. This being so, the most important source of competitive advantage are the resources and the strategy that promotes the value of these assets.

However, this only makes sense if competing companies cannot dispose of the same resources. In fact, according to Barney, generating competitive

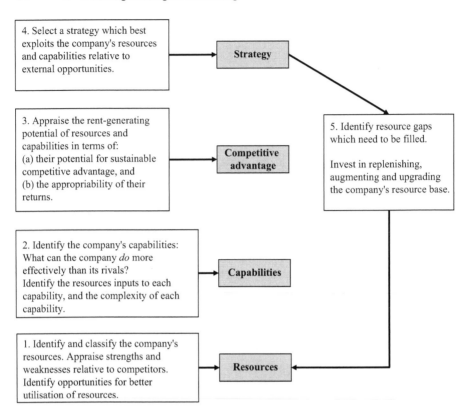

Fig. 3.2 Strategic formulation centred on resources
Source: Adapted from Grant Robert M., *op. cit.*, 1991

advantage relies on companies' implementing a value-creating strategy that is hard for competitors to imitate. Taking as a principle that no company can develop such a strategy in an industry characterised by resources that are perfectly homogenous and transferable among companies, Barney considers that to generate a real competitive advantage, a company's resources must be heterogenous and not transferable from one company to another. On the basis of Barney's model, we can identify five conditions for resources to generate lasting competitive advantage. These are combined in the acronym VRIST: value-creating, rare, inimitable, non-substitutable and non-transferable.

Value For a resource or a competence to create value it must contribute to generating a product or service that clients judge superior, thus resulting in higher profitability than that of competitors. The resource can contribute to value through:

- greater product sales than competitors from the same capital base;
- or higher margin sales than competitors.

Rare   If the resource or competence is easily accessible and widely shared by market actors, it can no longer be the basis of a distinctive strategic capability. On the other hand, if the resource is rare, the company can generate higher margins or sales volumes for the same cost base as the competition. To judge the rareness of a resource, a benchmark analysis can be carried out on a group of competing companies belonging to the same strategic group (see Sect. 3.2.2).

These first two criteria make it possible to evaluate the company's strategic capabilities at time *t*. The other criteria examined below are related more to durability and the lasting quality of the advantage generated.

Inimitable   If the competition does not possess resources and competences that are value-creating and rare, they may seek to imitate, reproduce or even improve (via creative imitation) the company's strategic capability. This capability will thus not offer a true competitive advantage unless the company's competences and resources are hard to imitate. Analysing this inimitability means seeking out the features of the capability in question and understanding how it emerged. Ingemar Dierickx and Karel Cool,[8] professors of strategy at INSEAD, identified three determinants that condition companies' inimitability:

- *"Historical determinants"*: If, over the years, the company has developed a unique experience in its market (as for example in the perfume and aroma industry, luxury, clinical development or specialised training), any competitor tempted by imitation has to fill the capability gap in such a short time that its competitiveness will suffer and the attempt is likely to fail.
- *"Causal ambiguity"*: If it is hard to identify the source of competitive advantage, it will be very difficult, time consuming and hypothetical for competitors and even for the company's collaborators and partners, to discover the factors (*i.e.*, the resources and competences) likely to generate that advantage and to find suitable means to replicate them.
- *"Social complexity"*: The company may have developed specific relationships with its clients, suppliers and advisors. It may have built up a specific image and reputation. It might have set up or encouraged the emergence of hard-to-copy organisational habits. This intangible combination of resources and know-how will give rise to an organisational capability that is complex and hard for competitors to imitate. This same complexity often causes difficulties when integrating new competences and resources during mergers and acquisitions

Non-substitutable This implies that the company's value-creating strategy cannot be countered by a substitute that would be easy for competitors to access and be at least as effective. Substitution is often sought in the field of technological innovations, and it is increasingly found in innovative marketing practices or new business models.

Non-transferable A resource or competence is transferable if it can be sold or acquired in the market. Equipment, material and patents are generally easily transferable. Consulting methodologies, business practices and personnel can easily be acquired. However, the capabilities related to organisational routines and the company's specific internal context are far harder to transfer. The non-transferable nature of strategic capabilities is essential in evaluating the lasting nature of the company's competitive advantage. Indeed, non-transferability generates the durable capture of this advantage, for the capabilities in question produce maximum value if, and only if, they are exploited by the company itself.

This approach to competitive advantage—based on resources—gives us a new perspective on the company's profitability and survival that completes the external/internal approach to environmental value. The internal/external approach defines competitive advantage as a company's aptitude to exploit its strategic resources (*i.e.*, its strategic capabilities) better than any competitor.

Best Consulting Practices in Brief

According to the approach above, the consultant should attempt to identify the company's set of strategic capabilities by distinguishing the "threshold" competences and resources (those needed to enter and expand in the target market on the same footing as competitors), from "distinctive" resources and competences (those that may create a specific value proposition, identified as such on the market and hard for competitors to imitate). In fact, threshold resources and competences refer to those that are able to master the market's key success factors, but that make no truly distinctive contribution compared to competitors. Distinctive strategic capabilities refer to competences and resources that the company possesses and its unique way of combining them to develop its activities. To distinguish between threshold and distinctive resources and competences, the consultant must first evaluate the company's environment as described in Chap. 2. A frequent mistake is to determine the company's strengths and weaknesses *a priori* without first considering its environmental context.

3.2.1.3   Strategic Intent

The resource-based approach to competitive advantage developed during the 1980s and 1990s results in a refined analysis of the company's strategic capabilities on which it can build up profitability and growth. Nevertheless, formulating strategy involves considering the fit of these resources to the environment, as suggested by Grant and shown in Fig. 3.2. Although during the 1980s the company was not yet prepared to modify and purposefully transform the environment to its advantage, this process was accelerated by the change in competitive intensity that occurred at the beginning of the 1990s.

This hypercompetitive context emerged towards the end of the 1980s. At that time, certain companies, well established in their market and with a perfect understanding and quasi-perfect mastery of their environment, saw their position challenged by new entrants who wanted to take advantage of these high value markets. In this context, the well-established companies defended their dominant position, obliging the new pretenders to innovate, thus modifying the rules of the game. This was followed by a permanent dynamic of evolution and transformation of competitors and markets that resulted in a particularly unstable environment. From then on, any competitive advantage was bound to deteriorate and be supplanted by a new value proposition from the competition. From 1989, Gary Hamel, founder of the consulting firm Strategos and professor of strategy at the London Business School and C.K. Prahalad, professor of strategy at the University of Michigan, called the (very) principle of a lasting strategic positioning into question. In various publications,[9] these authors highlight the notion of strategic intent that puts the company at the centre of strategy formulation and aims to transform the environment to create new competitive spaces.

Strategic intent rests on two prerequisites: one is to define a vision for a long-term, ambitious, inspiring mission; the second is to anchor the pursuit of this strategy firmly in the company's own central idiosyncratic competences. Defining the vision/mission in the sense of Hamel and Prahalad is one of the essential elements in drawing up strategy. This definition constitutes the main element in the reference framework phase of a strategic consulting mission. Indeed, it is at this stage that the company's CEO and top managers draw together the objectives of the company's competitive strategy as well as those of its development strategy (also known as growth strategy; see Chap. 4). Competences are described as central since they constitute the only stable basis on which to anchor the company's vision and mission and construct and deploy the strategy in an ever-changing competitive environment.

To this notion of central competences must be added the notion of capability and organisational learning needed to implement the strategic intent. The possession of unique strategic capabilities is not enough; it is also necessary to allow these to emerge, grow and above all be organised to reach the strategic objectives. Here it is a matter of organisational fit between the company's choices of strategic positioning and the organisational configuration supporting those choices.

3.2.1.4 Strategic Configurations

This requirement of double fit—external fit between the strategy and the company's environment and internal fit between the strategic choices, structure and processes—is an essential determinant of competitive advantage. The proponents of configuration theory – Danny Miller, Peter H. Friesen and Henry Mintzberg[10] as well as Robert Drazin and Andrew H. Van de Ven[11]—hold that for a given strategic positioning, there is an ideal combination of organisational choices—a configuration—that will generate superior performance.

The various streams of configuration theories have classified organisations according to their adopted strategy. The two dominant approaches to competitive strategies—being the most common and widely studied for their theoretical and managerial implications—are that of Raymond E. Miles and Charles C. Snow,[12] respectively, professors at the University of California at Berkeley and Penn State University, described in 1978 in their book *Organizational Strategy, Structure, and Process*, and that of Michael E. Porter,[13] detailed in *Competitive Strategy*, published in 1980.

Miles and Snow have described a systemic and dynamic approach to configurations based on the adaptive cycle of strategic choices that a company must initiate to pursue its intent to change its product/market positioning (see Fig. 3.3). From this internal/external approach to competitive strategy, they identify three viable configurations described as:

- "*Defenders*": Those who seek a stable competitive positioning in a perfectly understood and mastered competitive environment.
- "*Prospectors*": These are permanently on the lookout for new product or market opportunities.
- "*Analysers*": This group combines stability in their strategic business units, with the ability to exploit opportunities "with proven potential" provided by prospectors.

Miles and Snow defined a combination of strategic alignments among specific entrepreneurial, technological and organisational choices for each profile. A fourth category, "*reactors*," does not display consistent strategic choices. Companies adopting this reactor strategy are thus unable to develop a lasting competitive advantage. According to Miles and Snow, this configuration can only be transitional or it will result in company failure.

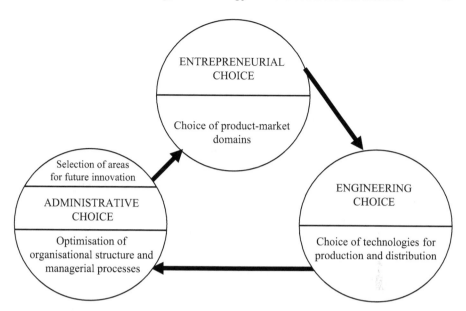

Fig. 3.3   Miles and Snow's adaptive cycle of strategic choices
Source: Miles Raymond E. & Snow Charles C., *op. cit.*, 1978

Porter's typology of configurations relies on an external/internal approach to strategic positioning towards clients and competitors. Porter identifies two generic strategies for overcoming competitors by "managing" market forces (see Chap. 2). He suggests that the company should construct its strategy according to how it creates value for clients in comparison to competitors (either through differentiating the offer or cost leadership) and depending on the envisaged market cover (either all the segments, or in some specific segments: see Fig. 3.4). A differentiation strategy emphasises the creation of a unique offer, recognised as such by the market. Such a positioning creates a feeling of loyalty and attachment on the part of clients and this generates higher margins, offering the company protection from threats and market forces in the form of new entrants, supplier pressure, substitutes or pressure on prices. A cost leadership strategy is based on an economically attractive offer made possible by optimising and mastering processes at all company levels. This quest for efficiency protects the company from market threats by weakening any competitor seeking to rival the company on its own territory: the efforts of such competitors will erode their own profitability and result in the downfall of the least efficient among them.

Although each of these two approaches to generic configurations provides a robust analytical framework for defining a strategy, Porter's generic strategies are the most commonly used in strategic management missions. However, from 1987 on, prefiguring strategic intent, Orville C. Walker and Robert W. Ruekert[14]

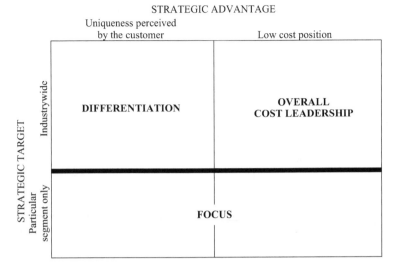

Fig. 3.4 Porter's generic strategies
Source: Porter Michael E., *op. cit.*, 1980

questioned Porter's "static" approach that emphasises the competitive strategies actually implemented by companies within their market context. Walker and Ruekert see this emphasis as an important limit to the pertinence of the guidance and recommendations companies require. A strategy's success depends as much on the right formulation with regard to the company's strategic capabilities and environment as on effective implementation. From this point of view, it is just as important to have a strategic intent that is consistent with the chosen configuration as to work on the "right formulation."

Miles and Snow's configurations alleviate this problem by proposing an analytical framework "in movement"; this focuses on the fit among strategic entrepreneurial orientation, competences, resources and efficient organisation. This framework makes the typology suggested by Miles and Snow particularly appropriate for strategic consulting missions with companies facing the previously described context of hyper-competition.

Nevertheless, Porter's and Miles and Snow's models should not be pitted against one another. In fact, they contribute complementary perspectives and are frequently combined in strategic management missions. For example, Walker and Ruekert present an extension of Miles and Snow's typology featuring companies' characteristics as prospectors, analysers, differentiated defenders and cost leadership defenders. Each perspective, whether centred on the environment or on the firm, provides deciders with tested typologies of differentiated configurations, characterised by their fit between strategic choices and organisational prerequisites (see Sect. 3.2.2).

3.2.1.5 Strategic Options and Piloting the Strategy

The combined evaluation of market value and the company's strategic capabilities derived from the strategic positioning diagnostic results in a portfolio of strategic development options. Peter J. Williamson,[15] professor at Cambridge Judge Business School, insists on the importance of this portfolio of strategic options for the company if it wants to avoid having its choices dictated by the market. Therefore, according to the same logic as strategic intent, he recommends continuous observation of the company's markets, developing new competences and resources to interact with their evolution.

Before setting up strategic options, these need to be assessed in terms of suitability, acceptability and feasibility (SAFe), in other words the following questions must be answered (see Sect. 3.2.2):

- Does the proposed strategy allow the company to make the best of opportunities and be equipped to combat threats from target markets?
- Is the strategy acceptable in terms of change, profitability and risk for the different stakeholders, *i.e.*, the clients, shareholders, company personnel and key actors in the ecosystem?
- Is the strategy feasible in practice, is it fundable, given the competences and resources available or to be acquired?

Once this evaluation has been completed and the strategic option chosen, the company has to prepare its implementation in a formalised and controlled process of strategic planning as described previously. In fact, the effective implementation of the strategy demands the organisation of the strategic capabilities aligned with the chosen strategy—the right strategic configuration; communicating this strategic intent to the company's main stakeholders (employees, shareholders, key partners, clients) to obtain their adhesion and motivation; using of financial and non-financial indicators that translate the deployment of the strategy; and, finally, implementing processes to watch the environment and, if necessary, adapt the strategic planning to changes in this environment.

3.2.2 Methodology and Tools for the Mission

The consultant's main challenge when defining the strategic positioning relevant to the company is to fit together the external environment, competitive strategy and organisational configuration. As mentioned previously, strategic

Best Consulting Practices in Brief

Analysing a company's strategic positioning is one of the most delicate and sensitive processes for a consultant. In fact, it constitutes the first step to elaborating possible options for strategic development and formulating the action plan to implement the strategy. Having identified the company's competences and resources, the consultant has to understand which strategic configurations and alignments to favour among strategic choices and how these capabilities should be used. Miles and Snow's typology will turn out to be particularly relevant because of the checklist it contains. The diagnostic of the strategic positioning provides guidelines for designing the strategic options for development and these should be assessed in the light of the company's strategic capabilities. Once the strategy is decided, the consultant has to suggest the realignments necessary before an effective strategy respecting the strategic planning can be implemented.

positioning refers to a double fit that allows the company to make the most of its strategic capabilities to adapt or even influence its market or markets. The available tools are complementary, whether developed by adepts of the structuralist, also called SCP (Structure-Conduct-Performance) approach (see Chap. 2), or by those in favour of the resource-based theory, and help to evaluate this fit. The question is not so much whether analytical tools exist as

Best Consulting Practices in Brief

Unlike the methodology used to diagnose the external environment, here the consultant should take a systemic approach, comparing and contrasting the analyses.

1. Identify the strategic capabilities that will allow the company to manage the key success factors of target market segments;
2. Undertake a strategic diagnostic of the company's competitive positioning by evaluating the chosen strategic posture for creating value from the company's competences and resources in view of the attractiveness of the targeted market segments;
3. Given the company's strategic capabilities, construct realistic strategic options in this posture, and assess their respective level of feasibility;
4. Include actions to compensate for feasibility gaps in the strategic plan for deploying the chosen option.

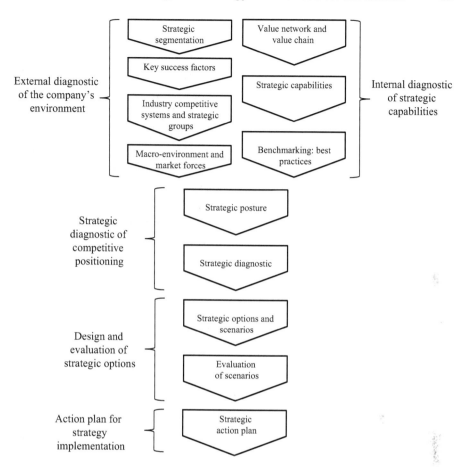

Fig. 3.5 The steps for diagnosing the company's competitive positioning and choice of strategic options
Source: Authors

how to use them appropriately according to a rational methodology that will result in coherence among all the data from the external diagnostic, the company's strategic configuration and its competences and resources. Figure 3.5 describes this methodological approach.

3.2.2.1 The Value Chain and the Value Network

Bringing to light the competences and resources upon which the company can build a competitive advantage is based on the external diagnostic, described in Chap. 2. This diagnostic of the company's environment should show up key success factors of market segments for the company's future development by highlighting the key factors specific to the strategic group to which the company belongs. In a resource-centred approach, the company's competitive advantage will depend on its capacity to better master these key success factors than its competitors by developing distinctive competences and resources. It is important here to clearly identify the internal value chain (*i.e.*, the different categories of the company's activities that finally result in creating a product or service) and the external value chain—the value network (*i.e.*, the fabric of inter-company relationships needed to create that product or service). Indeed, the key success factors of the segment's value network require the company to develop capabilities consistent with the actors both up and downstream. Similarly, it is important for the company to organise its internal activities so that it masters these key success factors as well as possible.

In his book *Competitive Advantage*, published in 1985, Porter[16] proposes a model of the value network and the internal value chain (see Figs. 3.6 and 3.7). The value network sheds light on the various levels of specialisation of actors involved in creating a product or service. As a rule, each actor specialises on the part(s) of the value network where it has a competitive advantage enabling to create a portion of relative value greater than the one other actors could create. The breakdown of the internal value chain shows up first, the primary activities directly linked to producing and launching a product or service on the market and second, the support activities that optimise the efficiency of the above. Porter's notion of value network can be approached from the more systemic angle of value actually captured by the company

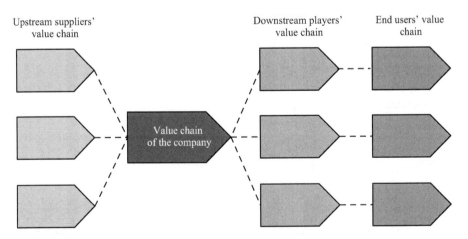

Fig. 3.6 The company's value network
Source: Adapted from Porter Michael E., *op. cit.*, 1985

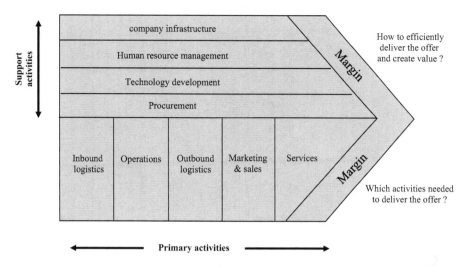

Fig. 3.7 The company's internal value chain
Source: Adapted from Porter Michael E., *op. cit.*, 1985

through its relations with the clients and suppliers of its existing network. It can also be seen from the angle of the value that it would have generated by modifying or enlarging its network to encompass other actors. In his article *The New Dynamics of Competition*, Michael D. Ryall[17] borrows from game theory to propose a new model of value capture. In this model, competition within an industry is expressed as a tension between the value generated by transactions that the company engages with certain actors (suppliers and clients) of its value network and the value that it could have generated by engaging these transactions with other actors outside its network. The company thus has an interest in proposing an offer that will also allow those actors to capture the potential value that exists outside the value network. Thus, when Apple, with its iTunes application, gave musical content suppliers access to its pre-existing client network, it increased its capability to capture value (its negotiating power) *vis a vis* these same suppliers. Furthermore, the density of the offer thus created was to attract new users that had until then been outside Apple's value network, enabling the company to generate a virtuous circle of value capture. In this perspective, capturing value makes it necessary to think in terms of complementarity of interest rather than in terms of bilateral transactions. This "ecosystem" view of the value network can be likened to the platform business model (see Sect. 7.2.1). Figure 3.8 illustrates this model of value capture.

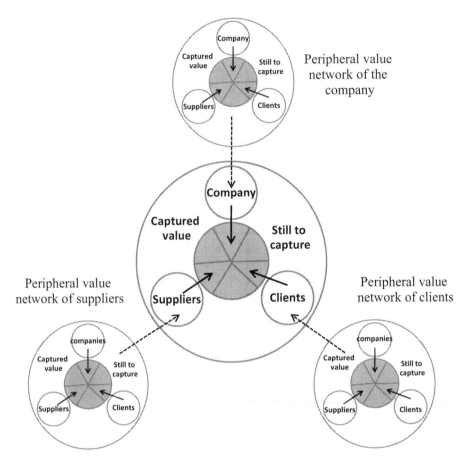

Fig. 3.8 The value capture model
Source: Adapted from Ryall Michael D., *op. cit.*, 2013

From Theory to Practice

Hightense (the fictitious name given to an existing company) is an SME active in the energy maintenance and management sector. Its main clients are industrial companies that consume a lot of electrical energy for their manufacturing processes. These include large chemical groups that use electrolysis processes, groups from the steel industry or major actors in the glass industry. The deregulation of the price of electricity in most European countries pushed these actors into not only a better position for negotiating the cost per kilowatt hour (kWh), but it also encouraged them to maximise their energy efficiency by paying particular

(continued)

(continued)

Upstream suppliers' value chain   Downstream players' value chain   End users' value chain

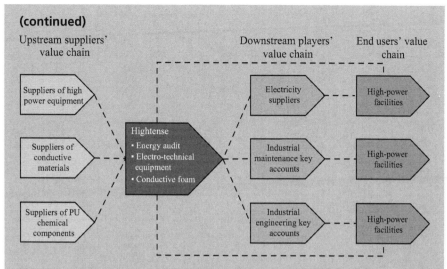

Fig. 3.9 Hightense's value network of energy maintenance

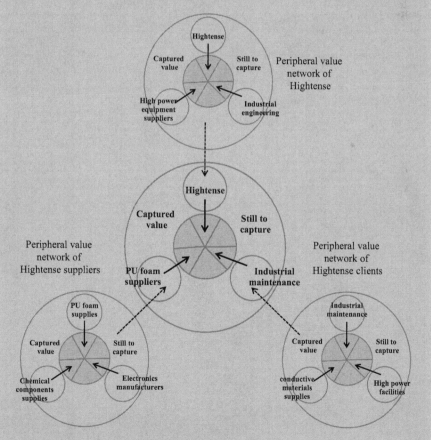

Fig. 3.10 Hightense's model of value capture
Source: Adapted from Ryall Michael D., *op. cit.*, 2013

(continued)

attention to energy losses in their industrial processes. It was precisely this need that Hightense decided to respond to by proposing a set of solutions for energy management, ranging from an energy audit to designing made-to-measure equipment, but also the production and installation of "physico-chemical" conductive devices to combat loss of electricity with interconnections. Given the processes of referencing implemented by its targeted clients, Hightense decided on a specific positioning within the value network of energy maintenance. This was based on securing the upstream sourcing of the constituents of the offer (materials, semi-finished products) as well as accessing major actors of the sector either directly or by prescription. Figure 3.9 positions the various actors from the viewpoint of Hightense's offer. Figure 3.10 illustrates Hightense's model of value capture. In this model, having patented a conductive polyurethane (PU) foam, Hightense allows its clients in industrial maintenance who buy this technology to enhance their offer to electricity producers. Hightense thus increases its negotiating power. Similarly, thanks to Hightense, suppliers of PU foam find outlets with manufacturers of electronics given the properties of this technology. Furthermore, Hightense's patent consolidates the company's negotiating power with its clients in electro-technical engineering, which in turn lends credibility to its offer to clients in industrial maintenance and its negotiating capabilities towards its PU suppliers. This creates a virtuous circle.

Figure 3.11 completes this ecosystem and describes the internal value chain of the activities required for positioning Hightense in its value network.

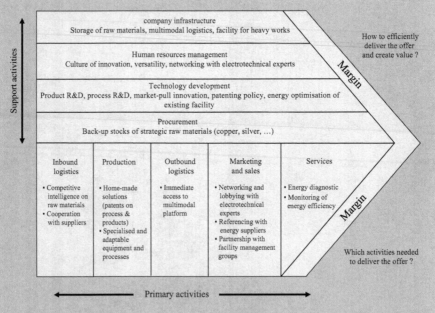

Fig. 3.11 The value chain of Hightense activities
Source: Adapted from Porter Michael E., *op. cit.*, 1985

3.2.2.2 Strategic Capabilities

The analysis of strategic capabilities consists of, first, identifying the indispensable competences and resources of any firm wishing to develop in one or several market segments of its choice. In this process, the accent should be on the company's competences and resources that will allow it to engage in activities on its specific value chain. As mentioned above, these strategic capabilities are identified as being the competences and resources the company develops in order to master the key success factors in its strategic segments. The company's prior positioning in its value network makes it possible to define the field of this analysis, while highlighting the determinants of the competitive advantage the company can generate within this network. Strategic capabilities are characterised on two levels:

- "Threshold capabilities" that any company of the same strategic group must possess to be able to enter the target market and exercise its activities.
- "Distinctive capabilities," specific to the company; these allow it to develop a more or less differentiating competitive advantage depending on their level of VRIST (value creation, rarity, inimitability, substitutability and transferability; see Table 3.1

3.2.2.3 Benchmarking

The evaluation of the soundness of the VRIST level of the company's strategic capabilities must be undertaken in tandem with a comparative analysis of the strategic capabilities of the company's competitors. The quality of this benchmark depends on the competitor companies chosen for analysis. There are two methodological approaches to benchmarking. The first aims to compare companies within a same industry or market segment. The detractors of this

Table 3.1 Levels of strategic capabilities

Strategic capabilities (Resources + competences)	Resources The assets that the company possesses or can call upon	Competences Ability to use and mobilise resources effectively
Threshold capabilities Required to be able to operate and compete in the market	Threshold resources Tangible assets Intangible assets	Threshold competences Required know-how to operate in the market
Distinctive capabilities Sources of competitive advantage (VRIST)	Distinctive resources Tangible assets Intangible assets	Distinctive competences Differentiating know-how

Source: Authors

approach argue that if the industry is not performing well overall, the comparative analysis will not really show up good practices. However, we believe that even in ailing sectors there are many particularly innovative companies that perform well. The theory of competitive advantage based on mastering market forces supports this counter-argument (see Chap. 2). Here again, the pragmatism of business reality prevails. The second approach consists of identifying the "best-in-class" of the activity in question. Thus, the best practices of a franchise in organic products may be inspired by those of a network of optical or cosmetic franchises. However, according to this same reality principle, it is important to look at the benchmark of the "best-in-class" while calibrating the company with competitors in a strategic group whose characteristics remain close to those of the company in question. In fact, according to the theory of strategic groups, these companies have in common their choice of identical strategic posture. The aim of identifying best practices, which can be presumed by looking at companies' economic performance, is to shed light on the organisational dimensions of the "ideal" strategic configuration for growth within a particular strategic group, and consequently to highlight not only competing firms' threshold competences, but also their distinctive competences and resources. In strategic consulting, it is particularly important to set the firm in its context because the postulate "all other things being equal" rarely holds true. To be useful and easy to exploit, benchmarking is thus, above all, a process of comparative analysis of the strategic capabilities and key activities deployed by companies with similar strategies in similar contexts.

From Theory to Practice

Hightense is in the value network of energy maintenance. This requires an internal value chain based on strategic capabilities to manage specific key success factors fulfilling the requirements of downstream actors. The following key success factors for these requirements have been identified according to the relevant actors: technical expertise in high voltage (prescriber + final client), guarantee of results (prescriber + final client), managing proposed technical solutions (final client).

A benchmark of the company's main competitors within the same strategic group positions Hightense in view of its threshold and distinctive capabilities. This comparative analysis shows that the strategic capabilities Hightense acquired to constitute and launch its offer result in its favourable positioning for developing a competitive advantage. Table 3.2 summarises these sources of competitive advantage. In this example, the benchmark shows clearly that Hightense manages most of the key success factors of energy maintenance better than its main competitors. The company's competitive advantage, however, lies essentially in the distinctive capabilities it has developed concerning the guaranteed results demanded by electro-intensive clients and its approach to optimising existing energy, a value proposition that is particularly welcome in a context of decreasing investments. Hightense's economic performance expressed through its ROI ratio translates this positioning that is based more on a strategic orientation of differentiation than on volume (see Chap. 4).

Table 3.2 Benchmark analysis of Hightense

Benchmark of strategic capabilities within the company's strategic group		FIRM			Competitor 1			Competitor 2			Competitor 3		
Key success factors	Threshold capabilities to manage KSF	Level of threshold capabilities (1–5)	Distinctive resources and competences	VRIST level (1–5)	Level of threshold capabilities (1–5)	Distinctive resources and competences	VRIST level (1–5)	Level of threshold capabilities (1–5)	Distinctive resources & competences	VRIST level (1–5)	Level of threshold capabilities (1–5)	Distinctive resources & competences	VRIST level (1–5)
Technical expertise in high-voltage electricity	Multi-sectors experts	5	Network of independent specialised experts	4	5	Internal staff of energy specialists	2	5	Internal staff of energy specialists and internal training unit	5	5	Network of independent specialised experts	4
	Product and process R&D in energy-saving	5	10% of revenues dedicated to R&D. Incentives for patenting	4	4	<5% of revenues dedicated to R&D. No intensive IP policy	2	5	8% of revenues dedicated to R&D. Incentives for patenting	4	5	10% of revenues dedicated to R&D. Incentives for patenting	4
	Prototyping laboratory for real conditions tests	5	Laboratory for long-term tests under industrial conditions	3	5	Test bench for prototyping	1	5	Test bench for prototyping	1	5	Laboratory for long-term tests under industrial conditions	3
	specialised industrial tools	5	Factory-like industrial tools	3	5	Factory-like industrial tools	3	5	Factory-like industrial tools	3	5	Factory-like industrial tools	3
	Mean of KSF 1	5.0	3.5		4.8	2.0		5.0	3.3		5.0	3.5	
Obligation of results on energy savings	Certified methodology for energy audit	1	Home-made methodology	2	5	Compliance with energy audit specifications	1	5	Compliance with energy audit specifications	1	5	Compliance with energy audit specifications	1
	Monitoring of energy performance	4	Full-web solution for telemonitoring of energy consumption	3	2	Regular energy audits	1	2	Regular energy audits	1	2	Regular energy audits	1
	Reactivity of maintenance and problem solving	4	Network of independent specialised experts	4	3	Based on internal staff workload	1	3	Based on internal staff workload	1	4	Network of independent specialised experts	4
	Revenue model based on energy savings	5	Invoicing based on % of energy savings	4	2	Invoicing based on audit days and cost of equipment	1	2	Invoicing based on audit days and cost of equipment	1	2	Invoicing based on audit days and cost of equipment	1

Table 3.2 (continued)

Benchmark of strategic capabilities within the company's strategic group		FIRM			Competitor 1			Competitor 2			Competitor 3		
Key success factors	Threshold capabilities to manage KSF	Level of threshold capabilities (1–5)	Distinctive capabilities — Distinctive resources and competences	VRIST level (1–5)	Level of threshold capabilities (1–5)	Distinctive capabilities — Distinctive resources and competences	VRIST level (1–5)	Level of threshold capabilities (1–5)	Distinctive capabilities — Distinctive resources and competences	VRIST level (1–5)	Level of threshold capabilities (1–5)	Distinctive capabilities — Distinctive resources & competences	VRIST level (1–5)
Mean of KSF 2		**3.5**	**(3.3)**		**3.0**	**1.0**		**3.0**	**1.0**		**3.3**	**1.8**	
Possibility for the client to take control of the solution	Customised solutions	5	optimisation of existing infrastructure as opposed to replacement of equipment	5	2	Replacement of failing devices and equipments	1	2	Replacement of failing devices and equipments	1	2	Replacement of failing devices and equipments	1
	Easy and safe maintenance	5	Limited production interruptions during maintenance. Sustaining solution (patented).	5	3	Regular maintenance operations and production interruptions	1	3	Regular maintenance operations and production interruptions	1	3	Regular maintenance operations and production interruptions	1
	Monitoring of energy performance	5	Shared telemonitoring web platform	3	4	Regular energy audits	1	4	Regular energy audits	1	4	Regular energy audits	1
	Quality certification on energy performance	5	ISO 14001 certification	2	5	ISO 14001 certification	2	5	ISO 14001 certification	2	5	ISO 14001 certification	2
Mean of KSF 3		**5.0**	**(3.8)**		**3.5**	**1.3**		**3.5**	**1.3**		**3.5**	**1.3**	
Relative positioning on strategic capabilities + source of competitive advantage		**(4.5)**	**(3.5)**		**3.8**	**1.4**		**3.8**	**1.8**		**3.9**	**2.2**	
Benchmark of economic performance (ROI)		22%			16%			19%			20%		

Best Consulting Practices in Brief

By analysing the strategic capabilities followed by a benchmark, the consultant is often able to highlight new key success factors stemming from particularly differentiating capabilities developed by the company. It is essential to identify such new key success factors if the company has chosen a "blue ocean" type of strategic posture (see Chap. 2) based on capturing and getting value from new product or market opportunities. This is done by identifying the soundness of the VRIST level of the strategic capabilities and the competitive advantage thus generated to construct entry barriers to actual or potential competition. Figure 3.12 summarises this process and the steps that the consultant has to undertake with his client.

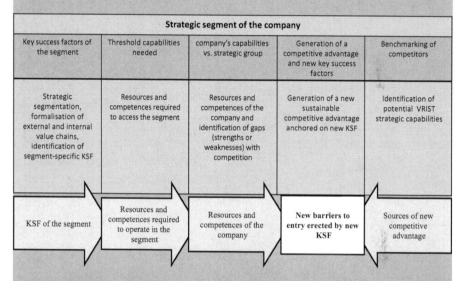

Fig. 3.12   Key success factors, strategic capabilities and competitive advantage
Source: Authors

3.2.2.4   Generic Models of Competitive Strategy

As previously mentioned, the most commonly used generic strategies for analysing or formulating a strategy of competitive positioning are the typologies of Porter and Miles and Snow (see Sect. 3.2.1). Porter's typology associates the type of strategic advantage chosen by the company (perceived uniqueness or low costs) and the scope of the target market (the whole market or certain segments). Miles and Snow propose a typology based on the differences of entrepreneurial intent as to the nature of the product/market domain chosen by the company (stable or dynamic, broad or narrow), and the organisational and technological adaptations related to each intent. Each typology (Porter or Miles and Snow) can be characterised according to the competences and resources necessary and the associated organisational prerequisites. We thus have a true "profiling" of a specific posture for each generic strategy; this provides a useful complement to the analysis of the company's capabilities because it replaces them in the context of the strategic choices. In fact, aligning the strategic choice of competitive positioning, strategic capabilities and associated organisation is a central element of generic strategies. It is a condition of the company's aptitude to use its resources effectively to generate a competitive advantage and construct performance. Tables 3.3 and 3.4 list these alignments by strategic posture for each typology.

Best Consulting Practices in Brief

The difficulty in analysing the company's competitive positioning lies in the consultant's ability to separate the analysis of the strategic choices in terms of their pertinence from that of the effective implementation of those choices. Often the consultant remains short sighted when faced by the company's performance, which he interprets as the sign of a good or bad strategy. The expert consultant, well-aware of the necessity of strategic fit, will take care to check the prerequisite alignments of the company's chosen strategic posture before any questioning of its competitive positioning.

3.2.2.5   Strategic Diagnostic

The diagnostic of the company's strategic positioning can now be carried out on the basis of the analysis of a company's external environment (see Chap. 2) and the internal analysis of the elements of its strategic posture. Now we need to evaluate the attractiveness of the targeted strategic segments through their specific characteristics and the company's capability to establish an advantageous competitive positioning of these segments by mastering the corresponding key success factors. There are many tools to establish this double positioning. Among the best known is the ADL matrix (Arthur D. Little), which takes looks at the degree of maturity of the company's business units (beginning, growth, maturity, decline), characterising them by needs for financing and industry risks (the influences of market forces). As shown in Fig. 3.13, the ADL matrix proposes a static portrait of the strategic business units. This means it is used less and less in missions of strategic consulting for companies that are more inclined to seek go/no go type aids for decision-making.

Table 3.3 Porter's characteristics of strategic postures

Strategic posture	Commonly required skills and resources	Common organisational requirements	Profit formula
Overall cost leadership	Sustained capital investment and access to capital	Tight cost control	Low cost to capture clients
	Process engineering skills	Frequent, detailed control reports	Scale and scope economies
	Intense supervision of labor	Structured organisation and responsibilities	Externalisation of low added-value activities
	Products designed for ease in manufacture	Incentives based on meeting strict quantitative targets	High frequency of repeat business or occurrence of new clients
	Low-cost distribution system		
Differentiation	Strong marketing abilities	Strong coordination among functions in R&D, product development, and marketing	Clients' loyalty to compensate high cost of clients' capture
	Product engineering		High value of esteem valued by a higher margin
	Creative flair	Subjective measurement and incentives instead of quantitative measures	
	Strong capability in basic research		
	Corporate reputation for quality or technological leadership	Amenities to attract highly skilled labour, scientists, or creative people	
	Long tradition in the industry or unique combination of skills drawn from other businesses		
	Strong cooperation from channels		
Focus	Combination of the above policies directed at the particular strategic target	Combination of the above policies directed at the particular strategic target	Combination of the above policies directed at the particular strategic target

Source: Adapted from Porter Michael E., *op. cit.*, 1998

Table 3.4 The characteristics of Miles and Snow's strategic postures

Strategic posture	Defender	Prospector	Analyser
Product-market strategy	Limited, stable product line on a stable market Cost efficiency through scale economies and process innovation Growth through market penetration	Broad, changing product line on various markets Product innovation and market responsiveness First in to new markets	Stable as well as changing product lines Process adaptation, planned innovation Second in with an improved product
Research and development	Process competences Product improvement	Product design Market research	Process and product adaptation
Production	High volume Low-cost specialised processes	Flexible, adaptive equipment and processes	Project development shifting to low-cost production
Organisational structure	Functional Dominant coalition functions: production and finance	Divisional (management by project) Dominant coalition functions: product R&D and marketing	Mixed project and functional matrix Dominant coalition functions: production, marketing and product development
Control process	Centralised, managed by plan	Decentralised, managed by performance	Stable units managed by plan Projects managed by performance
Planning process	Plan => Act => Evaluate	Evaluate => Act => Plan	Plan => Act => Evaluate Evaluate => Plan => Act

Source: Adapted from Miles Raymond E. and Snow Charles C., *op. cit.*, 1994 and 2003

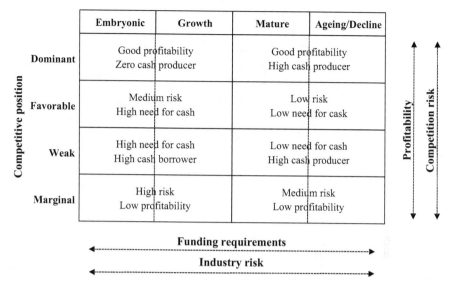

Fig. 3.13 Maturity/competitive position matrix (ADL)
Source: Adapted from Wright, Robert V. L. *A system for managing diversity.*
Arthur D. Little Incorporated, 1974

company's competitive position-Assets

		Strong	Medium	Weak
	High	**Development** Maintain position Invest to grow and create competitive gap Seek market power	**Selective growth** Focused investment Valorise via segmentation	**Selectivity** Test opportunities Seek niches or alliances
Industry attractiveness	**Average**	**Selective development** Maintain competitive advantage on segments with potential for growth	**Selectivity** Refocus on low-risk, profitable segments	**Selective divestiture** Seek niches with low risk or divest
	Low	**Selectivity** Focus on profitable segments Reduce risk	**Selective divestiture** Rationalise activities Divest non-profitable segments	**Divestiture** Minimise losses Stop investments Reduce fixed costs and plan exit

Fig. 3.14 Attractiveness/assets directional policy matrix (McKinsey)
Source: Adapted from McKinsey, Royal Dutch Shell, 1972

The directional policy matrix for strategic decision-making, initially developed by McKinsey and also called the attractiveness/assets matrix, measures the intrinsic attractiveness of each strategic segment depending on macroeconomic contingences gathered under the acronym PESTEL (political, economic, societal, technological, environmental, legal/regulatory), and sectoral contingences characterised by Porter's competitive market forces (see Chap. 2). The directional policy matrix also takes into account the relative attractiveness of each strategic segment by integrating the company's competitive positioning depending on its assets (strengths) and constraints (weaknesses) compared to the competition. As shown in Fig. 3.14, each strategic business unit is thus characterised by the strategic option associated with its segment-specific attractiveness, given the company's strategic capabilities.

From Theory to Practice

Hightense is mainly active on the market of high power energy maintenance and engineering, offering energy auditing and designing made to measure "single parts." Despite an intensive patenting policy, the company has hardly exploited the value created by its strategic capabilities in R&D and has not marketed the patented materials. Similarly, the conductive foam developed by the company to solve energy losses in high power electrical connections is in a recent launch phase, but the interest of accelerating this deployment, even of making it into an independent business unit, remains to be validated. Moreover, the company wishes to diversify its markets towards medium and low power segments that represent a promising growth potential where its strategic capabilities could generate a competitive advantage.

Hightense's entrepreneurial choice of product/market domain suggests a strategic posture of the prospector type. Yet, even if the company has stimulated technological innovation, it is not configured to capture signs of market opportunities or to seize such opportunities. The strategic fit of the prospector posture, as defined in Miles and Snow's typology, is thus not completely guaranteed.

The diagnostic of strategic positioning helps to guide the company in its development options in its various strategic business units (SBUs). The consultant will analyse these domains by appraising the level of attractiveness of SBU1 (high power engineering) and SBU2 (medium and low power engineering) and by positioning the company on the directional policy matrix of strategic decision according to its assets in each SBU. Tables 3.5 and 3.6 give examples of this process for SBU1. Figure 3.15 illustrates the output of the process for both SBU1 and SBU2.

(continued)

(continued)

The result suggests that Hightense should capitalise on its expertise in high power engineering (SBU1). Indeed, this sector is particularly attractive in a context where alternative energies have not yet come up with efficient responses in terms of benefits related to saving energy. The benchmark table supports this analysis by highlighting Hightense's capacity to master the sector's key success factors. Although SBU2 (medium and low power) shows interesting potential, it requires an intense policy of market and business monitoring as well as an organisational configuration that Hightense has not yet managed to implement. To enter this segment, the company must address sector niches that will allow it to capitalise on its high-power expertise while developing the strategic capabilities specific to the business.

Table 3.5 The attractiveness of SBU1 "High power engineering"

Characteristics of SBU 1	Attractiveness level	Total
Macro-economic context		**3.5**
Opportunities and threats that may impact the product/market domain of the company		
(1 = strong threat; 5 = strong opportunity)		
Political (stability, incentives, sectoral policy, …)	5	
Economic (growth, trade agreements, …)	2	
Socio-economic (trends, life styles, …)	3	
Technology (technological state of the art, disruptions, …)	4	
Environment (environmental contingences, …)	4	
Legal (laws, rules, standards, …)	3	
Sectoral context – market forces		**3.8**
Identify forces that may impact the competitive positioning and the level of protection of the company on the product/market domain		
(1 = weak protection; 5 = strong protection)		
Negotiation power of clients	5	
Negotiation power of suppliers	3	
Barriers to new entrants	3	
Risk of substitute products	4	
Intensity of competition rivalry	4	
Attractiveness of SBU 1		**3.65**

Source: Authors

(continued)

Table 3.6 Hightense's competitive positioning on SBU1 "High power engineering"

Capabilities of Hightense on SBU 1 High-power engineering	Level of capabilities	Total
Identify strengths and weaknesses of the company compared to competitors (VRIST) on the product/market domain		
R&D		5
Consideration for client needs	5	
Involvement of marketing	5	
Benchmarking	5	
Supply chain		4.5
Quality of relations with suppliers	4	
Permanent search for the best sourcing	4	
Respect of quality requirements	5	
Respect of delivery deadlines	5	
Marketing/sales		1.4
Business intelligence/market research	1	
Benchmarking	1	
Prospection	1	
CRM process and tools	2	
Client follow-up	2	

Capabilities of Hightense on SBU 1 High-power engineering	Level of capabilities	Total
Identify strengths and weaknesses of the company compared to competitors (VRIST) on the product/market domain		
Production		4.8
Efficiency	5	
Quality control	5	
Specialised production tool	4	
Finance – controlling		2.8
Analytical accounting	2	
Self-financing capacity	5	
Debt leverage capacity	1	
Cost control	4	
Planning	2	
Management of key success factors		4.5
High intensity expertise	5	
Guarantee of results	3.5	
Customised solution	5	

Level of competitive positioning   3.8

Source: Authors

(continued)

(continued)

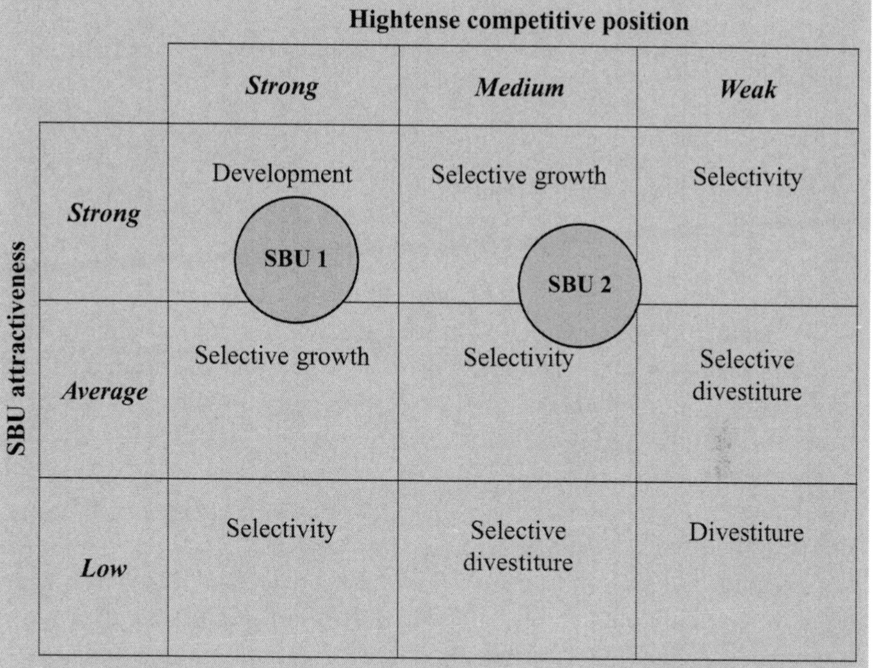

Hightense competitive position

		Strong	*Medium*	*Weak*
SBU attractiveness	*Strong*	Development (SBU 1)	Selective growth (SBU 2)	Selectivity
	Average	Selective growth	Selectivity	Selective divestiture
	Low	Selectivity	Selective divestiture	Divestiture

Fig. 3.15 Hightense's strategic decision matrix
Source: Authors

3.2.2.6 Assessing Strategic Options

A strategic diagnostic makes it possible to define the company's competitive positioning on each strategic business unit and detail options for strategic development related to this positioning. It is a key step in consulting because it constitutes the basis of decision-making for future investments, the company's organisational structure and its choices for growth. At this stage, the consultant faces a double challenge. First, he/she has to formulate possible scenarios for each option and second, the viability of each scenario must be assessed. Consultants neglect this double challenge all too often, considering that once the strategic options have been defined, it is easy to formulate and implement them as a natural extension of the preceding steps. However, even when the strategic choices make sense, implementing them effectively is complicated because it often involves organizational alignment towards the "ideal" strategic posture, developing new VRIST strategic capabilities and undertaking a delicate planning exercise in a context of market uncertainty and complexity.

Best Consulting Practices in Brief

In formulating scenarios, the consultant must avoid influencing the company while still guiding this formulation towards a path that considers the CEO's reference framework and the analysis that resulted in the chosen strategic option. It is a matter of "having the company act" by helping it to master the above analysis and build itself a new vision for the future. The more firmly the steps leading to the strategic diagnostic are rooted in solid theoretical bases backed by accurate, well explained data, the more the consultant can base her/his coaching on an approach that leaves little room for subjectivity.

The formulation of scenarios must take account of the company's internal value chain and its value network. This means defining the product/market domain, the targeted clientele, the related operational and financial resources, the actors both up- and downstream and the revenue model. The evaluation of each scenario must answer several key questions: Is the scenario "suitable" in the sense that it allows the firm to take up opportunities and guard against threats in the industry? Is it "acceptable" in terms of risk and profitability for all stakeholders (shareholders, financers, legislators, employees, local actors for economic development and…clients)? Is it conceivable on the level of operational and financial "feasibility"? Table 3.7 illustrates the different levels of scenario viability.

From Assessing Strategic Options to the Strategic Plan

In recent years, strategic planning has been criticised on the grounds that in a period of uncertainty, complex markets and hyper-competition, fixing objectives and planning how to implement and monitor a given strategy could hold back innovation, create inertia and thus decrease companies' capability to adapt to their environment. In fact, the real question is finding out if strategic planning should be a tool for formulating strategy and/or piloting its implementation. Several recent studies have shown that formalising a strategic plan requires prior understanding of the company's external and internal environment and that this understanding contributes to reaching the strategic objectives. Furthermore, when the strategic plan is contingent, *i.e.*, when it is built on the analysis of the company's markets and capabilities in a scenario process, it allows the company to plan while still adapting to the situation, thus permanently maintaining the double alignment of strategy/environment and strategy/resources.

Table 3.7 Criteria for analysing development scenarios

Analytical framework	Level of viability of scenario	Criteria of viability of scenario
Suitability	*Market*	Mid/long term positioning on the market segment
		Valorisation of strategic capabilities
		Influence on the positioning of the company in the value network
		Influence on the company's internal value chain
	Organisational	Reference framework of general management
		Company's culture and organisational routines
		Fit with the company's strategic posture
Acceptability	*Risk*	Reactions of competitors
		Reactions of clients
		Reactions of other external stakeholders
		Reactions of staff
		Changes in the market, disruptions
		Predictability of performance
	Profitability	Delay of ROI, delay of ROS, delay of ROE
		Expected economic profit (net profit – opportunity costs)
Feasibility	*Operational*	Human resources to be used
		Technical means
		Delay for implementation
		Resistance to change
	Financial	Breakeven point
		Related expenses
		Cash needed, financing requirements

Source: Authors

From Theory to Practice

The analysis of Hightense's competitive positioning highlighted the need to focus the development scenarios on the go-to-market strategy for each SBU. In this perspective, the consultant chose a formalisation framework based on the marketing mix of each SBU describing the portfolio of the offer, the pricing policy, the distribution model, the management of communication and customer relations and the resources needed for this go-to-market strategy. The formalisation must provide tangible elements for analysing the scenario's viability. All data gathered for the strategic diagnostic feed objective elements into the scenario. Table 3.8 formalises the go-to-market scenario of SBU1 "High power engineering" through organic growth achieved by its own sales force, given the nature of Hightense's technological strategic capabilities. Table 3.9 summarises the scenarios of SBU1 and SBU2, with two scenarios to address the medium and low intensity segment: First, energy engineering (SBU2.1), then trading of conductive foam (SBU2.2). The scenarios' assessment shows that the deployment proposed for SBU1 should be favoured. Conversely, scenario 2.2, based on a model of specialized trade, presents low viability. In carrying out this assessment, the consultant should take care to justify each ranking.

Table 3.8 Formalisation of the "high power engineering" scenario

Products-services	Pricing policy	Business development	Communication/customers relationship	Associated means
Energy audit	xx k€ for key accounts	Direct sales by technical-commercial binomial	Web site referencing according to the segmentation of the company's businesses	Business development
Expert report	yy k€ for SMEs (support on filing request for subsidies)	Target contact: technical and production management of key accounts	Energy audit and consultancy	x market managers for North Europe Nord, South Europe)
Advisory on energy management, technical and regulatory recommendations, safety at work	Breakeven point for audit: gross salary x 2.25	Referencing with prescribers, professional unions, insurance companies	Maintenance, Development, design, manufacturing,	Missions: business intelligence, prospection, quotations, negotiation, clients follow-up
Ancillary services: support on filing for energy savings reports	Daily price of audit: xxxx € key accounts yyyy € for SMEs	Prospection areas	Control and energy saving: Interconnection device	1 sales assistant
Energy maintenance (maintenance, facility optimisation)	xx% net margin on control	Priority 1: North Europe + South Europe (direct sales), North America (via distributor)	Scientific publications in professional journals.	Missions: sales administration, first level accounting
Control of installations (in situ or remote monitoring)	yy% net margin on maintenance	Priority 2: South America via Spanish distributor, Asia (China) via distributor	Attendance at trade shows (ELEC, INTEL…)	x engineers for technical support and development
Curative maintenance		Target clients A:	Introduction of the company's offering to prescribers for partnership	Missions: sales support + audit and consultancy
Preventive maintenance (remote monitoring)		Chemical plants with electrolysis process (xxx sites in Europe)	Referencing for energy savings certificates (national plans for energy savings: France, Italy, UK)	R & D unit on new applications (outsourced during the launch phase)
Predictive maintenance		Steel factories (xxx sites in Europe)	Accreditation with energy experts	Communication
Manufacturing of customised electro-technical equipment	xy% net margin	Target clients B:	Bilingual commercial presentation materials with:	Web + communication agency (web site, referencing, commercial and technical brochures, professional fairs)
Disconnecting switches, jumper-switches, Automatic connectors …		Nuclear (xx sites in Europe, xx worldwide)	Descriptions of electro-technical expertise (examples)	R&D: product and process
		Interconnection foam device installed on all connections maintained (integral part of the service) + tests on other installations	Simulation of energy gains	Test benches for laboratory and industrial tests,
		Business decision lead time: 3–6 months on maintenance and audit contracts, 8–12 months for interconnections	Customer references	R & D team (outsourced during the launch phase)
Sale and installation of conductive foam device	Price per m²: xxxx € Incentives on energy savings	Business intelligence on clients, markets, regulatory affairs, calls for tender		Operating budget
				Sales (staff, cost of sales): xxx k€
				Communication: xx k€
				R&D: (staff + laboratory): xxx k€
				Overheads: xx k€
				Total operating budget: xxx k€

Source: Authors

Table 3.9 Evaluation of scenario viability

Scenarios ranking scale: 5 = very high risk on viability, 1 = no risk on viability	Offering	Market suitability	Organisational suitability	Risk acceptability	Profitability acceptability	Operational feasibility	Financial feasibility	Total
SBU 1 High power energy engineering	Energy audit Energy maintenance Manufacturing of electro-technical equipment Sales/Installation of interconnection devices	1	1	3	3	1	1	1.7
SBU 2.1 Medium and low power energy engineering	Energy audit Energy maintenance Manufacturing of electro-technical equipment Sales/Installation of interconnection devices	2	2	2	2	2	2	2
SBU 2.2 conductive foam for medium and low power connections	Wholesale of interconnections foam to manufacturers and suppliers of electricity Wholesale of conductive foam to electricians Wholesale of conductive foam to manufacturers of electrical hardware and equipment	4	3	1	4	4	3	3.2

Source: Authors

From Theory to Practice

The strategic plan must result from the analysis of the company's strategic business units and their present and future viability in the current state of knowledge and information available. For the plan to be used efficiently and contingently as mentioned above, it must be applied to both the primary and support activities of the company's internal value chain. This renders the strategic objectives operational by optimizing the use of VRIST strategic capabilities and taking corrective action on the capabilities that need developing. In the case of Hightense, Table 3.10 formalises this process by operational objective aimed at deploying scenarios 1 and 2.1. Hightense's strategic plan translates the need to pursue intensive R&D while taking more account of market opportunities. The model also shows the need to work on organisational efficiency in production as well as in business development. Each operational subobjective has then to be translated into a timed action plan with regular due dates (here, every three months). The right deployment of the different action plans is measured with appropriate performance indicators.

Table 3.10 Hightense's strategic action plan

Strategic activities	Strategic operational objectives	Q1	Q2	Q3	Q4
R&D	Increase innovation performance: novelty, differentiation, quality				
	Increase market-based innovation				
KPI (key performance indicators)	R&D intensity				
	Nb of product patent applications				
	Nb of process patent applications				
	Patents/applications				
Production	Increase product quality				
	Increase productivity				
KPI (key performance indicators)	% of non-conformities				
	% clients claims				
	Unit cost				
Marketing/ communication	Increase awareness on high-power sectors				
	Increase incoming calls				
KPI (key performance indicators)	Internet referencing				
	Nb of incoming calls				
	Request for proposals after professional fairs				
Sales	Increase field presence				
	Increase sales of equipment				
KPI (key performance indicators)	Nb of visits to clients				
	% proposals/visits				
	% deals/proposals				
	Request of proposals after professional fairs				

(continued)

Table 3.10 (continued)

Strategic activities	Strategic operational objectives	Q1	Q2	Q3	Q4
Human resources	Secure key competences Improve quality of customer relationship				
KPI (key performance indicators)	% staff turnover Training budget (negotiation, CRM, ...)				
Finance	Increase commercial performance Decrease of working capital needed				
KPI (key performance indicators)	Sales/product portfolio Profitability/product portfolio ROS, AT Days of account receivables, days of account payables Value of stocks				

Source: Authors

Notes

1. Gunther McGrath Rita, "Transient Advantage", *Harvard Business Review*, vol. 91, no 6, 2013, p. 62–70.
2. Ansoff H. Igor, *Corporate Strategy: Business Policy for Growth and Expansion*, McGraw-Hill, New York, 1965.
3. Mintzberg Henry and Lampel Joseph, "Reflecting on the Strategy Process", *Sloan Management Review*, vol. 40, no 3, 1999, p. 21–30.
4. Grant Robert M., "The Resource-Based Theory of Competitive Advantage: Implications for Strategy Formulation", *California Management Review*, vol. 33, no 3, 1991, p. 114–135.
5. Penrose Edith, *The Theory of the Growth of The Firm*, John Wiley & Sons, New York, 1959.
6. Wernerfelt Birger, "A Resource-Based View of the Firm", *Strategic Management Journal*, vol. 5, 1984, p. 171–180.
7. Barney Jay, "Firm Resources and Sustained Competitive Advantage", *Journal of Management*, vol. 17, no 1, 1991, p. 99–120.
8. Dierickx Ingemar and Cool Karel, "Asset Stock Accumulation and Sustainability of Competitive Advantage," *Management Science*, vol. 35, no 12, 1989, p. 1504–1513.
9. Hamel Gary and Prahalad Coimbatore K., "Strategic Intent", *Harvard Business Review*, vol. 67, no 3, 1989, p. 148–161. *Id.*, "The Core Competence of the Corporation", *Harvard Business Review*, vol. 68, no 3, 1990, p. 79–90. *Id.*, "Strategy as Stretch and Leverage", *Harvard Business Review*, vol. 71, no 2, 1993, p. 75–84.

10. Miller Danny, Friesen Peter H. and Mintzberg Henry, *Organizations: A Quantum View*, Prentice-Hall, Englewood Cliffs, 1984.
11. Robert Drazin and Andrew H. Van de Ven, "Alternative Forms of Fit in Contingency Theory", *Administrative Science Quarterly*, vol. 30, 1985, p. 514–539.
12. Miles Raymond E. and Snow Charles C., *Organizational Strategy, Structure and Process*, McGraw-Hill, New York, 1978.
13. Michael E. Porter, *Competitive Strategy: Techniques for Analyzing Industries and Competitors*, Free Press, New York, 1980.
14. Walker Orville C. and Ruekert Robert W., "Marketing's Role in the Implementation of Business Strategies: A Critical Review and Conceptual Framework", *Journal of Marketing*, vol. 51, 1987, p. 15–33.
15. Williamson Peter J., "Strategy as Options on the Future", *Sloan Management Review*, vol. 40, no 3, 1999, p. 117–126.
16. Porter Michael E., *Competitive Advantage: Creating and Sustaining Superior Performance*, Free Press, New York, 1985.
17. Ryall Michael D., "The New Dynamics of Competition", *Harvard Business Review*, vol. 91, no 6, 2013, p. 80–87.

Further Reading

On Strategic Capabilities

Barney Jay, "Organizational Culture: Can it be a Source of Sustained Competitive Advantage?", *Academy of Management Review*, vol. 11, no 3, 1986, p. 656–665.
Penrose Edith, *The Theory of the Growth of the Firm*, John Wiley & Sons, New York, 1959.

On Strategic Configurations

Miles Raymond E. and Snow Charles C., *Fit, Failure and the Hall of Fame*, Free Press, New York, 1994.
Miles Raymond E. and Snow Charles C., *Organizational Strategy, Structure and Process*, Stanford University Press, Redwood, 2003.

On Value Networks and Value Capture

Ryall Michael D., "The New Dynamics of Competition", *Harvard Business Review*, vol. 91, no 6, 2013, p. 80–87.

On Matrices of Competitive Positioning

Hofer Charles and Schendel Dan, *Strategy Formulation: Analytical Concepts*, West Publishing, St. Paul, 1978.

Sudharshan Devantham, *Market Strategy: Relationships, Offerings, Timing & Resource Allocation*, Prentice-Hall, Englewood Cliffs, 1995.

Wright Robert, V. L., *A System for Managing Diversity*, Arthur D. Little Incorporated, 1974.

On Strategic Planning

Martin Roger L., "The Big Lie of Strategic Planning", *Harvard Business Review*, vol. 92, no 1, 2014, p. 79–84.

Mbengue Ababacar and Laid Ouakouak Mohamed, "Planification stratégique ratio-nnelle et performance de l'entreprise: une étude internationale", *Management International*, vol. 16, no 4, 2012, p. 117–127.

Näsi Juha and Aunola Manu, "The Language and Actors of Strategic Planning Systems: Empirical Evidence on Utilized Instruments and Consultants from Large Finnish Corporations", *Academy of Strategic Management Journal*, vol. 2, 2003, p. 61–72.

4

Choosing a Growth Strategy

4.1 The Consulting Mission

Growth is a company's leitmotif. It lies at the heart of company CEOs' thinking and discourse, it governs communication to shareholders and is managers' main preoccupation. However, as well as preoccupying a company's top managers, growth is also a central concern for all company stakeholders, from employees and shareholders to governments, investment funds or trade unions. This obsession with growth is sometimes described as a true addiction.[1] It is nourished by the idea that the competition is increasingly subject to the "*red queen*" effect,[2] according to which "I have to run faster than the others if I don't want to keep in the same place." The quest for growth is therefore the logical continuation of the imperative for speed, agility and movement that is widespread across companies.

Companies manage their growth daily, whether measured with the increase in number of products sold or larger market share. Even though this quest for growth might seem like a kind of obsession, it is also a source of anxiety. Indeed, growth cannot be taken for granted. To ensure growth a company must be able to develop a unique product (or service) offer and then find a market for this (or conversely). For company top managers, not a day goes by without facing operational and multifaceted issues related to managing the company's offer and its associated markets. This involves, for example, launching new products, organising and training the salesforce, monitoring competitors' products, adjusting sales prices, promoting existing products, prospecting new clients or even opening up new markets—and these often must be done simultaneously.

© The Author(s) 2018
P. Chereau, P.-X. Meschi, *Strategic Consulting*, DOI 10.1007/978-3-319-64422-6_4

However, when the company's growth is analysed over the long term, it is clear that growth results from strategic choices. These choices may be deliberately taken by top managers who formalise the details, steps and implementation process in the context of a strategic plan. On the other hand, these choices may be "emerging" and decided on "along the way," in the light of arising opportunities. In this event, CEOs and top managers must seek to align strategic vision with strategic action, constantly going back and forth between the two.

As regards their content, strategic choices for company growth are developed from a valuable basis for reflection: the company's strategic business unit (SBU) portfolio. Indeed, whether a growth strategy is deliberate or emerging, it requires an extremely refined, intricate, not to say "granular" knowledge of the pairs combining product/service/solution offer with specific customer segments. From these offer/segment pairs, otherwise known as strategic business units (SBUs), the company top managers can embark on the process of devising a growth strategy for their company. The first step in this process is an evaluation of the SBUs, both one by one and as a group. After this review, CEOs and top managers must define a precise vision of the level of current and potential growth not only of the whole portfolio, but also of each SBU. In a second step, CEOs and top managers must ask whether the portfolio should be maintained and supported in its current configuration or whether it should be profoundly restructured. If the latter, the portfolio can be transformed by developing new SBUs and/or by divesting some units. In other words, the growth strategy corresponds to a set of choices intended to give the company's SBU portfolio a specific configuration. The strong or weak level of growth in number of products sold, market share or turnover, results from the configuration chosen for this SBU portfolio.

Consulting missions related to choosing a growth strategy are often an extension of the missions presented in the two previous chapters. Indeed, a mission of assessing the environment for each SBU or a mission of strategic positioning (*i.e.*, assessing the company's capability to effectively respond to the SBU's key success factors) often lead to a new consulting mission devoted to choosing a (new) growth strategy.

A first series of missions deals with reconfiguring the company's SBU portfolio. Such a need often begins with the simple observation that the current portfolio configuration no longer generates increased turnover. This growth crisis, which two consultants from Bain & Company (Chris Zook and James Allen) named "*stall-out*,"[3] is a pathology affecting most grown-up companies. According to these two consultants, strong growth often goes hand in hand with an excessive organisational structure, complex administrative routines and bureaucratic fossilisation. Consequently, the growth machine that made the company successful stalls; the stalled company being more a victim of its own incapacity to seize market opportunities than any drying up of these opportunities. Companies may also face a paradoxical situation where increasing turnover has no positive effect on profits. Worse still, and with the same idea of connecting growth to profitability, the turnover may increase while profits actually decline. Less easy to observe directly, but just as worrying, this situation of unprofitable growth warns top managers of the need to review the company's SBUs individually and as a group. This lack of growth and/or of profitable growth must be seen as related to a negative (and worrying) evaluation of the value and attractiveness of the market segments pertaining to the SBUs, and/or to a problem of strategic fit between the company's competences and resources on one side and market segment key success factors on the other. Here, the key questions for CEOS and top managers are:

Which SBUs have an issue of growth and/or of profitable growth? Why do they have this issue? Is it due to negative changes in one or several market segments, increased competition or a loss of competitiveness of the product/service offer?

A second series of missions plunges right into the definition of strategic choices for growth by proposing new directions for configuring a new SBU portfolio. These new directions may constitute a continuation of existing offer/segment pair, implying that the portfolio will remain within its current boundaries but the SBUs will be revisited to create a true solid competitive advantage or to strengthen the existing one. These new directions can also be defined by focusing on the periphery of the current offer/segment pairs. Here, the main idea is to detect the product (service and/or solution) ranges and the market segments that could complement or renew the current SBUs. To define these strategic choices for growth, the consultant can start by analysing the existing situation. In this case, the consultant will identify product ranges and market segments that have high growth potential but that are not yet exploited by the company and could easily be added to its current offer/segment pairs. The consultant can also comprehensively anticipate and construct the future along "*blue oceans*" lines (in the sense of W. Chan Kim and Renée Mauborgne[4]) to define the boundaries of new product ranges and new high growth potential market segments. Finally, these new directions may include a complete breakthrough with the current boundaries of the SBU portfolio. This means seeking growth by leading the company to diversify into radically new businesses. In this second series of missions, the consultant must be able to answer the client company's following key questions:

Which direction should the SBU portfolio take? Which as yet unexploited market segments would be receptive to my current offer? Should I change my product offer with regard to the new characteristics of my current market segments? For which new markets could the company's competences and resources develop a new offer? Should my company embark on a diversification strategy?

A final series of missions specifically concerns the pertinence and choice of a diversification strategy. This is a particularly risky growth strategy because it will take the company outside its traditional boundaries and businesses and lead top managers outside their frame of reference. Implementing a diversification strategy is often experienced as disruptive, with its advantages (questioning and renewing core businesses and exploring new solutions and businesses) and its pitfalls (excessive costs and slow development of new businesses, insufficient competences and resources to respond effectively to the SBU's key success factors). For a company whose growth has stalled, the choice to diversify may be a more dangerous "cure" than the disease itself. This choice is therefore not to be made lightly and needs to be evaluated with regard to the expected synergies between the current and new businesses. Here, the key questions for CEOS and top managers are:

Before embarking on a diversification project, has my company exhausted all the growth possibilities offered by keeping its SBU portfolio within its current boundary? What is the cost of diversifying into a new business? In other words, what investment is needed to develop the competences and resources that are key for the company to build a sustainable competitive advantage in this new business? What competences and resources are similar to my core and diversification businesses? What cost economies could I expect from these synergies?

4.2 Theory, Methodology and the Tools for the Mission

4.2.1 Theoretical Background

A consultant seeking to formalise a growth strategy for a client company must rely on the indispensable growth (or product/market) matrix. Whether the consultant refers to this explicitly or not, he/she needs to use the growth

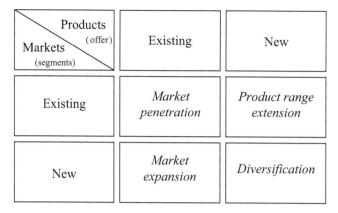

Fig. 4.1 Growth matrix and strategies
Source: Adapted from Ansoff H. Igor, op. cit., 1965

matrix for several reasons. First, its associated growth strategies have become part of managers' common knowledge: market penetration, product range extension, market expansion and diversification. Next, the growth matrix has an easily accessible two-dimensional structure: products (offer) and market (segments). These are divided into "existing" and "new" and reflect possible directions for the company's SBUs (see Fig. 4.1).

The growth matrix was formulated by H. Igor Ansoff, professor of management at Carnegie Mellon University, in his book *Corporate Strategy*, published in 1965. This volume sets out one of the first conceptualisations of company strategy. According to this first conceptualisation, strategy only deals with defining objectives and "*governing rules*" to ensure "*regular and profitable growth*" for the company. For Ansoff, company strategy and growth strategy are one and the same.

Ansoff's growth matrix, shown in Fig. 4.1 and Table 4.1, recapitulates the main directions that a company can take to ensure a strong growth for its turnover.

The first direction the company can take for its SBUs is market penetration. The objective here is to increase turnover by building a sustainable competitive advantage within the existing boundaries of its SBUs. Market penetration requires a double assessment of the company's strategic fit: first, it consists of assessing its existing capability to effectively respond to the SBUs' key success factors (see notions of external fit and strategic positioning in Chap. 3); then, it consists of assessing the degree of fit between the strategic positioning and the competences, resources, structure and organisational processes supporting the implementation of this positioning (see notion of internal fit in Chap. 3). This double assessment should lead the

Table 4.1 The characteristics of the growth matrix

Strategy/ direction	Market penetration	Product range extension	Market expansion	Diversification
Strategic objective	Seeking a better strategic position and strengthen competitive advantage in existing markets	Complementing and/or renewing product offer associated with SBUs	Generating new market segments and/ or testing existing but unexploited segments	Seeking growth outside core SBUs
Competitive rules (or key success factors)	Exploiting the rules better than the competition in existing SBUs			Exploring and/ or creating new rules
Strategic action	Acquiring direct competitors enjoying strong growth, investing in product differentiation, seeking size effect and economies of scale, and organisational restructuring	Launching new products and services, innovating, imitating, scanning the competitor's products/ services	Prospecting new market segments and emerging modes of distribution, and expanding internationally	Developing new competences and resources in-house, corporate venturing, acquiring and/ or partnering with start-ups in new businesses

Source: Authors

company to a strategic realignment on its existing markets. This realignment often goes hand in hand with the company's increased competitive aggressiveness: initiating price wars, exerting stronger pressures over suppliers and clients, optimising manufacturing and distribution costs and/or further differentiating current products/services/solutions. This strategic realignment and the resulting competitive aggressiveness cannot be achieved without additional investments in competences and resources as well as organisational restructuring.

Extending product ranges (product range extension) and adding new market segments (market expansion) are two directions that provide the company with new room for manoeuvring in its existing SBUs. The growth engine of the company may have stalled because it has exploited the possibilities of market penetration to the maximum or simply because its respective markets have reached maturity. Without fundamentally questioning both its strategic positioning and internal fit, the company may find ways for its SBUs to grow by introducing new product ranges or adding new market segments. By following these expansion strategies, the SBUs are complemented or slightly renewed, but their boundary remains almost unchanged. Extending the product range and expanding the market can be seen as strategies aiming to stretch the boundaries of existing SBUs without modifying the competitive rules, nor the company's strategic positioning and internal fit. These strategies translate into launching new products and services, investing in innovation (innovation related to products and services or to their distribution), scanning competitor's products that might be imitated, prospecting new market segments and expanding internationally.[5]

Diversification is the last direction the company can take to ensure regular and profitable growth. Building on the growth matrix, diversification is defined as the company's entry into new SBUs. It often occurs that the company has been diversifying over time without knowing it or planning for it. By regularly introducing new product ranges and new market segments into its portfolio, the company may have been knocking on the door of diversification, step by step without really having explicitly decided to do so. But such a diversification "along the way" is rare. Many companies make the choice to diversify deliberately, knowing just what it takes, for once again, it is all a question of fit between the company's external environment, strategy, competences and resources.

As mentioned previously, diversification is risky because developing new SBUs will lead the company outside its core and traditional businesses. By definition, a business is a combination of different but complementary competences and resources (technological, marketing, financial, organisational…). All SBU portfolios rely on the company's mastering one or several businesses. Those lying at the heart of the company's SBU portfolio and ensuring the company's competitiveness are known as core businesses.

Best Consulting Practices in Brief

The presentation of the growth matrix leads to using similar terms: products, services, offer/segment pairs, SBUs and now, businesses. This semantic profusion can be confusing for client companies. At this stage, it may be useful for the consultant to explain these terms, specifying how they are related and how they connect to each other. To this end, we recommend the tree diagram proposed by Coimbatore K. Prahalad and Gary Hamel[6], professors of strategy at the University of Michigan and at the London Business School, respectively. A company can be

(continued)

(continued)

represented as a tree (see Fig. 4.2): products, services and solutions are fruits, SBUs are branches, businesses are the trunk, and competences and resources are the roots. Behind this metaphor, Prahalad and Hamel defend the idea that a company must primarily invest in its competencies and resources rather than in its products or SBUs. By regularly nourishing its competencies and resources, the company will strengthen its SBUs and develop competitive products and services.

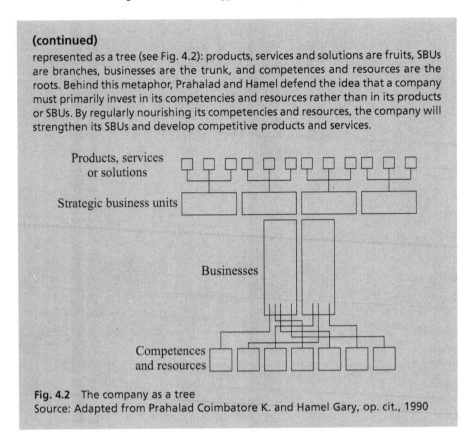

Fig. 4.2 The company as a tree
Source: Adapted from Prahalad Coimbatore K. and Hamel Gary, op. cit., 1990

Diversification leads to creating a new business, called a diversification business, which adds new SBUs to the existing portfolio. The success of a diversification move implies that the company has managed to both develop and integrate this diversification business internally. More specifically, the company must be able to identify the competences and resources it lacks to create the new business, develop these internally or acquire them externally and above all, graft them onto the company, making sure they are synergistic and coherent with its other businesses, organisational culture, structure and internal routines. It is easier to develop and integrate the diversification business if the new business possesses certain competences and resources in common with the company's core businesses. These common competences and resources may be used as diversification pivots. When the company leverages on these pivots to develop new businesses, the diversification is defined as related.[7]

Developing and integrating a diversification business internally involves high financial investments, which are often greater than the investments required for market penetration or (product range/market) expansion. Therefore, a high return on investment in the new business is conditioned by the resulting growth in turnover and the company's capability to minimise the direct and indirect expenses incurred when implementing the diversification strategy. In this event, sharing competences and resources across the company's core and diversification businesses plays a key role. Sharing competences and resources across several businesses helps to relieve cash flow by reducing investment needs and the associated financial expenses; it also reduces operational expenses by benefiting from economies of scale and size effect. The cost economies induced by sharing competences and resources across the company's core and new businesses are known as diversification synergies. Before diversifying into a new business, the return on investment must be anticipated by evaluating as closely as possible the additional growth in turnover and profitability, the level of investment required and above all, the amount of expected synergy.

Best Consulting Practices in Brief

Can my company engage in several growth moves at the same time? Client companies often ask this after they have seen Ansoff's growth matrix. In principle, it is indeed possible to act differentially on the company's SBU portfolio. For example, a portfolio may be reconfigured with the joint effect of market penetration for one SBU in particular, a product range and/or market expansion for another and diversification with the introduction of new SBUs. However, one must bear in mind that implementing several growth strategies simultaneously may damage the coherence of the SBU portfolio and, above all, it may need investments that could have destabilising effects on the cash flow balance, thus endangering the company's very survival. It is therefore recommended to adopt the following sequential approach: penetrate existing markets, expand the product range/market and finally, diversify. In this way, the company seeks growth in its portfolio by exploiting each move to the utmost before proceeding to the next.

4.2.2 Methodology and Tools for the Mission

A consulting mission to help the client company choose and implement a growth strategy can be divided into two steps. In the first step, the consultant should identify the nature of the company's growth issue and understand how the company will be able to achieve profitable growth. This first step, known as profitable growth analysis, is based on two tools: the profitable growth test and the strategic model for profitability.

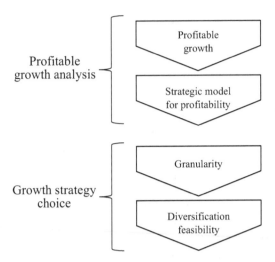

Fig. 4.3 Profitable growth analysis and growth strategy choice
Source: Authors

In the second step, the consultant should propose a new configuration for the company's SBU portfolio. With a view to this reconfiguration, the consultant and the client company must choose whether to implement one particular growth strategy or possibly, a sequence of several growth strategies over time. This second step, known as growth strategy choice, is also based on two tools: the granularity test and the diversification feasibility test. Overall this consulting mission is organised around four steps, which are summed up in Fig. 4.3.

4.2.2.1 The Profitable Growth Test

For a long time, growth and performance as well as growth and profitability were conflated. The idea of a virtuous circle whereby sales growth mechanically induced profit growth was widespread across companies and consultants. This idea came about through considering that growth had a leverage effect on profit, occurring through size effect and economies of scale, which resulted from the continuous increase in turnover. However, observing the paradoxical situation of failing companies with strong growth showed that the relationship between growth and profit was far from being as mechanical as it first appeared. Indeed, growth is not always profitable. In this situation, the company may find itself trapped inside a vicious circle where sales growth is accompanied by profit deterioration or even financial losses. Indeed, growth

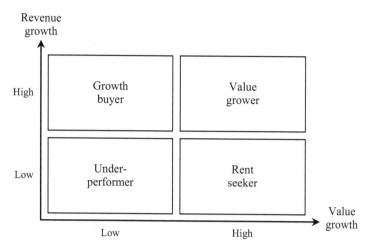

Fig. 4.4 The profitable growth matrix
Source: Adapted from Deans Graeme K. and Kroeger Fritz, *op. cit.*, 2004

must be managed properly; neglecting this may rapidly produce negative effects on the company's profit: significant external funding needs, cash flow deterioration, increase in financial expenses (related to the poor management of current assets), rapid progression in administrative expenses related to the increase in a company's size or even overestimating operational synergies.

From these observations, two consultants from A. T. Kearney, Graeme K. Deans and Fritz Kroeger, published *Stretch! How Great Companies Grow in Good Times and Bad* in 2004. In this volume, they formalised the notion of profitable growth and defined different company profiles according to growth and profitability. These growth and profitability profiles are divided into four quadrants in a two-dimensional matrix (see Fig. 4.4) and are summarised in Table 4.2.

As regards growth measurement in this matrix, consulting firms (notably A. T. Kearney and the Boston Consulting Group) agree on using annual sales growth, often averaged over five years. As regards profitability, two measures are mostly used: an averaged (over five years) total shareholder return,[8] and an averaged (over five years) return on investment (net profit-to-assets ratio), which is a measure of economic value creation. The analysis of the four growth and profitability profiles is generally carried out by comparing companies operating in the same industry. This comparison makes it possible to calculate an average level of growth and profitability for the industry, thereby distinguishing weak from strong growth and low from high profitability.

Table 4.2 The characteristics of profitable growth profiles

Profile	Value grower	Growth buyer	Rent seeker	Underperformer
Approach to growth	Seeking a balance between growth and profitability. Investing in core and new businesses, seeking to limit additional fixed costs (what James Kilts, Gillette's CEO from 2001 to 2005, called "ZOG" or "zero overhead growth"), and exploiting as many inter-business synergies as possible	Strongly seeking additional turnover. Investing in existing (through innovation, acquisition of market shares, launching new products, prospecting new clients, competitive aggressiveness) and new businesses	Little propension to seek additional turnover. Reducing investments	No additional turnover
Approach to profitability	Strong profitability related to exploiting synergies and high asset productivity	Weak profitability related to poor management of investments and asset growth	Strong profitability related to minimising assets, restructuring the SBU portfolio and reducing financial and operational expenses	Weak profitability related to poor management of assets and costs
Strategic objective	Preparing the future and seeking profitable growth in existing businesses	Preparing the future and building a new competitive advantage	Consolidating and maximising profits from current competitive advantage	No clear strategic objective

Source: Authors

Best Consulting Practices in Brief

The profitable growth analysis is an essential step in a consulting mission. Beyond the joint financial analysis of growth and profitability, the client company must understand that the quest for profitable growth is the "alpha and omega" in the choice of a growth strategy. For this reason, consultants are advised to introduce the results of the Boston Consulting Group study, showing the difficulty of building long term competitive advantage, right at the start of the mission.[9] Figure 4.5 summarises this with the evolution of the total shareholder return (used as a performance measure) of 2056 companies from different countries between 1996 and 2005. Specifically, this graph shows the number of years in a row with companies delivering an annual total shareholder return above the industry average. Based on these results, it seems impossible to maintain an above average performance for over nine years. In other words, the lifetime of a competitive advantage is at most nine years. After showing client companies this graph, consultants should tell them Kilts' rule,[10] according to which after five years, the company that stands out as uncontested leader in an industry is the one that manages to be in the top third every year for growth and profitability. Once client companies have seen the Boston Consulting Group graph and Kilts' rule, they will have no problem understanding the relevance of profitable growth and the strategy needed to attain this.

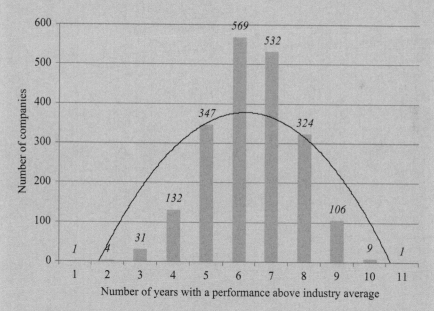

Fig. 4.5 The lifecycle of a competitive advantage
Source: Adapted from Olsen Eric, Plaschke F. and Stelter D., the Boston Consulting Group, 2006

From Theory to Practice

The luxury industry is a good illustration of the profitable growth test. This industry is analysed in Fig. 4.6, for European companies that today own the main world famous luxury brands. Growth and profitability are evaluated over five years (2008–2012) for six companies: LVMH, Kering (that notably owns Gucci and Yves Saint Laurent brands), Hermès, Richemont (Cartier), Tod's and Burberry. Growth is calculated using the averaged annual sales growth and profitability with the averaged ROI (net profit-to-assets ratio). Each company is represented by a circle proportional to its averaged market-to-book ratio[11].

Three companies deliver high profitable growth: Burberry, Richemont and especially Hermès. Indeed, Hermès stands out as the uncontested champion of profitable growth. Kering also stands out as the underperforming company in this industry. Comparing position of companies in the profitable growth matrix and their respective stock market performance highlights that shareholders and stock market investors particularly value profitable growth. From this viewpoint, we can learn a lot from Hermès about the importance of combining high growth and profitability: in 2012, compared to LVMH that is by far the largest world player in the luxury industry, the stock market value of Hermès was three times smaller, but with fifteen times fewer assets!

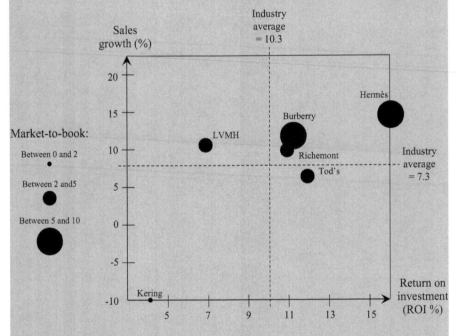

Fig. 4.6 European luxury companies in the profitable growth matrix (2008–2012)
Source: Authors

4.2.2.2 The Strategic Model for Profitability

As an extension to the profitable growth test (and if the company has still decided to invest strongly in its business growth), the consultant must ensure that these investments and the resulting modification of the SBU portfolio will not be detrimental to the company's profitability. In other words, investments for growth must lead to increased profitability. For this to happen, a necessary prerequisite is to understand how the company "produces" its profitability and more specifically, to highlight the company's strategic leverages of profitability.

A strategic model of the company's profitability can be obtained by aligning these strategic levers and integrating them into a synthetic framework. In this step, the consultant uses accounting and financial data to respond to the following questions:

What strategic levers does the company use to increase its profitability? Which of them are not exploited, and why? Will investing in growth strengthen or conversely, destabilise, these strategic leverages?

To our knowledge, the DuPont model for performance analysis is the best suited to helping consultants grasp these strategic levers both individually and as a group. The model was developed during the First World War by F. Donaldson Brown (at the time, chief financial officer of the American chemical group DuPont de Nemours). This model has the considerable advantage of using accounting and financial data to understand the company's strategic choices. It integrates both financial and strategic views of performance analysis.

The DuPont model requires two variables from the income statement (total sales and net profit) and two others from the balance sheet (total assets and shareholder equity). Different combinations of these variables allow calculation of ratios that are organised into four interrelated levels of company performance: commercial performance, economic performance, debt and financial performance (see Fig. 4.7).

The first level of analysis focuses on commercial performance. This level is based on two ratios: return on sales (or ROS) and asset turnover (or AT). The ROS is calculated using the net profit-to-sales ratio. This is above all an indicator of the company's capability to generate margin. In other words, it indicates to what extent the company leverages on the margin effect. First, it provides information on how the company manages its different (operational, financial, administrative…) costs. Second, it gives an indication about the level of a company's pricing power. In other words, by evaluating the company's capability to maintain or even increase its sales prices, the ROS

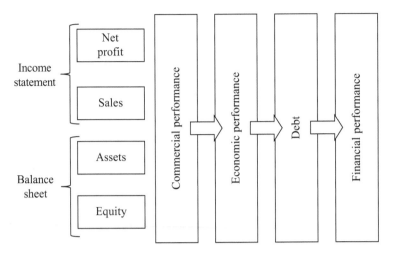

Fig. 4.7 The DuPont model structure
Source: Adapted from the DuPont Model

indicates whether its products, services or solutions are successfully differentiated and more generally, the success of its differentiation strategy. This margin effect can also be calculated at the segment or industry level by averaging the ROS of the main players. This averaged ROS gives information on the nature of the competitive system of the segment or industry in question (see Chap. 2). In this way, a low ROS (under 5%) would indicate both that sales price is a primary key success factor and the absence of a companies' pricing power. Here we find the important features of the volume competitive system. On the contrary, an average to high ROS (over 10%) would indicate the strong pricing power enjoyed by some companies. In this event, we can deduce that some companies in this segment or industry enjoy a solid competitive advantage based on successful differentiation. Furthermore, we may conclude that such a segment or industry is highly likely to be a specialised competitive system.

The AT (asset turnover) coefficient is the second ratio used to assess the company's commercial performance. It is obtained by dividing total sales by total assets. As its name indicates, this ratio measures above all the company's capability to leverage its assets and generate a maximum turnover. In other words, it is a ratio that evaluates the asset productivity as well as the company's use of the volume effect. It can also be seen as an indicator of the company's capital intensity. A high AT coefficient often reflects high asset productivity but it may also indicate low capital intensity (*i.e.*, few fixed assets with little or no inventory). A low AT coefficient may be explained by poor asset productivity but this might also indicate high capital intensity (*i.e.*, important fixed assets with large inventory and cash).

The second level of analysis in the DuPont model pertains to economic performance. This level is based on a single ratio, which is defined as the return on investment (or ROI).[12] This ratio is obtained by dividing the net profit by total assets. It is a key indicator of economic value creation as it provides information on the company's capability to optimise the exploitation of its assets and associated (operational, financial, administrative…) costs so as to extract a maximum margin. In the interrelated approach to performance levels in the DuPont model, the ROI may also be calculated as the product of the two previous commercial performance ratios (see Fig. 4.10):

$$ROI = ROS \times AT$$

In other words, companies' economic value creation results from two joint effects or leverages: margin (see ROS) and volume (see AT). By breaking down the ROI in this way, we can deduce the company's generic strategy (in the sense of Michael E. Porter, see Chap. 3). The analysis of the extent to which companies use margin and volume leverages allows us to formalise a matrix whose quadrants can be partly associated with Porter's generic strategies (see Fig. 4.8). To distinguish the four quadrants in the matrix, the industry average is generally used for the ROS and the value of 1 is often taken as a cut-off point for distinguishing between low and high AT.

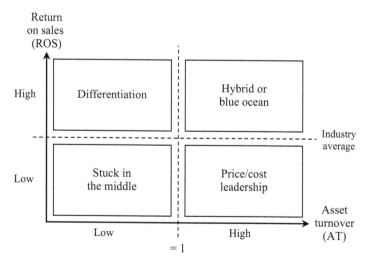

Fig. 4.8 ROI and Porter's generic strategies
Source: Authors

Best Consulting Practices in Brief

Choosing a cut-off point for ROS and AT is a delicate question. Indeed, according to the values chosen, the resulting strategic analysis may be different. For AT, it is advisable to use the value 1 as a cut-off point. This is easy to justify, as in the breakdown of ROI (ROI = ROS × AT) in the DuPont model, the AT coefficient can be presented as a multiplier of the margin effect (ROS); if its value is lower than 1, it reduces the margin effect, and its impact on ROI is negative. On the contrary, if its value is higher than 1, it amplifies the margin effect and its impact is positive on economic value creation. For ROS, the choice of cut-off point is more difficult to justify. An industry average may be satisfactory for companies with heterogenous strategic choices, which will be reflected in the associated ROS. However, for some segments or industries which are highly homogenous (like luxury or paper/pulp), the average ROS can either be very low (in the paper/pulp industry) or very high (in the luxury industry), and this could bias the strategic analysis. To avoid this, our experience of using the DuPont model in different industries and over different periods has led us to think that a value under 5% reflects a low ROS and value over 10% reflects a strong ROS.

A first quadrant, differentiation, corresponds to companies with a strong ROS and a weak AT. Here, companies favour margin leverage over volume leverage. Companies in this quadrant have managed to develop products and/or services that customers perceive as unique. In general, these companies enjoy strong pricing power. On the other hand, neither the effective exploitation of their assets nor the aggressive conquest of market share are priorities for these companies. A second quadrant, price/cost leadership, refers to the opposite strategic profile: a weak ROS and a strong AT. Here, companies favour volume leverage over margin leverage. This translates into a continual quest for increased market share that will generate economies of scale and the necessary size effect to reduce companies' full cost of products, services or solutions. This reduction in full cost offers these companies room for manoeuvering for their pricing policy. A third "hybrid" quadrant combines strong ROS and AT. This combined positioning offers companies the highest level of economic value creation. Indeed, companies in this quadrant exploit volume and margin leverages jointly. This very profitable positioning, is however, hard to reach as it requires companies to possess numerous competences and resources, allowing them to differentiate their products, win market share and exploit/explore new competitive spaces or "*blue oceans*" (in the sense of Kim and Mauborgne, see Chap. 2). A last quadrant is characterised by weak ROS and a weak AT. In other words, here we find companies with low level of economic value creation. This weak ROI is the outcome of the absence of clear strategic positioning, which leads companies to under-exploit (or even not exploit at all) margin and volume leverages. This lack of clear and deliberate strategy results in the "*stuck in the middle*" situation described by Porter in his book *Competitive Advantage*, published in 1985: "*a company that engages in each generic strategy but fails to achieve any of them is 'stuck in the middle.' It possesses no competitive advantage. This strategic position is a recipe for below-average performance.*"

The third level of analysis concerns debt. This level is based on a single ratio, which is debt leverage (or DL). This ratio is obtained by dividing total assets by shareholder equity. This is an indicator of the company's level of debt. However, its use to analyse debt is not straightforward. In fact, it is not a direct measure of debt such as gearing (financial debt-to-equity ratio). For example, a DL of 1 means that the company has no debt and a value of 2 corresponds to a debt equivalent to half the company's assets. Interpreting the favourable or unfavourable nature of debt leverage depends on the competitive system operated by the client company (see Chap. 2). DL plays its profit multiplier role only in volume segments and industries. In a volume competitive system, the profit-leveraging effect of debt plays out fully, allowing the company to grow fast—much faster than the competition—benefiting from a strong size effect and increasing its profit. Here, we can talk about a virtuous circle of debt (see Fig. 4.9). Bruce H. Henderson, the founder of the Boston Consulting Group, was a specialist of debt leverage and his advice to companies operating in a volume competitive system was very clear[13]: "*use more debt than your competition or get out of the business. Any other policy is either self-limiting, no-win, or a bet that the competition will go bankrupt before they displace you*" (p. 1). On the other hand, in other competitive systems, an average-to-high DL (above 2[14])

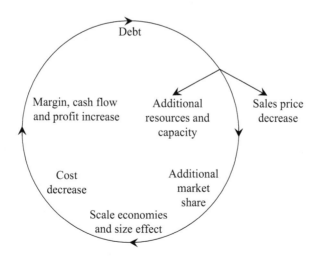

Fig. 4.9 The virtuous circle of debt
Source: Authors

is either ineffective (in fragmented and specialised competitive systems where companies easily finance their growth with quick, comfortable margins) or dangerous (in dead-end competitive systems where the market is mature or declining). In the particular context of a dead-end competitive system, the profit-leveraging effect of debt no longer works, turning the virtuous circle into a vicious one.

The fourth and final level of analysis in the DuPont model concerns financial performance. This level is based on the return on equity (or ROE). This ratio is obtained by dividing net profit by shareholder equity. It is a key indicator for the company's shareholders. Indeed, it informs about the company's capability to create value for shareholders, whether the company is listed on the stock market or not. Interpreting this ratio depends on the nature of the company's profit allocation policy:

- If the company applies a dividend policy (profit is fully distributed to shareholders), ROE may be interpreted as a shareholder return.
- If the company applies a retained earning policy (profit is fully retained and invested in the company), ROE may be interpreted as an asset growth rate.
- If the company applies a mixed profit allocation policy (profit is shared between shareholders and the company), ROE may be interpreted both as a shareholder return and an asset growth rate; the value of each depending on the proportion of profit allocated to shareholders and the company.

In the DuPont model's interrelated approach to performance levels, the ROE may also be calculated as the product of the economic performance and debt leverage performance ratios (see Fig. 4.10):

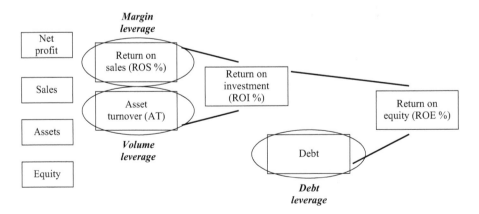

Fig. 4.10   The DuPont model's "Russian dolls"
Source: Adapted from the DuPont model

$$ROE = ROI \times DL$$

In other words, the financial value creation of any company is the outcome of three effects or leverages: margin, volume and debt. This value creation, which is key for both shareholders (as well as potential investors) and the company, is determined by the company's capability to exploit one, two or all three of these strategic levers.

Best Consulting Practices in Brief

The DuPont model's "Russian Dolls" aspect is one of its most notable characteristics. The consultant should underline this, as it is important that the client company understands that its financial performance results from the (good or poor) management of the margin, volume and debt leverages. The company's financial performance results from how (well or not) the three leverages mentioned above are adjusted.

From Theory to Practice

Table 4.3 summarises the DuPont model applied to six European companies in the luxury industry in 2012[15]: LVMH, Kering, Hermès, Richemont, Tod's and Burberry. To identify the strategic levers used by each company and establish their strategic model for profitability, we used the following cut-off points: 10% for ROS, 1 for AT and 2 for DL.

The figures in italics in Table 4.3 indicate the strategic levers used effectively by each company, thereby showing their strategic approach to profitability. Table 4.3 shows that most companies rely almost exclusively on strong margin leverage to create financial value. Only Kering (using both margin and debt leverages) and Burberry (using both margin and volume leverages) differ slightly from the other companies. Figure 4.11 completes the previous analysis by showing that all the companies in question are positioned in the differentiation quadrant of the ROI graph.

Table 4.3 The DuPont model of European luxury companies (2012)

Company	LVMH	Kering	Hermès	Richemont	Tod's	Burberry	Cut-off point
ROS	12.18%	10.76%	21.23%	19.75%	14.76%	12.71%	> 10%
AT	0.57	0.39	1.09	0.72	0.95	1.23	> 1
ROI	6.94%	4.19%	23.14%	14.22%	14.02%	15.63%	
DL	1.99	2.16	1.35	1.37	1.35	1.60	> 2
ROE	13.81%	9.05%	31.23%	19.48%	18.92%	25.00%	

Source: Authors

(continued)

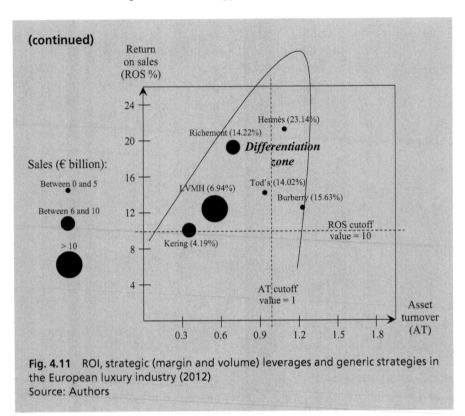

Fig. 4.11 ROI, strategic (margin and volume) leverages and generic strategies in the European luxury industry (2012)
Source: Authors

4.2.2.3   The Granularity Test

Once the profitable growth analysis has been completed, the consultant may decide to engage in choosing a growth strategy with the client company. To this end, the consultant must think about a new configuration of the client company's SBU portfolio. The following questions are generally asked at this stage:

> *Where can we find new directions for profitable growth? Can we find them within the existing (or slightly modified) SBUs or in new ones? In other words, should the company grow by remaining within the traditional boundary of its core business(es) or on the contrary, should it diversify into one or several new businesses?*

The granularity test can help the consultant answer these questions more thoroughly. Originally, the idea of granularity applied to the field of photography and images. In its initial technological aspect, granularity referred to the size of the grain or number of pixels of a photo or image. The idea of granularity comprises that of clarity and precision. This notion was then transferred into the military field by General David Petraeus.[16] He used the term in many interviews to describe the need for a detailed (or granular) approach to what was going on on the ground in Iraq and Afghanistan where American troops were engaged. Recently, the idea of granularity was used in company strategy where it has since been widely applied. Mehrdad Baghai (an independent consultant), Sven Smit and Patrick Viguerie (both consultants at McKinsey) proposed adopting a granular approach to company growth.[17]

Baghai, Smit and Viguerie's original idea is that organising and analysing companies by division, business or product line does not result in making the right strategic choices for growth. Indeed, division-, business- or product line-based organisations, which are supposed to reflect the SBU portfolio, restrict the strategic choices for growth as these organisational sets of the company are too broad and not sufficiently pertinent. As Baghai, Smit and Viguerie remark in their article published in the *Harvard Business Review*, *"growth is granular, but most companies aren't"* (p. 87). Therefore, CEOs and top managers often make strategic choices for growth with a very broad idea of their company's organisation in mind. These strategic choices and their resulting implementation with mergers & acquisitions, market share gains or divestments, are rarely taken using a granular approach to the company and its SBUs. On the contrary, these strategic choices are applied to the level of a business or a combination of SBUs. In the end, whole areas of SBUs can disappear from the company's portfolio although some of them entail profitable "pockets" of growth.

Taking a granular approach to the company and its strategic choices for growth means adopting a much more detailed and precise level of analysis than businesses or product lines. A first review can be made for each SBU. On this basis, top managers must define a clear vision of the existing and potential level of growth for each SBU. Next, a second review must be made focusing especially on the SBUs with weak growth prospects. This second review is based on the micro-segmentation of the company's SBU portfolio. Indeed, it may be necessary to refine the granularity beyond the SBUs or the pairs associating a product and/or service offer to specific market segments. An SBU can be divided up by detailing the product offer and/or the market segments. The end result defines micro-segments from which top managers can initiate the process of formulating the growth strategy to be carried out in their company.

Putting the businesses and SBUs under the microscope often reveals that the growth drivers no longer need to be sought outside the company's portfolio. Rather than diversifying in new businesses, the company may find profitable growth by identifying the pockets of growth within its own portfolio and allocating them the necessary (technological commercial, marketing, financial, human…) competences and resources to achieve and consolidate their potential. This precision engineering, which must be used to remodel the company's

SBU portfolio, not only applies to the pockets of growth within SBUs whose growth has stalled, but also to the declining micro-segments within fast-growing SBUs. With this granular approach to the company and its growth, top managers can rapidly give (back) to the company new room for manoeuvering its SBUs. Here, it is more a matter of remodelling the portfolio with SBUs that have redefined boundaries than of totally disrupting the portfolio by simultaneously divesting one or several businesses and diversifying in new SBUs.

From Theory to Practice

As an illustration, we applied the granularity test to the Kering group and its different divisions. Since the beginning of his tenure as CEO, François-Henri Pinault placed the issue of profitable growth at the heart of his group's strategy.[18] In 2016, this group was split into two divisions: luxury (including Gucci, Bottega Veneta and Saint Laurent as the main brands) had an overall growth of 7.6%. This level of growth is even more comfortable since the associated profitability is high. This profitability, calculated using ROS (see the DuPont model), amounts to 22.8%.[19] As a whole, the luxury division is an example of profitable growth, suggesting that no changes need be applied to its associated SBU portfolio. A more granular approach to Kering's main luxury brands offers directions for considering how to increase and consolidate this strong profitable growth (see Fig. 4.12). For example, the Gucci brand has an intermediate level of growth relative to the two other brands analysed. Although still comfortable, the annual turnover progression of 12.3% in the luxury division hides pockets of strong growth, such as Eastern Europe, ready-to-wear and shoes. Following the same line of reasoning, Bottega Veneta has possibilities of ultra-growth, with niches in jewellery and perfume (see other products in Fig. 4.12) and Saint Laurent with Japan and leather goods. Special attention in terms of allocating competencies and resources should therefore be paid to these segments whose perspectives for growth are high.

Fig. 4.12   The granular approach to Kering's luxury division (2016)
Source: Authors [on the basis of Kering's annual reports]

(continued)

(continued)

The sport and lifestyle division (including Puma and Volcom as main brands) showed an overall growth of 5.4% in 2016. This is satisfactory, even though it is lower than the luxury division's growth. In reality, Kering's concern is the gradual deterioration in the growth and profitability of this division's flagship brand (Puma): in 2016, its growth was amounting to 7.0% whereas in 2012 it was 8.7% and its profitability was still positive (ROS = 3.4%) but still down relative to 2012 (8.8%). If this downward trend is not turned around and profitability not accelerated over the coming years, there will clearly be an issue of unprofitable growth for this brand and more generally, for the division as a whole. A granular approach to Puma brand gives an accurate view of the opportunities for growth and also certain threats that hang over that growth (see Fig. 4.13). The Puma brand has stronger growth (at 7.0%) than the average of the sport and lifestyle division, but its profitability is relatively close to that of the division (3.1%). The question that should be asked for Puma concerns its prospects for growth. The brand has an extremely contrasting portfolio in terms of product segments and regions/countries: on one side, there are pockets of strong growth, especially for segments, which are historically within Puma's preserve (Eastern Europe and Germany) and associated to its flagship product (footwear); on the other side are poorly oriented segments (emerging economies and accessories). Applying the granular approach to this division underlines the imperative of restructuring the division's SBU portfolio and points to possible directions for re-allocating competencies and resources.

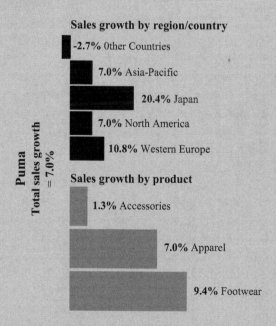

Fig. 4.13 The granular approach to Kering's sport and lifestyle division (2016) Source: Authors [on the basis of Kering's annual reports]

Best Consulting Practices in Brief

It would be a mistake to reduce the granular approach to a simple reorganisation of divisions, product lines and SBUs. As the promoters of this approach have shown, using a finer grain is a first step that should make it possible to identify both pockets of growth and declining micro-segments. The next step consists of evaluating whether the three growth drivers in the sense of Baghai, Smit and Viguerie ("*market momentum*" or the intrinsic dynamic of market growth, "*market share gains*" or the conquest of market share and "*mergers & acquisitions*" or buying market shares through mergers and acquisitions) are well oriented for the company. These three growth drivers are reviewed for both pockets of growth and declining micro-segments; corrective decisions regarding competences and resources reallocation should follow.

4.2.2.4   The Diversification Feasibility Test

If the client company has covered all the previous steps and decides that its portfolio should be renewed by developing one or several new businesses, the question must be asked as to the practical feasibility of such a diversification move. One important aspect of this is how to finance such a move. Indeed, many diversifications fail because the companies neglect to appreciate the exact amount of investment required to ensure the success of developing a new business. First of all, the investment must cover the entry into the new business whether this be through acquisition, joint venture or organic development. Next, all the investment required for developing competences and resources and subsequently building a sustainable competitive advantage in the new business must be added up. Finally, one must not forget the possible costs of restructuring the organisation, in order to facilitate the internal alignment between core and new businesses.

Even though the financial aspects may have been addressed, there remains a number of questions that are more strategic in nature. These questions, which should be looked at with a go/no go logic, were proposed by Constantinos C. Markides, professor of strategy at London Business School, in an article published in 1997 in the *Harvard Business Review*.[20] Figure 4.14 presents an adaptation of Markides' go/no go questionnaire. The higher the number of negative no go–type responses, the higher the likelihood that the diversification move will fail, even though the company has the required financial resources to conduct such a move.

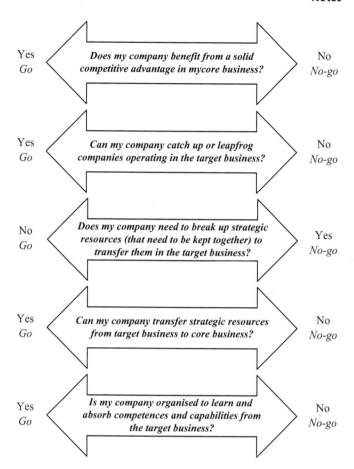

Fig. 4.14 The diversification feasibility questionnaire
Source: Adapted from Markides Constantinos C., *op. cit.*, 1997

Notes

1. Fisher Marshall, Gaur Vishal and Kleinberger Herb, "Curing the Addiction to Growth", *Harvard Business Review*, vol. 95, no 1, 2017, p. 65–74.
2. This refers to the red queen in Lewis Carroll's *Alice Through the Looking Glass*. He explains how Wonderland works to Alice in the following terms: "*here, you see, it takes all the running you can do, to keep in the same place. If you want to get somewhere else, you must run at least twice as fast as that!*" (Lewis Carroll and Martin Gardner, *The Annotated Alice: Alice's Adventures in Wonderland and Through the Looking Glass*, New American Library, New York, 1960, p. 345).
3. Zook Chris and Allen James, "Reigniting Growth", *Harvard Business Review*, vol. 94, no 3, 2016, p. 70–76.

4. Kim W. Chan and Mauborgne Renée, "How Strategy Shapes Structure", *Harvard Business Review*, vol. 87, no 9, 2009, p. 73–80.

5. International expansion, which is a specific type of market expansion, will be addressed within its own chapter (see Chap. 5).

6. Prahalad Coimbatore K. and Hamel Gary, "The Core Competence of the Corporation", *Harvard Business Review*, vol. 68, no 3, 1990, p. 79–90.

7. This form of diversification is distinct from unrelated or conglomerate diversification in which the new business does not share any competences and resources with the core business. In developed economies, companies rarely embark on such diversification as the likelihood of failure is very high. For listed companies, unrelated diversification is highly likely to lead to a drop in share value. This adverse stock market reaction to unrelated diversification is known as diversification discount. Indeed, unrelated diversification results in strategic and organisational rupture. Only a few European or American groups with a specific conglomerate profile (like General Electric in the U.S., Bombardier in Canada or Bolloré in France) will find this form of diversification valuable. The diversification motives here are more financial than strategic: Adopting a financial portfolio approach to SBUs in order to reduce overall risk and leverage on the financial synergies for SBUs having different lifecycles. Nevertheless, a renewal of interest for conglomerates has come about recently in the light of the success of diversified groups in some emerging economies. Whether it be *business houses* in India (like Tata or Mahindra) or *holdings* in Turkey (like Koç or Sabanci), they all have in common that they are family conglomerates, which have a dominant position ("*local champions*") in their home country and expand very rapidly in world markets. Chin Vincent and Michael David C., *How Companies in Emerging Markets are Winning at Home*, The 2014 BCG Local Dynamos Report, the Boston Consulting Group, 2014. Ramachandran J., Manikandan K.S. and Pant Anirvan, "Why Conglomerates Thrive (Outside the U.S.)", *Harvard Business Review*, vol. 91, no 12, 2013, p. 110–119.

8. The annual total shareholder return of a listed company is calculated for a year by adding all the dividends distributed to shareholders and the share value appreciation (equal to the difference between the company's stock market value at the start and end of the year).

9. Olsen Eric, Plaschke Frank and Stelter Daniel, *The Role of Growth in Achieving Superior Value Creation: Spotlight on Growth*, The 2006 Value Creators Report, the Boston Consulting Group, 2006.

10. James Kilts was Gillette's CEO from 2001 to 2005. Under his leadership, the company was profoundly modified: in 2001, when he was recruited, Gillette's growth was not profitable and both sales and profits had dropped continuously over several years. When Kilts left in 2005, the company was once again on the rails, with annual growth of 9% for turnover and 16% for profit. For more

information about James Kilts' transformation of Gillette, we recommend the following article by three consultants from Booz & Company: Favaro Ken, Meer David and Sharma Samrat, "Creating an Organic Growth Machine", *Harvard Business Review*, vol. 90, no 5, 2012, p. 97–106.

11. A company's market-to-book is calculated by dividing its stock market value (equal to the number of shares in circulation at a given period multiplied by share price), by the amount of its shareholder equity. The market-to-book ratio is often used to measure the stock market value creation.

12. We consider ROA (return on assets ratio) and ROI (return on investment ratio) as quasi-identical, given that the investments accumulated by the company over time correspond to its total assets.

13. Henderson Bruce H., *"More Debt or None?"*, bcg.perspectives, the Boston Consulting Group, 1972.

14. A debt leverage (DL) of 2 is often considered as a sufficient cut-off point to distinguish low from high debt. Indeed, a DL of 2 means that the debt corresponds to half the asset value or equivalent to the shareholder equity value. This level of debt is judged as "reasonable" by banking and financial services companies since if the company is financially distressed, shareholder equity will cover the debt.

15. The illustration of the DuPont model with European luxury companies is taken from the case study *Bulgari, Burberry, Gucci... Strategy and Value Creation of the European Luxury Companies*, Centrale de Cas et de Médias Pédagogiques, Paris, G1697(GB). This case study was written and published by Philippe Chereau and Pierre-Xavier Meschi in 2011 (updated in 2014).

16. On this topic, we can quote as an example the interview given by General David Petraeus to *The Wall Street Journal* (2 September 2010): *"we have never had the granular understanding of local circumstances in Afghanistan that we achieved over time in Iraq [...]. One of the key elements in our ability to be fairly agile in our activities in Iraq during the surge was a pretty good understanding of who the powerbrokers were in local areas, how the systems were supposed to work, how they really worked."*

17. Baghai Mehrdad, Smit Sven and Viguerie Patrick, "Is Your Growth Strategy Flying Blind?", *Harvard Business Review*, vol. 87, no 5, 2009, p. 86–96.

18. Pinault François-Henri, "Kering's CEO on Finding the Elusive Formula for Growing Acquired Brands", *Harvard Business Review*, vol. 92, no 3, 2014, p. 43–46.

19. Due to missing information on the Kering group and its two divisions, ROS was calculated here by dividing operating profit (and not the net profit) by total sales.

20. Markides Constantinos C., "To Diversify or not to Diversify", *Harvard Business Review*, vol. 75, no 6, 1997, p. 93–99.

Further Reading

On the Ansoff's Growth Matrix, Diversification and the Success of Conglomerates from Emerging Economies

Ansoff H. Igor, *Corporate Strategy: Business Policy for Growth and Expansion*, McGraw-Hill, New York, 1965.

Chin Vincent and Michael David C., *How Companies in Emerging Markets are Winning at Home*, The 2014 BCG Local Dynamos Report, the Boston Consulting Group, 2014.

Markides Constantinos C., "To Diversify or Not To Diversify", *Harvard Business Review*, vol. 75, no 6, 1997, p. 93–99.

Ramachandran J., Manikandan K.S. and Pant Anirvan, "Why Conglomerates Thrive (Outside the U.S.)", *Harvard Business Review*, vol. 91, no 12, 2013, p. 110–119.

On Profitable Growth, Its Measures and Leverages

Deans Graeme K. and Kroeger Fritz, *Stretch! How Great Companies Grow in Good Times and Bad*, John Wiley & Sons, New York, 2004.

Zook Chris and Allen James, "Reigniting Growth", *Harvard Business Review*, vol. 94, no 3, 2016, p. 70–76.

Ersek Barrett, Weisenbach Keller Eileen and Mullins John, "Break your Industry's Bottlenecks", *Harvard Business Review*, vol. 93, no 7, 2015, p. 99–105.

On James Kilts, the "*ZOG*" and Gillette's Growth Strategy

Favaro Ken, Meer David and Sharma Samrat, "Creating an Organic Growth Machine", *Harvard Business Review*, vol. 90, no 5, 2012, p. 97–106.

On Granularity and Its Application to the Strategic Choices for Growth

Baghai Mehrdad, Smit Sven and Viguerie Patrick, "Is Your Growth Strategy Flying Blind?", *Harvard Business Review*, vol. 87, no 5, 2009, p. 86–96.

5

Expanding Internationally

5.1 The Consulting Mission

"The solution is international expansion. But what exactly was the problem?" Apart from this wisecrack, today, all companies of all sizes and industries are strongly advised to expand internationally. Political leaders, consultants, investment funds, shareholders and the highest spheres of government all repeat the same credo: strong growth can only come about through international expansion.

Exploiting new directions for growth, transferring distinctive capabilities into new geographical markets, creating a world base for organisational learning, generating global network effects for digital platforms, accessing new clients and markets, producing additional economies of scale, increasing profit and creating value for shareholders... International expansion brings about all that and sometimes much more for companies that engage in this specific growth strategy. With all these promises, it is not surprising if other growth strategies (such as market penetration, product range expansion, market expansion or diversification, see Chap. 4) pale by comparison.

However, these promises are often hard to fulfil for local companies that see themselves (too) quickly as multimarket, multinational and multicultural entities. The transformation from a local to an international company is not plain sailing. A recent study in France on 127 first-time small and medium-sized export enterprises showed that about 35% failed and went bankrupt in the five years following their first export operations.[1] Of course, their failure

© The Author(s) 2018
P. Chereau, P.-X. Meschi, *Strategic Consulting*, DOI 10.1007/978-3-319-64422-6_5

was not entirely due to the decision to expand internationally. Nevertheless, this high failure rate indicates that internationalisation is a growth strategy whose difficulties should not be underestimated.

The first difficulty is knowing where the frontiers lie between local and international. Many companies with no direct international links access foreign markets indirectly through being referenced by globalised omnichannel or online distributors that sell these "local" suppliers' products in their foreign networks. Other companies with local B-to-B contracts manufacture and sell components to large groups that assemble, transform and sell the finished products internationally. But do the above examples illustrate companies operating on a purely local basis or companies that have begun to internationalise? In fact, many of these companies internationalise, without knowing or planning it. In other words, they are aware that they have embarked on a process of internationalisation, but have not specifically organised for this. They adopt a reactive (not proactive) strategic attitude, seizing market opportunities as they come up. Finally, these companies are no longer truly local but not yet fully international and they do not reap all the potential benefits of a more thoughtful and deliberate approach to internationalisation.

A second difficulty comes from the paradoxical situation of foreign markets and customer behaviour in different parts of the world. For the uninitiated, the trends and characteristics of globalisation are disconcerting. It is as if two parallel worlds were simultaneously pulling in opposite directions. On one side, there is the world of globalisation where customer tastes, habits and behaviour are homogenising alongside converging modes of consumption. This is the borderless world described by Kenichi Ohmae (former consultant at McKinsey in Japan) in *The Invisible Continent*[2] or by Thomas L. Friedman, the *New York Times* journalist, in *The World is Flat*.[3] It is a world in which global brands like Apple, Samsung, Google, Facebook, Gucci and Louis Vuitton prosper by selling identical products, services and solutions throughout the whole planet. But beside this globalised "flat world," another world exists. In this world, religion, ethnicity, claims for nationalism and sovereignty are exacerbated with local governments frequently intervening in the economic sphere. To use the terms of Pankaj Ghemawat, professor of international strategy at the IESE in Barcelona and New York University's Stern School of Business, this is the world of "*distance*," the world of cultural, administrative, geographical and economic (or "*CAGE*") differences. The fault lines described by Ghemawat in a series of articles published in the *Harvard Business Review* run through both emerging and developed economies. In this fractured and compartmentalised world, "*guarded globalization*"[4] prevails. This makes it very difficult for foreign entrants to address not only customers, but also suppliers, distribution networks, State and government institutions, or indeed the entire society with global brands, identical products and solutions and standardised approaches to communication and distribution. This paradoxical co-existence makes Ghemawat say that we have entered an age of semi-globalisation, the age of "*World 3.0*" to quote the title of his latest book.[5] The difficulty of internationalising causes for companies is how to manage this paradoxical situation and this world of distance. Should companies adapt to this distance? Should they try to reduce it? Or should they take advantage of it by disaggregating their value chain regionally and adopting a specific international organisation?

The third difficulty of internationalisation is finding and achieving the double fit (see Chap. 3). First, with a view to external fit, otherwise known as the strategy/environment fit, internationalising companies must find the strategic response most suited to their own international markets in this paradoxical, semi-globalised environment. This is where the challenges of adapting to different foreign markets, integrating into the business networks of each host country, standardising its offer globally or disaggregating its value chain regionally, take on their strategic importance. After finding and achieving the fit with its international markets, the internationalising company must obtain the second fit: aligning its international organisation with its international expansion strategy. This involves organisational and operational choices that are just as important as those for the internationalisation strategy. Companies must rapidly come up with relevant answers to these important questions, without necessarily having the resources, experience or time to make the right decision.

To help companies overcome the difficulties inherent to international expansion, strategy consultants may be entrusted with various missions. These are organised around the four main questions that Lorraine Eden, professor of management at Texas A&M University, poses when analysing internationalisation of companies[6]: Why? Where? How? When?

A first set of missions deals with the "why" of internationalisation. What are the company needs or issues that internationalisation will address? Is it defensive internationalisation for the company facing a decline in its local market, reduced turnover or increased competition? Or, on the contrary, is it offensive internationalisation for the company willing to benefit from global economies of scale, exploit a unique know-how and expertise in foreign markets, accelerate the network effects needed for the success of its digital platform or optimise its value chain? Analysing the "why" should allow consultants to confirm the pertinence of their client companies' motives for internationalisation. Such analysis can also help client companies clarify motives that were previously vague or veiled. Formalising these and transforming them into objectives allows the companies to monitor the performance of the internationalisation process regularly. Apart from this, the first set of missions should serve to identify the non-economic motives for internationalisation and thus spot any flawed choices for international expansion, namely choices dictated by imitation, bandwagon or fashion effect.

A second set of missions focuses on the "where" of internationalisation. Here the question lies in the choice of target countries or regions. The geographical target of export and/or investment projects has serious consequences for the internationalising company. There are many risks of incompatibility or even refusal and these can endanger the whole internationalisation process. In fact, the company's offer in its local market is not automatically transposable to any foreign market. Similarly, the company's internationalisation strategy, including its management of distance as well as its degree of aversion to uncertainty will lead it to favour some foreign markets and (temporarily or permanently) leave others aside.

The "how" of internationalisation brings a third set of missions. The targeted markets or countries have already been selected and the consultant's role is to help the company choose a mode of entry and ensure that it will be successfully implemented. The mode of entry serves as an organisational interface that manages the set of transactions between the internationalising company and the host market. A first challenge is choosing between equity or non-equity entry modes. Equity modes include setting up a wholly owned subsidiary, forming a joint venture with a local partner or acquiring a local company. Non-equity modes include exporting, using local representatives, franchising or signing distribution licences with local companies. The consultant must help the internationalising company by analysing the advantages and disadvantages of the different entry modes available in the target country. This analysis takes into account the characteristics of the target market, the company's competences and resources and its internationalisation strategy. A second challenge concerns setting up the conditions that will ensure the launch and effective implementation of the chosen entry mode. Here, the consultant is especially useful when the equity entry mode is chosen. This concerns missions aiming to accompany client companies for international expansion. These usually focus on the transactional aspects of two common equity entry modes: forming a joint venture with a local partner and acquiring a local company. If the company opts for a joint venture, the mission consists of helping it to select a local partner, assessing the respective contributions of each partner, negotiating the terms of the alliance contract and setting up the mode of governance and control. If the company decides to acquire a local entity, the mission will focus instead on finding a target, conducting due diligence, setting a price for the acquisition and defining a post-acquisition integration plan.

The final set of missions concerns the "when" of internationalisation. The timing of the internationalisation process brings up questions that a strategy consultant can help to answer. When should the company start its internationalisation? Should it latch onto opportunities for international expansion as soon as these come up or should it wait to have reached a minimum size, implying that it has already accumulated locally sufficient competences and resources to expand abroad? As well as the issue of how long to wait before internationalising, timing also poses the question of the speed and pace of internationalisation: should internationalising companies enter as many foreign markets as possible to obtain global coverage for their activities as fast as possible or should they go step by step, leaving time to digest each new foreign entry before going onto the next?

5.2 Theory, Methodology and the Tools for the Mission

5.2.1 Theoretical Background

The consulting missions mentioned above can be conducted using theoretical frameworks specifically developed to involve companies in a dynamic mechanism, allowing them to shift from local to international. This dynamic mechanism, also known as internationalisation process, is made up of causal links and steps that must be respected if the company intends to internationalise successfully.

The first theoretical framework for analysing the internationalisation process was developed in 1977 by Jan Johanson and Jan-Erik Vahlne, professors of management at the University of Uppsala.[7] This theoretical framework is also defined as the Uppsala model. It is based on the premise that any company initiating an internationalisation process is adversely affected by its "liability of foreignness."[8] This international first mover does not know how to manage the CAGE differences between its home country and the target country, so it cannot fully exploit and transfer the distinctive capabilities and resources that it has created, developed and exploited locally. If the internationalising company neglects or minimises this handicap, it may endanger the success of its first international expansion moves.

To face this liability and internationalise successfully, the Uppsala model analyses the company's internationalisation process as resulting from a double sequence of evolution in the "*psychic distance*" and the "*establishment chain*" (to use Johanson and Vahlne's terms). Psychic distance can be defined by the set of CAGE dimensions that alter the internationalising company's perceptions of a foreign market or country. As a consequence, the psychic distance may be greater or smaller according to the extent of CAGE differences between the home and target countries. The establishment chain refers to the different entry modes (equity and non-equity) that the company can use to enter the foreign market. Johanson and Vahlne's establishment chain begins by selecting the entry modes with the lowest level of risk and investment (exporting and/or using a local agent). The chain continues with modes requiring greater resource commitment (local distribution subsidiary) and ends up with modes characterised by the highest level of investment and resource commitment (manufacturing subsidiary or joint venture). Following this double sequence of evolution, the internationalising company progresses incrementally along the psychic distance and establishment chain. Figure 5.1 depicts this double sequence of international evolution more precisely: first, the company has to start its internationalisation process by choosing a foreign market with weak psychic distance (see evolution sequence type A). Once this choice has been made, the company then enters and expands into the foreign market, following the different steps of the establishment chain (see evolution sequence type B).

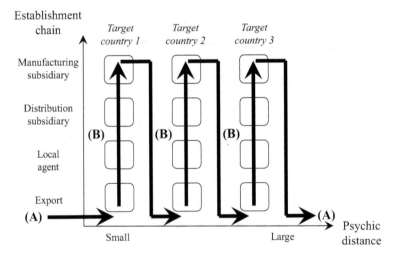

Fig. 5.1 The double evolution sequence of the Uppsala model
Source: Authors

This double sequence of evolution in both psychic distance and establishment chain takes place over a long timeframe. Going from one step to another in this double sequence is triggered by what Johanson and Vahlne call the *"basic mechanism of internationalization."* For each target country, this mechanism works in two steps: first, it is based on the starting situation of the internationalising company, as described by its level of resource commitment to the country (see establishment chain) and its knowledge of the country (its markets, distribution networks, culture, regulatory framework, competition…). Next, by working and accumulating various experience in the target country, over time, the foreign entrant will gradually increase its knowledge of the target country and reduce its *"liability of foreignness."* The accumulation of this *"experiential knowledge"* and the successful local implantation with a first entry mode will lead the foreign entrant to increase its resource commitment to the target country, shifting to an equity entry mode and advancing along the establishment chain. Finally, when the foreign entrant has developed a refined knowledge of the target country and reached the last steps of the establishment chain, it can decide whether to start again with this gradual mechanism of internationalisation, setting up in another foreign market whose psychic distance is somewhat greater.

Since its original version in 1977, the Uppsala model has been supplemented over time. An updated recent version contains the new component of *"guarded globalization"* with its fault lines and fragmentation. Here, Johanson and Vahlne defend the idea that foreignness is less of a liability than *"outsidership,"*[9] i.e., a company entering a country where it has no access and links to local business networks (clients and distributors, suppliers, competitors, government and State institutions).

A second theoretical framework of the internationalisation process was proposed in 1994 by Benjamin M. Oviatt and Patricia Phillips McDougall, professors of management at Georgia State University and Georgia Institute of Technology, respectively. Before developing their own model of internationalisation, Oviatt and McDougall examined and put forward the shortcomings of the Uppsala model. They criticised it as having a deterministic, gradual, slow and relatively inflexible approach to company internationalisation. Nevertheless, they recognised that the Uppsala model at least protects internationalising companies from country risk and the high uncertainty inherent to internationalisation. However, in their view, its major disadvantage is to neglect market opportunities, the specific features of certain highly value-added businesses and the possession by the internationalising companies of VRIST resources (see Chap. 3 for the definition of resources that are valuable, rare, inimitable, non-substitutable, and non-transferable). On the basis of their criticism of the Uppsala model, Oviatt and McDougall elaborated an alternative internationalisation model: the "*International New Venture*" (or INV) model.[10] This INV model is particularly suited to companies that from inception, may reach a wide clientele base on a global scale. These "*born global*" companies, to use the terms created by McKinsey in a study of Australian exporters,[11] are largely made up of start-ups that have developed a new and unique technology, a digital platform or an e-business model. To ensure their early and accelerated internationalisation, whatever their country of origin or business, these start-ups often hire managers with solid international experience acquired in multinationals. Although the INV model is applicable to a narrower business context than the Uppsala model (whose application is intended to be more universal), it does approach the internationalisation process from perspectives that until then had been neglected or considered risky for internationalising companies: early and rapid foreign entries, accelerated global reach, value maximisation and systematic exploitation of market opportunities.

5.2.2   Methodology and Tools for the Mission

For companies willing to expand internationally, a step by step process can be applied to help reach this objective (see Fig. 5.2). It is important to note that the first steps of this process will differ depending on whether the client company has already embarked upon internationalisation or not. Companies whose geographical operations have so far been strictly local must first follow a preliminary

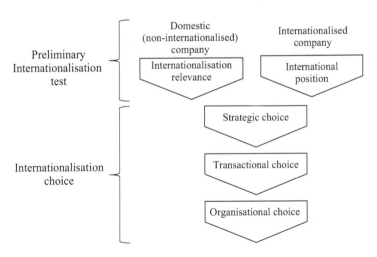

Fig. 5.2 Steps of the internationalisation process
Source: Authors

step if this is the first time they aim to expand abroad. This preliminary step takes the form of a test known as "*RAT/CAT*" (Relevant, Appropriate and Transferable/ Complementary, Appropriate and Transferable). The outcome of the RAT/ CAT test either confirms the company's intent to internationalise or leads it to reconsider the interest and timing of such a strategic move. If the company has already launched its internationalisation process, the preliminary step takes the form of an analysis of its current international position.

After applying the appropriate test, a three-step process can be initiated. Each step corresponds to a choice that is key to the company's successful international expansion: strategic choice, transactional choice and organisational choice. The first step, or *strategic choice* step, uses the 3A test to validate or devise an internationalisation strategy. The second step, or *transactional choice* step, offers a grid to help select an appropriate entry mode for each target market. The third and final step, the *organisational choice* step, details the architecture of the company's international organisation.

5.2.2.1 The RAT/CAT Test for Examining the Pertinence of Internationalisation

As mentioned at the beginning of this chapter, internationalisation is not a compulsory stage in the lifecycle of a company. Many companies prosper on their local markets and neither need to internationalise nor have the capabilities to do so. As noted by Ghemawat in his 2011 article in the *Harvard Business Review*,[12] "*less than 1% of all U.S. companies had foreign operations, and of those, the largest fraction operated in just one foreign country [...]. Among the U.S. companies that were in one foreign country, that country was Canada 60% of the time*" (p. 94).

Before venturing into foreign territory and expanding internationally, all companies must enquire as to the pertinence of initiating this growth strategy. There are many reasons for putting off its internationalisation for a few years or even ruling it out for a longer period, but these reasons are not always clear in the mind of the company's top management. Donald Lessard, Rafael Lucea and Luis Vives, professors of management at MIT Sloan School of Management, George Washington University and the ESADE in Barcelona, respectively, developed an original method to allow CEOs and top managers to examine the pertinence of expanding abroad. The method's originality is to establish the potential benefits of the company's internationalisation from the classic angle of transferring a local competitive advantage to foreign markets, but also from the more innovative angle of identifying the positive effects of the international on the local and more generally, on building a solid competitive advantage both locally and globally. Each of these aspects raises a specific question, which the authors express as follows[13]:

1. *"Will a company's current capabilities provide a competitive advantage in a target market?"*
2. *"Will that new location give the company an opportunity to enhance its capabilities?"* (p. 62)

This method is adapted from James March's model of *"exploitation/exploration"* organisational learning and applied to a company's internationalisation process. Thus, deciding whether to engage in the internationalisation process or not is conditioned by the company's capacity to transfer and exploit its distinctive capabilities in international markets, and to explore the development of new capabilities in these markets, which in turn will renew the company's capability portfolio.

Each new foreign entry will trigger a new cycle and will thus incrementally enrich the company's capability portfolio, thereby increasing its differentiation and strengthening its local and global competitive advantage. However, this cycle can only be incremental and value-creating if the internationalising company manages to pass successive RAT/CAT steps. The RAT test corresponds to questions posed at the cycle's first step when the company is seeking to transpose its local competitive advantage internationally. The CAT test corresponds to questions at the second stage, when the company intends to benefit from the subsequent renewal of its distinctive capability portfolio. These questions should be seen as indicative of a go/no go decision about internationalisation (see Fig. 5.3).

Best Consulting Practices in Brief

Before proposing the RAT/CAT test to a client company, it is important to bear in mind that this test is particularly suited to companies pursuing a differentiation strategy and running an activity with high added value that is strongly linked to innovation or based on exploiting unique know-how and expertise. In this event, transferability, appropriability, imitation and additional learning are key criteria for the company and must guide its decision on whether to internationalise or not. On the other hand, this test should be applied with caution for companies pursuing a price/cost leadership strategy and whose activity involves less added value. In that case, the main concern is not the capability's transferability or appropriability, nor additional learning, but rather optimising the regional disaggregation of the value chain, delocalising efficiently the company operations and achieving global economies of scale.

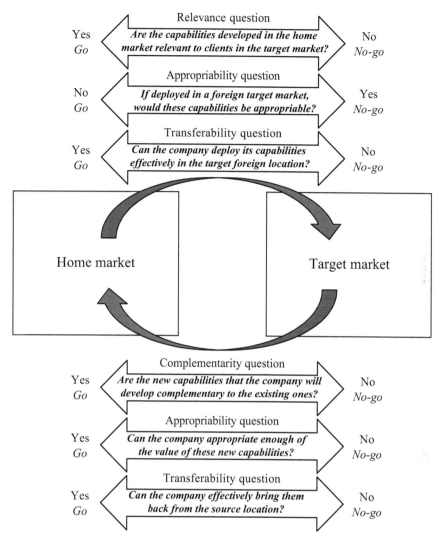

Fig. 5.3 The RAT/CAT test
Source: Adapted from Lessard Donald, Lucea and Vives Luis, *op. cit.*, 2013

5.2.2.2   Analysing the Company's International Position

Companies that have already ventured abroad differ greatly in the paths they have taken. Some have only just embarked on internationalisation, testing the export of a few products on their first foreign market, while others have been active for many years in the world's main regions and have an international turnover far higher than that of achieved in their local market. Between these extremes lies a whole range of distinct and intermediary positions regarding internationalisation.

The company might have internationalised without any purposeful guiding strategy, seizing opportunities as they came up. In this case, it may need to give more strategic, transactional and organisational coherence to its international expansion. Companies that are in an advanced phase of internationalisation may also ask for an assessment of the value of their geographical market portfolio. This should help CEOs and top managers decide about future investments abroad, reallocating resources among the different geographical markets and possibly deciding to exit certain countries or regions.

With a view to defining the company's international position, consultants must first use the "*GRI/GCI*" test (*global revenue index/global capability index*). This test, developed by Philippe Lasserre, professor of international strategy at INSEAD, maps the company's position regarding different profiles of internationalised companies.[14] The underlying idea of this mapping is to distinguish several internationalisation profiles for companies according to how they choose to manage their value chain internationally. This map has two dimensions: the first gives the company's position as regards the geographical distribution of its international sales. This is measured using the GRI. The second dimension assesses the geographical distribution of the company's manufacturing, assembly and R&D operations. It is measured using the GCI. The GRI and GCI are based on the same calculation method, which compares the geographical distribution of the company's sales (for the GRI) and assets (for the GCI) to the geographical distribution of sales for the industry. The closer the company's geographical distribution of sales and assets is to those of the sales in its industry, the closer the indices will be to the maximum 100%. Conversely, the larger the difference between these geographical distributions, the lower the indices. Lasserre proposes the following formula to estimate these two indices:

$$GRI = \Sigma\, I_n \left[CumS_n + \left(CumS - S\right)_n \right]$$

and

$$GCI = \Sigma\, I_n \left[CumA_n + \left(CumA - A\right)_n \right]$$

where I_n corresponds to sales in the region n as a percentage of total sales for the industry, S_n to the company's sales in region n as a percentage of its total sales and $CumS_n$ to the company's cumulated sales (in ascending order) for all regions; A_n corresponds to the company's assets in region n as a percentage of its total assets and $CumA_n$ to the company's cumulated assets (in ascending order) for all regions.

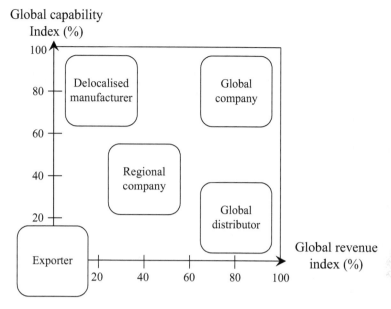

Fig. 5.4 Map of internationalised company's profiles
Source: Adapted from Lasserre Philippe, *op. cit.*, 2003

Table 5.1 The characteristic profiles of internationalised firms

Profile	Exporter	Global distributor	Global producer	Regional company	Global company
GRI	Weak (< 20%)	Strong (> 60%)	Weak (< 30%)	Average (between 30% and 60%)	Strong (> 60%)
GCI	Weak (< 20%)	Weak (< 30%)	Strong (> 60%)	Average (between 30% and 60%)	Strong (> 60%)
Characteristics	Firm beginning internationalisation and/or favouring cautious entries in few countries	Firm exporting its products and services in the main regions of the world	Firm delocalising a large part of its value chain but whose sales are mostly achieved in its local market	Firm developing a strong business presence in one region of the world	Firm developing a strong business presence in the main regions of the world

Source: Adapted from Lasserre Philippe, *op. cit.*, 2003

The map derived from the GRI and GCI shows several profiles of internationalised companies (see Fig. 5.4). The main characteristics of these profiles are summarised in Table 5.1.

From Theory to Practice

Below, we illustrate the analysis of an internationalised company's profiles by applying it to the Chinese computer maker Lenovo.[15] After being created as NTD in 1984 by a group of researchers from the Chinese Academy of Sciences, the Chinese company grew very rapidly. Until 2004, Lenovo was above all interested in building up a strong competitive advantage in its local market. Once it had consolidated its local position, the company got off the ground internationally with the acquisition of IBM's computer division in 2004. That year marked a significant turning point in Lenovo's growth and the start of its accelerated international expansion. Thus, the group grew from a 2% global market share in 2003 to 21.3% in 2016. Today, Lenovo has taken over from Hewlett-Packard as leader in the computer industry and is about to follow the same path in smartphones, having acquired Motorola's mobile phone division in 2014. In analysing Lenovo's approach to internationalisation, it is useful to position the Chinese computer maker in the map of internationalised company's profiles. We have chosen to focus on the early 2010s, years corresponding to Lenovo's accelerated international expansion. Table 5.2 presents the geographical distribution of Lenovo's international sales and that of the global computer industry for 2011.

Table 5.3 details the different steps of the GRI calculation. Even at a glance, it is easy to see that Lenovo's sales distribution is relatively close to that of the global computer industry. The GRI in Table 5.3 is 75.6%. Using the same calculation method, Lenovo's GCI is 66.4%. These figures position Lenovo in the category of global companies.

Table 5.2 Geographical distribution of Lenovo's international sales and of the computer industry in 2011

Geographical markets	Lenovo (unit sales as percentage of total sales)	Computer industry (unit sales as percentage of total sales)
Asia-Pacific (except Japan)	58	34
North America	12	21
Japan	8	4
Latin America	5	11
Eastern Europe	5	7
Middle-East and Africa	2	6
Western Europe	10	17
Total	100	100

Source: International Data Corporation (IDC), 2013

(continued)

(continued)

Table 5.3 Lenovo's GRI in 2011

	Middle-East and Africa	Latin America	Eastern Europe	Japan	Western Europe	North America	Asia-Pacific (except Japan)
I_n	0.06	0.11	0.07	0.04	0.17	0.21	0.34
S_n	0.02	0.05	0.05	0.08	0.10	0.12	0.58
$CumS_n$	0.02	0.07	0.12	0.20	0.30	0.42	1.00
$(CumS - S)_n$	0.00	0.02	0.07	0.12	0.20	0.30	0.42
$CumS_n + (CumS - S)_n$	0.02	0.09	0.19	0.32	0.50	0.72	1.42
$I_n[CumS_n + (CumS - S)_n]$	0.12	0.99	1.33	1.28	8.50	15.12	48.28
GRI = $\sum I_n[CumS_n + (CumS - S)_n]$	75.62%						

Source: Vidal Pascal and Meschi Pierre-Xavier, *op. cit.*, 2013

Best Consulting Practices in Brief

Defining the map of internationalised company's profiles and more specifically, calculating the GCI (global capability index) using company's assets is suitable for industrial companies. On the other hand, using a company's assets and their geographical distribution to calculate the GCI is not suited to service companies. In this specific context, it is advised to use a different measure based on the geographical distribution of employees.

To complement the analysis of the company's international position, it can be useful to position the company's geographical markets on a BCG, Arthur D. Little or McKinsey matrix (see Chap. 3). Here this type of matrix must be adapted to analysing the company's portfolio of geographical markets. The construction and interpretation are the same, but the company's strategic business units are replaced by its geographical markets or the world regions where it is active. The choices for investing, divesting and reallocating resources among geographical markets and regions follow the same rationale as those resulting from a traditional BCG, Arthur D. Little or McKinsey matrix.

5.2.2.3   Defining a Strategic Choice for Internationalisation or the 3A Test

Once the pertinence of expanding internationally or the company's international position has been established, the client company must initiate the three-step process whose first step is intended to either validate its internationalisation strategy or devise one from scratch. This important step can be seen as a set of choices (organisational, transactional, marketing, industrial…) aiming to ensure the profitable growth of the company's international sales. Strong or weak international growth, measured with the number of products sold abroad, global market share or international sales, results from the company's strategic choices for its internationalisation and the configuration of its portfolio of geographical markets.

Devising an internationalisation strategy first requires the company to assess three specific pressures. Each of these induces a specific choice and response by the company when defining its international expansion. These three pressures are developed by Ghemawat in a 2007 article published in the *Harvard Business Review*[16] (see Fig. 5.5).

Each of these pressures corresponds to one specific strategic choice for internationalisation, which is distinct from other choices in the way it addresses the issues of distance and CAGE differences between the home and target markets (see Table 5.4).

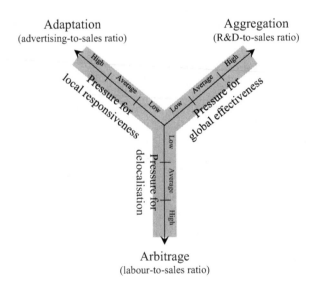

Fig. 5.5 Strategic choices for internationalisation
Source: Adapted from Ghemawat Pankaj, *op. cit.*, 2007

Table 5.4 The characteristics of CAGE differences[a]

Culture	Administration	Geography	Economy
Differences in language, values, norms, religions and social system	Differences in legal, institutional, regulatory and political systems	Physical and shipping distance, differences in time and climate	Differences in economic factors (exchange rates, customs barriers, natural and financial resources, infrastructure, taxation, labour costs, capital costs, and foreign direct investment)

Source: Adapted from Ghemawat Pankaj, *op. cit.*, 2001
[a]Ghemawat Pankaj, "Distance Still Matters: The Hard Reality of Global Expansion", *Harvard Business Review*, vol. 79, no 8, 2001, p. 137–147

These pressures result from the company's resources, product and market portfolio, corporate strategy and the structure of its industry at the global level. To assess these pressures and help companies position themselves, Ghemawat proposes a specific measure for each pressure, as shown in Fig. 5.5. Each of these measures is easily accessible from the company's financial and economic documents. In addition to Ghemawat's measures, we suggest using the degree of global concentration, or CR4. In a 2011 article in the *MIT Sloan Management Review*,[17] Chris Carr and David Collis, professors of strategy at the University of Edinburgh Business School and Harvard Business School, respectively, developed the idea that CEOs and top managers aiming to define an international expansion strategy would want to know the global industry structure and, notably, the degree of concentration for companies operating in that industry. The CR4 is a measure of concentration applied to an industry at the global level. It is calculated by adding up the global market share of the four largest competitors in the industry. Carr and Collis defend the idea that a high degree of global concentration, *i.e.*, above 40%, indicates an industry where the competitors are largely present in the main world regions and are therefore highly interdependent. This high competitive interdependence reflects the integration of the world's main geographical markets. Conversely, a low degree of global concentration indicates regional or national fragmentation of the competition and low global integration of international markets.

From the different elements mentioned above, it is possible to characterise the three pressures in Fig. 5.5 and the AAA (adaptation, aggregation and arbitrage) internationalisation strategies as follows (see Table 5.5): a first pressure, defined as *local responsiveness*, refers to the need for the internationalising company to adapt its offer to local conditions and consumer needs. This pressure for local responsiveness is especially strong for companies whose activities place them in direct relationship with end consumers (B-to-C activities). Obviously,

Table 5.5 The AAA internationalisation strategies

Characteristics	Adaptation		Aggregation	Arbitrage
Pressure	Local responsiveness	Local integration	Global effectiveness	Delocalisation
Managing CAGE differences	Reduce differences by adapting locally	Reduce differences by integrating locally	Reduce differences by finding a common denominator among different foreign markets	Benefit from differences by playing on comparative advantages of each foreign market
Main action	Adapt offer to different foreign markets	Integrate local business networks	Standardise offer on different foreign markets	Disintegrate value chain internationally depending on comparative advantages of foreign markets
Objectives	Create brands perceived as local	Be perceived as a quasi-local player	Produce economies of scale worldwide	Produce economies linked to international specialisation of operations
Organisation	By foreign markets, countries or world regions		By business units, product lines or key accounts	By functions, operations or divisions of the value chain

Source: Authors

this is relevant to companies operating in the consumer goods industry, but also and more generally to many industries that are poorly concentrated globally (*i.e.*, with a CR4 well below 40%), which Carr and Collis call "*regional and national terrains.*" Ghemawat recommends assessing the pressure for local responsiveness by estimating the company's advertising-to-sales ratio. In fact, a company seeking to build up a strong local image in a foreign market must invest significantly in communication, branding and advertising. Thus, an advertising-to-sales ratio above 6% reflects a strong propensity to local adaptation, a ratio between 2% and 6% indicates an average propensity and a ratio below 2%, a weak propensity.

The *local adaption* strategy, which responds to this first pressure, is defined as the set of actions allowing the internationalising company to be perceived as quasi-local by the target country's customers, distributors, suppliers, and government and State institutions. More specifically, the company will try to respond to the expectations, characteristics and needs of the customers of each foreign market by the local development of a specific brand, communication, product range and distribution and/or after-sales service.

Local adaptation is not always a sufficient strategic response when the company internationalises towards *"regional and national terrains"* whose logic is *"guarded globalization,"* as observed in many industries located in emerging economies and *"frontier economies."*[18] In these industries, listening to local customers and proposing products and brands adapted to their needs is not enough. It is not only products and brands that must blend into the host market, but more generally, the foreign entrant and its organisation. It has to get embedded in the local business network (including suppliers, distributors and competition). In emerging economies where public institutions and State-owned companies have a major influence on business, the foreign entrant's transformation into a quasi-local player also involves joining wider networks, including political and government players, the social economy, lobbies and society at large.[19] The "immersed" foreign company reaps many benefits from such a *local integration* strategy. It creates a good local image and reputation, reduces its liability of foreignness, sells its products more easily to local clients; it also gains access to public tenders, opens new markets, co-develops products with local partners and in the longer term, encourages the emergence of a legal framework protecting foreign investors thereby contributing to filling in the *"institutional voids"*[20] in these countries. Samuel Palmisano, former CEO of IBM, summarised this view in an interview in the Indian newspaper *The Economic Times* (July 25, 2014): *"and we didn't simply enter markets. As IBM has done throughout its history, we made markets, working with leaders in business, government, academia and community organizations to help advance their national agenda and address their societal needs."*

Best Consulting Practices in Brief

In any analysis conducted prior to formulating an entry strategy into an emerging or frontier economy, the consultant must identify local champions[21] in the targeted industry, which have inflicted strategic reversals on multinationals. A quick and easy measure of relative local concentration—for example, a cumulated market share of the two largest local competitors that is significantly higher than that of the two biggest multinationals established in the country—will shed light on the industries that are likely to be difficult and risky for the foreign investor. If such a case comes up for a client company, it is important to devise an entry strategy that will facilitate its local integration.

(continued)

(continued)

The example of the food distribution industry in South Africa and the entry strategy of the American group Wal-Mart illustrates the difficulty of challenging these local champions in certain emerging economies. In the early 2010s, Wal-Mart was almost absent from the African continent and sought an entry point that would enable it to expand rapidly. In May 2011, Wal-Mart thought it had found the solution in acquiring the South African distributor Massmart, a minor local player with only 1.2% of market share but with subsidiaries in most African countries, including the one with the highest population, Nigeria. The American multinational entered a difficult industry, strongly dominated by two local distributors, Shoprite (18.3% market share) and Pick 'n' Pay (14.4%). Neither of these had been overtaken by the foreign companies already present in South Africa, largest amongst them Dutch SPAR with 9.2% of the market and the Australian Woolworths with 3.6%. Wal-Mart made its entry in this environment, intending to challenge the two local champions, owned by the richest and most influential families in South Africa (the Wiese family for Shoprite and the Ackerman family for Pick 'n' Pay). Wal-Mart's entry in South Africa has, so far, not been what the American multinational hoped for, with Massmart's market share dropping to 1% in 2015. Numerous industry analysts anticipate Wal-Mart's divestment by 2018 if its South African market share does not significantly progress by then.

The second pressure, defined as *global effectiveness*, corresponds to the need to reduce costs and generate economies of scale globally. This pressure for global effectiveness is often associated with companies operating B-to-B activities or getting involved in a vertical supplier-client relationship. This requirement may also concern companies with a high level of fixed administrative, financial, R&D and/or distribution expenses. Finally, the pressure for global effectiveness is very frequent in industries that are highly concentrated globally (with a CR4 above 40%), defined as "*global oligopolies*" by Carr and Collis. Ghemawat recommends evaluating this pressure by estimating the company's R&D-to-sales ratio. In fact, a company that invests highly in R&D activities must rapidly increase its global sales to spread these fixed costs over a larger amount of sales. Thus, a R&D-to-sales ratio above 5% is considered as representing a strong pressure for global effectiveness, a ratio between 2% and 5% an average pressure and a ratio below 2% a low pressure. If the company's financial and economic documents allow, it is also possible to use the total amount of fixed expenses and compare this with the company's sales.

In response to the pressure for global effectiveness, the "*global aggregation*" strategy aims to offer a standardized product, service or solution to a maximum number of foreign markets. This strategy leads the internationalising company to develop a world brand associated to a product range, distribution and after-sales service, which are identical from one market to another.

The third and final pressure, defined as *"delocalisation,"* which incites the company to take advantage of the CAGE differences specific to each foreign market and to do this through the international disaggregation of its value chain. The pressure for delocalisation is high for companies operating in labour-intensive industries. It may also concern industries with high added value (such as biotechnologies, information technologies, software engineering or R&D consulting), and industries with less added value (textile and garment, call-centres and transportation logistics). To evaluate the pressure to exploit the CAGE differences among foreign markets, Ghemawat proposes using the company's labour-to-sales ratio. In fact, a company with a high labour-to-sales ratio will seek to reduce it or a least control it by benefiting from the differences in labour costs from one country to another. Thus a ratio between 50% and 80% is considered to be a strong pressure to delocalise, a ratio between 20% and 50% an average pressure and a ration below 20% a low pressure.

The *"international arbitrage"* strategy that corresponds to this pressure is based on different delocalisation operations that will result in the internationalising company's spreading its value chain over several countries or foreign markets. The company facing strong pressure for delocalisation will develop internationally by establishing some of its operations in countries presenting advantageous differences in costs relative to the home country. Thus, the international arbitrage strategy may lead the company into the "traditional" delocalisation of manufacturing and assembly operations to countries with low-cost labour, but this strategy can just as well concern tax optimisation, transfer of certain R&D activities (as observed in India for certain European or American IT companies) or transportation logistics (as observed in Eastern Europe for certain German and French logistics suppliers).

The international arbitrage strategy is particularly suited to companies that can easily disentangle operations within their value chain and make delocalisation decisions for each of these. This means that the company can compare the cost of its main operations in its country of origin to that of equivalent operations in other regions of the world. Furthermore, it implies that certain operations are "delocalisable" without generating excessive transaction and coordination costs.

In sum, the international arbitrage strategy provides guidance to the company in its choice of international entries by seeking comparative geographical advantages. The arbitrage strategy proposed by Ghemawat is an updated form of the theory of comparative advantages. This theory, formalised at the beginning of the 19th century by the British economist David Ricardo, encourages countries to specialise in activities where they benefit from a comparative advantage. The source of this advantage might be a natural resource (such as the sun or fertile terrain, in his example of wine being manufactured in Portugal) or a labour resource (such as the qualified manpower and productive workshops in Ricardo's example of sheets made in Great Britain).

From Theory to Practice

We applied the 3A test to the Chinese computer maker Lenovo. The information gleaned from the company's executive managers[22] placed the company under medium/high pressure for local responsiveness, high pressure for global effectiveness and low/medium pressure for delocalisation. As a result, Lenovo should favour a strategic response to the pressure for global effectiveness. This means opting in priority for global aggregation in its internationalisation strategy (see Fig. 5.6).

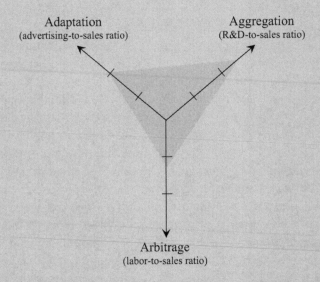

Fig. 5.6 The 3A test and Lenovo's strategic choices for internationalisation (To position Lenovo in relation to the three pressures, we used approximate measures for the adverting-to-sales, R&D-to-sales and labour-to-sales ratios that we obtained through a series of interviews carried out in 2012–2013 with two executive managers at Lenovo: Sam Dusi (*Vice-President Market Analysis & Intelligence*) and Dan Stone (*Vice-President Strategy & Corporate Development*)). Source: Authors

Best Consulting Practices in Brief

The implications of the 3A test are easy to formulate when only one pressure stands out clearly. In that case, it is easy to align the appropriate internationalisation strategy (whether it be local adaptation, global aggregation or international arbitrage) and the international organisation choices (see Table 5.5). However, if not one but two or three strong pressures act simultaneously, this

(continued)

(continued)

strategy/organisation fit is much harder to reach. Therefore, combinations of adaptation/arbitrage, aggregation/arbitrage or adaptation/aggregation must be considered, but the associated international organisation is not evident. Many organisational questions have to be answered: How should competences and resources be allocated to foreign subsidiaries? To what degree should these subsidiaries be autonomous? What coordination and control mechanisms need to be set up and diffused internationally? Answers exist with matrix organisations (country/product, country/function or function/product), flexible systems of integration and *ad hoc* management styles. But so far, no best way has appeared and this remains relatively unknown territory for strategy consultants.

5.2.2.4   Selecting an Entry Mode

After defining the internationalisation strategy and the target foreign markets, there remains the question of selecting an entry mode for each market. The main function of the entry mode is to handle the (finance, technology, human resources, knowledge…) transactions between the company and the foreign market as effectively as possible. In other words, the entry mode must be considered as an interface or a mode of transactional governance.

Selecting an entry mode has consequences for any company that decides to enter a foreign market. The first level of selection is between equity and non-equity entry modes. Companies with little international experience and/or privileging risk minimisation for their foreign entries, should first engage in export operations, work with local agents or sign distribution agreements or licences with local companies. More experienced companies, with some knowledge of the foreign market gained through a first entry with a non-equity mode and/or that are less risk averse, might consider shifting to an equity entry mode. This will involve a second level of selection between the different equity entry modes. In general, the choice is between setting up a local, wholly owned subsidiary, forming a joint venture with a local partner or acquiring a local firm.

The foreign entrant can select an equity entry mode by positioning itself relative to five needs that may be fulfilled partially or fully by the three equity modes (wholly owned subsidiary, joint venture and acquisition). These needs often reflect the value system of the company's top management and make it possible to define criteria to help select the right entry mode (see Fig. 5.7). These selection criteria were developed in 2009 by Pierre-Xavier Meschi.[23]

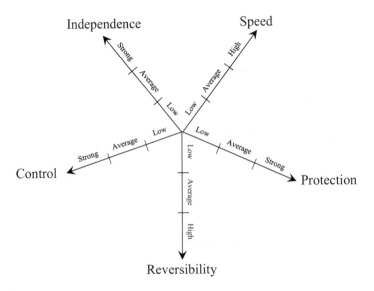

Fig. 5.7 Criteria to select an equity entry mode
Source: Adapted from Meschi Pierre-Xavier, *op. cit.*, 2009

The first need related to entry mode is *"independence" vis a vis* local compa-nies in the target market. This means knowing whether the foreign investor considers it a priority to enter the target market without having to negotiate, collaborate and work with a local company. More specifically, this need for independence is conditioned by the foreign company's willingness to mini-mise transaction costs. These costs are high with the joint venture and acquisi-tion modes. In fact, forming a joint venture incurs transaction costs through finding a local partner, evaluating a partner's contributions to the joint ven-ture and negotiating and drawing up an alliance contract. In the context of an acquisition of a local company, transaction costs arise from selecting a target, conducting due diligence, estimating the target's value, and negotiating and drawing up an acquisition contract.

As shown in Fig. 5.8, the wholly owned subsidiary is the entry mode that ensures the highest degree of independence from local companies in the target market. Transaction costs are reduced to a minimum as this entry mode is based on the organic development of a subsidiary from scratch in the target market. For the two other equity entry modes, joint venture and acquisition, the transaction costs are high. However, for joint ventures, they can be reduced by sharing them with the local partner.

The second need relates to the *"speed"* of operation on the target market. The foreign company may expect an entry mode to enable the company to be

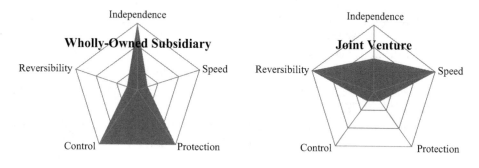

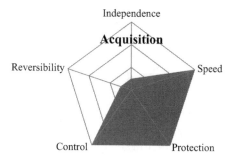

Fig. 5.8 Compared advantages and disadvantages of equity entry modes
Source: Adapted from Meschi Pierre-Xavier, *op. cit.*, 2009

operational and active in the target market as quickly as possible. This need is associated with the foreign entrant's willingness to seize opportunities rapidly, be faster than (or catch up to) the other foreign entrants and/or leverage from its entry on the target market as soon as possible. Thus, the entry mode must, in particular, give the foreign company and its products rapid access to the target market's distribution channels.

To respond to this need for speed, Fig. 5.8 underlines that the joint venture and the acquisition are favoured entry modes compared to the wholly owned subsidiary. In fact, with a joint venture or an acquisition, the company can rely on a local third party (partner or target) whose contribution is specifically to allow the foreign entrant to access key local resources: human, manufacturing and marketing resources as well as a detailed knowledge of distribution networks, markets and clients. When opting for a wholly owned subsidiary, the foreign entrant has to develop these assets, competences and resources locally from scratch. This entry mode therefore requires a certain amount of time to be fully operational.

The third need is related to the *"protection"* of competences and resources that the foreign entrant will transfer and exploit in the target market.

The foreign company may benefit from distinctive competences and resources whose exploitation ensures its solid competitive advantage in its local market. From one point of view, the foreign entrant is tempted to transfer and exploit these distinctive competences and resources in other geographical markets than its local market. But from another point of view, a risk exists that certain companies operating in the target markets might appropriate or imitate these competences and resources when they are transferred internationally. The choice of entry mode is key to minimising this risk of appropriation and imitation.

Figure 5.8 shows that some entry modes ensure stronger protection than others. This is notably the case for the wholly owned subsidiary and acquisition modes that completely internalise the transfer and use of competences and resources. Contrary to the joint venture mode, in which assets and resources are shared and managed jointly with the local partner, the wholly owned subsidiary and acquisition modes do not involve other local players internally, thus avoiding their possible access to transferred competences and resources.

The fourth need is "*control*" over local decisions. The foreign entrant may want to control decisions made in the entry mode to its advantage. Choosing an internationalisation strategy often results in companies eager to keep a close watch on local decisions. A company pursuing a global aggregation strategy must control the decisions made by its foreign subsidiaries, making sure that these rigorously meet the global standardization of products and operations. In this context, the internationalising company must favour an entry mode that allows it to check the alignment of local decisions with its internationalisation strategy.

Just like protecting competences and resources, strong control over local decisions is expected with wholly owned subsidiaries and acquisitions (see Fig. 5.8). The ownership of the equity as well as the management dominance of the wholly owned subsidiary or the target allow the foreign entrant to exercise full control over local decisions. This is not possible for joint ventures whose equity and management are shared between foreign and local partners. This results in two-headed management and decision making that although collaborative in theory, in practice often lead to long and sometimes conflicting negotiations between partners.

The fifth and final need is "*reversibility*." From the outset of its entry into the target market, the foreign company must anticipate the possibility of its local subsidiary's failure and have a clear view on the conditions of exit from this market. If the target market presents strong potential but also high risks, this need for reversibility may be high and the company will then favour an entry mode that minimises possible exit costs. The entry mode here must be envisaged as a real option.[24] Similar to options in financial markets, the entry mode must allow the company to invest more and take full control (*call* option) if the venture succeeds or to divest easily (*put* option) if it fails.

Figure 5.8 shows that the joint venture mode gives the best guarantee of reversibility and minimises exit costs. In fact, many joint ventures include detailed exit clauses in their contracts under which the foreign entrant and its local partner can easily sell off their equity stake to the other partner or to a third party. This sale can occur at specific periods in the joint venture's life-cycle and at a price previously agreed in the contract. Conversely, wholly owned subsidiaries or acquisitions do not offer this flexibility. Their eventual divestment will involve a long and random process entailing the same difficulties and transaction costs that were applicable to the original acquisition: finding an acquirer, conducting due diligence and evaluating the value of the subsidiary, negotiating and drawing up a divestment contract.

5.2.2.5   Organising Internationally

The final step in the internationalisation process consists in choosing an international organisation that is aligned with the internationalisation strategy. Three types of international organisations can be envisaged to ensure the effective implementation of the strategies for local adaptation, global aggregation and international arbitrage. These are presented below as possible architectures for the value chain of companies expanding internationally. Here we present stereotypical organisations and many variations are possible depending on the industry, management style, size and, above all, the company's choice of combining different internationalisation strategies (such as adaptation/arbitrage, aggregation/arbitrage, or adaptation/aggregation).

The first architecture for the international value chain corresponds to the local adaptation strategy. This requires strong autonomy for the management of foreign subsidiaries and the international transfer of much of the value chain: distribution, marketing, manufacturing, logistics and sometimes even R&D (see Fig. 5.9). This choice results in foreign subsidiaries being highly endowed with competences and resources that allow them to engage in varied and autonomous actions for local adaptation. In this organisational configuration, the parent company exercises light and flexible control over its different subsidiaries in the world. This control is based on an annual reporting. This reporting checks whether the financial objectives assigned to each subsidiary at the beginning of the year have been met and if there are any deviations from these objectives. This control may also aim to ensure the coherence and alignment of the product

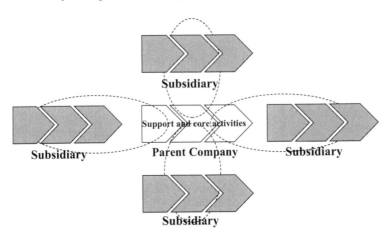

Fig. 5.9 Adaptation strategy and international organisation of the value chain
Source: Authors

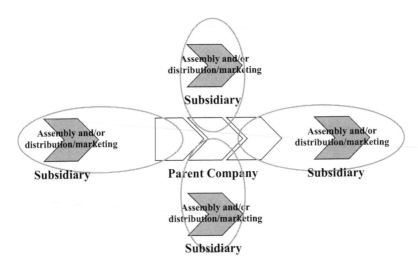

Fig. 5.10 Aggregation strategy and international organisation of the value chain
Source: Authors

and brand portfolios worldwide. More specifically, the control procedures of a company engaged in a local adaptation strategy should avoid product and brand cannibalisation issues or uncontrolled proliferation in the number of products and brands in different geographical markets.

The global aggregation strategy is associated with strong geographical concentration of the core and support activities (see Fig. 5.10). Most of these

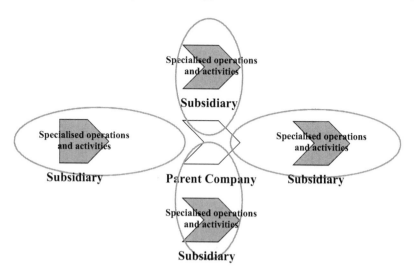

Fig. 5.11 Arbitrage strategy and international organisation of the value chain
Source: Authors

activities are grouped in the company's country of origin or may be spread over a few countries in an organisation centralised by main regions. In this organisational configuration, foreign subsidiaries are submitted to close control over their decisions and are not endowed with strategic competences and resources. The foreign subsidiaries' main role is either the local distribution of products made in the home country or low-cost assembly of different components for a finished product that can be sold locally or in other geographical markets. In general, these foreign subsidiaries contribute limited added value to the company's products or services.

The international arbitrage strategy is associated with companies organised into functions or main competences (see Fig. 5.11). More specifically, this organisation requires the transformation of certain operations, functions or main competences into autonomous cost centres. In this organisational configuration, foreign subsidiaries are endowed with competences and resources required to efficiently run the delocalised value chain operations. These subsidiaries are subject to the parent company's close control over the costs of their operations. The cost of delocalised operations is regularly benchmarked against what the company could obtain in other regions of the world. This control procedure is also focused on monitoring transaction and coordination costs among the different delocalised operations.

Notes

1. Meschi Pierre-Xavier, Ricard Antonin and Tapia-Moore Ernesto, "Fast and Furious or Slow and Cautious? The Joint Impact of Age at Internationalization, Speed and Risk Diversity on the Survival of Exporting Firms", *Journal of International Management*, vol. 23, no 3, 2017, p. 279–291.

2. Kenichi Ohmae had a long career as a consultant with McKinsey in Japan. He published many books in which he presents strategies for a borderless world with convergent customer behaviour. In this line, two of his books were highly successful: *The Borderless World: Power and Strategy in the Interlinked Economy*, Harper Business, New York, 1990 and *The Invisible Continent: Four Strategic Imperatives of the New Economy*, Harper Business, New York, 2000.

3. Friedman Thomas L., *The World is Flat: A Brief History of the Twenty-First Century*, Farrar, Straus & Giroux, New York, 2005.

4. Bremmer Ian, "The New Rules of Globalization", *Harvard Business Review*, vol. 92, no 1/2, 2014, p. 103–107. This new movement of globalisation was initiated by several emerging economies that *"have become wary of opening more industries to multinational companies and are zealously protecting local interests. They choose the countries or regions with which they want to do business, pick the sectors in which they will allow capital investment, and select the local, often State-owned, companies they wish to promote"* (p. 104).

5. Ghemawat Pankaj, *World 3.0*, Harvard Business School Press, Cambridge, 2011.

6. Eden Lorraine, "Letter from the Editor-in-Chief: Time in International Business", *Journal of International Business Studies*, vol. 40, no 4, 2009, p. 535–538.

7. Johanson Jan and Vahlne Jan-Erik, "The Internationalization Process of the Firm: A Model of Knowledge Development and Increasing Foreign Market Commitments", *Journal of International Business Studies*, vol. 8, no 1, 1977, p. 23–32.

8. Zaheer Srilata, "Overcoming the Liability of Foreignness", *Academy of Management Journal*, vol. 38, no 2, 1995, p. 341–363. The notion of *"liability of foreignness"* was defined by Srilata Zaheer, professor of management at the University of Minnesota, as the *"costs of doing business abroad"* (p. 342). These costs incurred by new entrants on foreign markets result from several sources: CAGE differences, lack of knowledge of the local environment or local players' negative perceptions of the new entrant's country of origin.

9. Johanson Jan and Vahlne Jan-Erik, "The Uppsala Internationalization Process Model Revisited: From Liability of Foreignness to Liability of Outsidership", *Journal of International Business Studies*, vol. 40, no 9, 2009, p. 1411–1431.

10. Oviatt Benjamin M. and Phillips McDougall Patricia, "Toward a Theory of International New Ventures", *Journal of International Business Studies*, vol. 25,

no 1, 1994, p. 45–64. Oviatt and McDougall define this specific category of internationalising companies as follows: "*a business organization that from inception, seeks to derive significant competitive advantage from the use of resources and the sale of outputs in multiple countries*" (p. 49).

11. McKinsey Australia, *Emerging Exporters: Australia's High Value-Added Manufacturing Exporters*, Australian Manufacturing Council, Melbourne, 1993.

12. Ghemawat Pankaj, "The Cosmopolitan Corporation", *Harvard Business Review*, vol. 89, no 5, 2011, p. 92–99.

13. Lessard Donald, Lucea Rafael and Vives Luis, "Building your Company's Capabilities through Global Expansion", *MIT Sloan Management Review*, vol. 54, no 2, 2013, p. 61–67.

14. Lasserre Philippe, *Global Strategic Management*, Palgrave Macmillan, New York, 2003.

15. The information used here is derived from the case study *Lenovo: A Chinese Dragon in the Global Village*, Ivey Publishing, Ivey Business School, 9B13M029. This case study was written and published by Pascal Vidal and Pierre-Xavier Meschi in 2013

16. The analysis proposed by Ghemawat in this article builds on the different internationalisation strategies defined first by John M. Stopford and Louis T. Wells and second by Christopher A. Bartlett and Sumantra Ghoshal. Ghemawat Pankaj, "Managing Differences: The Central Challenge of Global Strategy", *Harvard Business Review*, vol. 85, no 3, 2007, p. 58–68.

17. Carr Chris and Collis David, "Should You Have a Global Strategy?", *MIT Sloan Management Review*, vol. 53, no 1, 2011, p. 21–24.

18. Musacchio Aldo and Werker Eric, "Mapping Frontier Economies", *Harvard Business Review*, vol. 94, no 12, 2016, p. 41–48.

19. This necessary extension of a local adaptation strategy to a local integration strategy was detailed by José F.P. Santos and Peter J. Williamson, professors at INSEAD and the University of Cambridge respectively, in the following article: Santos José F.P. and Williamson Peter J., "The New Mission for Multinationals", *MIT Sloan Management Review*, vol. 56, no 4, 2015, p. 45–54.

20. The notion of "*institutional voids*" was developed by Tarun Khanna and Krishan Palepu, professors at Harvard Business School, to describe emerging economies and define them, presenting them as markets with strong potential growth but also associated with a number of risks for foreign investors. This idea refers to markets and competitive spaces that lack government, regulatory and legal institutions to protect foreign investors and their assets (especially contracts, brands and intellectual property), sheltering them from possible expropriation, extortion or nationalisation, and guaranteeing competition deprived of manipulation and distortion. These institutional voids may be partial in many emerging economies or total in "*frontier economies.*" Khanna Tarun and Palepu Krishna, "Why Focused Strategies may be Wrong for Emerging Markets", *Harvard Business Review*, vol. 75, no 4, 1997, p. 41–54.

21. The BCG qualified these local champions in emerging countries as "*local dynamos*": these are local companies with a strong domination over a particular industry, even when faced with other local companies but especially when confronted by large multinationals. Online distribution in Russia with Ozon, in India with Flipkart and China with Alibaba is often put forward to illustrate the local domination of these "*local dynamos*" over Amazon. Chin Vincent and Michael David C., *How Companies in Emerging Markets are Winning at Home*, The 2014 BCG Local Dynamos Report, the Boston Consulting Group, 2014.

22. To position Lenovo in relation to the three pressures, we used approximate measures for the advertising-to-sales, R&D-to-sales and labour-to-sales ratios that we obtained through a series of interviews carried out in 2012–2013 with two executive managers at Lenovo: Sam Dusi (*Vice-President Market Analysis & Intelligence*) and Dan Stone (*Vice-President Strategy & Corporate Development*).

23. Meschi Pierre-Xavier, "Les coentreprises", *in Management Stratégique de la Concurrence*, in Le Roy Frédéric and Yami Saïd, Chapter 12, Dunod, Paris, 2009, p. 133–143.

24. Stalk Jr. George and Iyer Ashish, "How to Hedge your Strategic Bets", *Harvard Business Review*, vol. 94, no 5, 2016, p. 80–86.

Further Reading

On Distance, CAGE Model, Semi-Globalisation and Questioning Globalisation and the Global Integration of Geographical Markets

Bremmer Ian, "The New Rules of Globalization", *Harvard Business Review*, vol. 92, no 1/2, 2014, p. 103–107.

Ghemawat Pankaj, "Distance Still Matters: The Hard Reality of Global Expansion", *Harvard Business Review*, vol. 79, no 8, 2001, p. 137–147.

Ghemawat Pankaj, *World 3.0*, Harvard Business School Press, Cambridge, 2011a.

Ghemawat Pankaj, "The Cosmopolitan Corporation", *Harvard Business Review*, vol. 89, no 5, 2011b, p. 92–99.

Musacchio Aldo and Werker Eric, "Mapping Frontier Economies", *Harvard Business Review*, vol. 94, no 12, 2016, p. 41–48.

On Internationalisation Strategies, International Organisations, the Sources of Ghemawat's AAA Strategies and Local Integration as an Extension of Local Adaptation

Bartlett Christopher A. and Ghoshal Sumantra, *Managing Across Borders: The Transnational Solution*, Harvard Business School Press, Cambridge, 1989.

Ghemawat Pankaj, "Managing Differences: The Central Challenge of Global Strategy", *Harvard Business Review*, vol. 85, no 3, 2007, p. 58–68.

Santos José F.P. and Williamson Peter J., "The New Mission for Multinationals", *MIT Sloan Management Review*, vol. 56, no 4, 2015, p. 45–54.

Stopford John M. and Wells Louis T., *Managing the Multinational Enterprise: Organization of the Firm and Ownership of the Subsidiary*, Basic Books, New York, 1972.

6

Combining Strategy and Innovation

6.1 The Consulting Mission

During a strategy consulting mission, the question of strategic management of innovation is one that consultants often deal with. Indeed, innovation is the prime concern of company strategy; an innovative offering, a more efficient manufacturing process or a different way of organising with a new business model, may better stand up to competition and win a distinctive lasting competitive advantage or more generally, support company growth.

Fariborz Damanpour and William M. Evan[1] see innovation as adopting measures, systems, policies, programmes, processes, products or services to maintain or expand competitive advantage. These are either generated internally or purchased and they are new for the organisation in question.

This definition shows that when a company innovates, it embarks on a process that affects every part of the organisation and all aspects of operations. It is important that the company durably captures the positive outcomes of the efforts it makes throughout this complex process. Indeed, the competences required to achieve innovation are rather different from those that allow the long-term exploitation of the innovation's benefits. Consultants focus on implementing the strategic options defined during the competitive positioning diagnostic (see Chap. 3). In a market context of ever increasing change and turbulence, they must therefore think about the company's capacity to propose new solutions in terms of offering or business practice that will be of lasting benefit.

With this in mind, it is helpful to look at the different typologies of innovation in relation to the characteristics of the company's chosen strategic posture. These typologies are usually described in terms of:

© The Author(s) 2018
P. Chereau, P.-X. Meschi, *Strategic Consulting*, DOI 10.1007/978-3-319-64422-6_6

- The "nature" of innovation: sustaining innovation that aims to improve or renew the offer on the existing market. Or disruptive innovation that aims to overturn the field rendering competing offers obsolete, or that proposes a new offer, (or one considered as such), for instance in a new market.
- The "source" of innovation—from a technological or market opportunity.
- The innovation "activity" in itself, either in terms of products and processes or more fundamentally, through modifying the company's business model.

Here again, the notion of alignment or fit between the company's strategic posture and its associated innovation behaviour is essential. The conclusions of many studies converge, underlining that when CEOs and top managers choose and implement their competitive positioning strategy, they should consider the innovation nature, source and activities that correspond to their strategic posture, the characteristics of their target markets and their available capabilities likely to influence the fit between strategy and innovation. In other words, companies cannot afford to expand or adopt innovation behaviours that are not in line with their strategic objectives. In a critical analysis of the shared enthusiasm of researchers, CEOs and top managers for disruptive innovation, Andrew A. King and Baljir Baatartogtokh[2] warn about the need to "keep within reason" and adopt a strategic approach to innovation: when the rules are upended by disruptive innovation, the first question to ask is whether the new market forces maintain the attractiveness of this market, given the company's resources, or whether it might not be better to reposition the company where its resources would still represent real strategic capabilities. Similarly, rather than modifying the company's strategic posture and innovation behaviour, it might be wiser to cooperate with the new entrant in a logic of complementary assets.

The consultant should guide the CEO and top managers towards the strategy/innovation alignment offering the best fit in the company's market context. The following questions should be answered:

Is there a specific innovation behaviour suited to the company's chosen competitive positioning that would make it easier to reach its strategic objectives? If so, are there any gaps between the company's current innovation behaviour and the ideal target behaviour? What would be the impact of a change in entrepreneurial, technological or organisational strategic choice on the strategy/innovation fit? More specifically, what levers of strategic posture should the company use to innovate efficiently and reach its innovation objectives?

These questions lead to different missions or parts of missions regarding strategic management of innovation. For example, an innovation diagnostic must be undertaken to assess the company's innovation practices to take advantage of technological or market opportunities according to its strategic capabilities. Possible gaps would lead to another type of mission with a complete review of the company's business model that would result in its innovation (see Chap. 7).

Another type of mission consists of accompanying the company in its decision to use innovation to support internal growth while making optimal use of its competences and resources to expand existing activities or its strategic product/market domain. Consultants must then provide answers to the following central question of innovation strategy:

Should the company encourage efforts to better exploit existing resources or on the contrary, should it develop new strategic capabilities to explore new paths to expansion?

Whatever the mission of strategic management of innovation, consultants must attempt to combine strategy and innovation according to the company's market context, internal competences and resources, strategic posture as well as its typology.

Today it is commonly accepted that large companies and SMEs make different strategic choices to introduce their respective innovations. Moreover, it seems that market characteristics influence innovation practices differently in large and small companies.

6.2   Theory, Methodology and the Tools for the Mission

6.2.1   Theoretical Background

6.2.1.1   Strategy and Innovation: The Need for Fit

Implementing a company's strategy requires solid strategic choices in terms of the capabilities to be developed and the type of technology and organisation that best serve these capabilities. These strategic choices tend towards permanently making optimal use of the company's resources. In their article published in the *Harvard Business Review*,[3] Gary Hamel and Coimbatore

K. Prahalad insist that such a strategic intent must be supported by an organisational structure and processes suited to its implementation. Hamel and Prahalad underline that strategic intent obliges the company to be innovative and make the most of its resources to create new competitive advantages.

In the hypercompetitive context that characterises most industries, teams in strategy consulting are increasingly in demand. CEOs and top managers seek advice on their choices for expanding or refocusing their activity portfolio, diversifying their markets or even rethinking the company's business model and being tempted to create a new competitive space.

Indeed, companies need to design and implement competitive strategies that are "adaptive," where innovation plays a central role combining diversity with coherent strategic options. There is strong demand for consulting in strategic management of innovation. Faced with this demand, consultants can rely first, on solid theoretical frameworks on strategic management, and second on innovation. The real issue is to link these theoretical frameworks into a coherent combination of these two distinct but strongly related concepts.

Based on the results of much research, Shaker A. Zahra and Jeffrey G. Covin[4] agree that a key variable of economic performance is the relationship between a company's strategy and its innovation practices. It can also be said that the market environment and the company's resources influence its strategic choices and that these same choices determine the type of innovation to be undertaken. In other words, strategy conditions innovation and some strategy/innovation fits are preferable to others.

Unfortunately, the influence of the determinants of competitive strategy on the determinants of innovation, as well as specific fits between strategic posture and the nature of innovation are parameters that are often neglected in the field of innovation management and more specifically, in consulting in strategic management of innovation. As a result, the "one size fits all" argument predominates, with decision criteria being more easily applied to company size, the R&D intensity of the industry, innovation best practices in the industry or the resources used. Furthermore, most of the analyses and tools available focus on technological innovation, leaving aside marketing or organisational innovation and limiting the scope and effectiveness of recommendations to company level. Finally, the distinction is rarely made between large companies and SMEs, while as shown in many studies, for example those of Andrea Vaona and Mario Pianta,[5] large and small companies follow different innovation strategies and use different strategic determinants to develop and launch their innovations. Product innovation is rooted in a growth strategy through opening new markets, while process innovation is rooted in a strategy of market penetration and flexible production. Opening new markets thanks to product innovation seems easier and more widespread in large companies. As for process innovation, small companies tend to focus on production flexibility while large ones go in for market expansion.

Keith K. Pavitt[6] highlights the existence of technological trajectories that imprison companies in sectoral schemas that obscure certain innovation opportunities. One can wonder whether SME's possess the capabilities to create and develop the appropriate structure and resources to escape from their schema and modify the boundaries of their competitive space as large companies do. Among SMEs, the essential properties inherent to companies' size seem to generate innovation characteristics derived from the strategic posture. Indeed, small size confers potential flexibility and closeness to clients while hampering economies of scale, perimeter of action and the experience effect. Certain studies on small companies' production and dissemination of innovation insist on the specific behaviours of small companies compared to large ones, such as their greater capability to transpose technology in a variety of new technology/product/market combinations. Furthermore, other studies have shown that market characteristics also influence innovation differently in large and small companies. In this case, the strategic management of innovation rests on a dual assumption:

- There are specific fits between competitive strategy and innovation behaviour that are preferable in terms of efficiency and performance.
- The relationship between strategy and innovation is influenced by the company's external environment (market forces) and its internal environment (competences and resources).

However, a lack of coherence between strategic posture and innovation behaviour is often a source of failure in implementing companies' competitive strategies. This failure is linked to the fact that the perception of environmental uncertainty and complexity impacts companies' strategic posture, the allocation and development of resources and consequently, the management and organising of innovation.

The theory of strategic configurations combined with the structuralist approach and the resource-based view of competitive advantage allows us to design the reference framework of the logic of strategy-innovation alignments, as illustrated in Fig. 6.1.

Given the complexity of the process, public policy to foster innovation, especially in SMEs, tends to support and disseminate this type of approach to strategic management of innovation. Nevertheless, recent studies on the effectiveness of local innovation systems in the European Union have pointed to a lack of guidance for companies and an absence of contextualisation in transfers of good innovation management practices.[7]

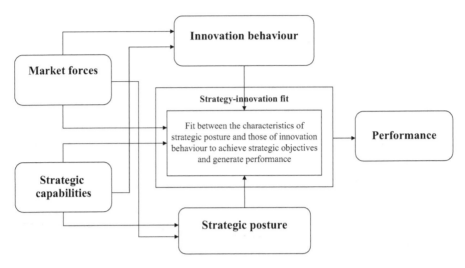

Fig. 6.1 Strategy/innovation alignments in context
Source: Authors

Best Consulting Practices in Brief

The consultant in strategic management of innovation should strive to align the company's competitive strategy and innovation practices by choosing strategy/innovation domains that are coherent with the company's context—its market characteristics, competences and resources. To do this, it could be very useful to refer to Miles and Snow's generic model of the predictive alignments between the company's characteristics of innovation behaviour and entrepreneurial, engineering and organisational choices, and Porter's contextual approach to strategic positioning. This approach is particularly suitable because it takes account of external and internal parameters that influence choices both of strategy and of innovation. The expert consultant can therefore approach the problem from an analytical and methodological basis that both the consulting team and the company's CEO and top managers find familiar.

6.2.1.2   Innovation Behaviour: Innovation Nature, Source and Activity

Many typologies have been put forward to identify innovation "nature" (notably considered as incremental, radical, continuous, discontinuous, modular or architectural), "sources" (from technological or market opportunities) or "types of activity" (product, process, marketing, organisational). Nevertheless, as Fariborz Damanpour[8] has underlined, organisational performance depends more on the fit among these different innovation categories than on each category taken separately. According to the same view, Joe Tidd, John Bessant and Keith K. Pavitt[9] insist that innovation is a process that combines different types of knowledge to create new knowledge. This new knowledge can influence the company's internal or external environment to different degrees, depending on whether it modifies the components of a value proposition or is a systemic combination of these components; the degree of novelty of the components or of this new combination constituting either minor changes (known as incremental) or major changes (known as radical). Figure 6.2 illustrates the different degrees of combination and novelty resulting from these combinations.

Because this knowledge is not static but continuously evolving, innovation management is particularly uncertain regarding performance and even regarding the innovation itself in real terms. The main challenge companies face regarding the result of the innovation process is that their knowledge development is often a reflection of their organisational configuration and its associated strategic posture. Indeed, the strategic posture itself brings about the company's innovation behaviour. So, when the innovation concerns only a limited number of components of the company's value proposition, the resources concerned exchange naturally with each other and integrate the new knowledge, feeding it back into the strategic posture. On the contrary, when the innovation is at the systemic level of the organisation (influencing various resources, complementary competences, external actors...), the organisational configuration may not be suitable and may damage the company's innovation performance. Rebecca M. Henderson and Kim B. Clark[10] describe his type of innovation as "*architectural innovation.*"

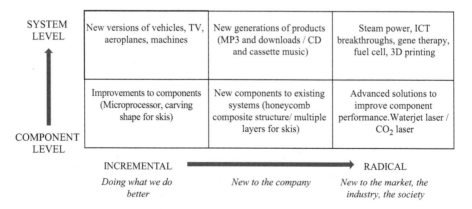

Fig. 6.2 The dimensions of innovation
Source: Adapted from Tidd Joe, Bessant John and Pavitt Keith K., *op. cit.*, 2005

Figure 6.3 illustrates the relationship between the level of closeness or distance of knowledge elements needed for innovation and the degree of closeness or distance of the innovation compared to the existing core value proposition.

The Nature of Innovation

In his book *The Innovator's Dilemma*, published in 1997, Clayton M. Christensen distinguishes between two fundamental profiles of innovation nature: "*sustaining innovation*," which continues to improve the offer for existing clients and markets, and "*disruptive innovation*," whose characteristics are likely to address a very different market segment by questioning the very practices of that market. Sustaining innovations may be radical or not, but they are generally better exploited by companies already well-established in the market targeted by the innovation. On the other hand, the potential of disruptive innovation is better exploited by new entrants whose strategic orientation consists of taking advantage of new markets or technological opportunities.

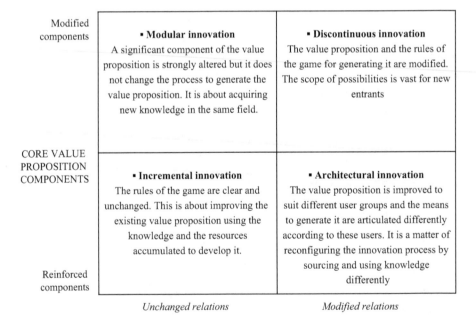

Modified components	• **Modular innovation** A significant component of the value proposition is strongly altered but it does not change the process to generate the value proposition. It is about acquiring new knowledge in the same field.	• **Discontinuous innovation** The value proposition and the rules of the game for generating it are modified. The scope of possibilities is vast for new entrants
CORE VALUE PROPOSITION COMPONENTS Reinforced components	• **Incremental innovation** The rules of the game are clear and unchanged. This is about improving the existing value proposition using the knowledge and the resources accumulated to develop it.	• **Architectural innovation** The value proposition is improved to suit different user groups and the means to generate it are articulated differently according to these users. It is a matter of reconfiguring the innovation process by sourcing and using knowledge differently
	Unchanged relations	*Modified relations*

RELATIONS BETWEEN KNOWLEDGE ELEMENTS NECESSARY TO INNOVATION

Fig. 6.3 The challenges of innovation
Source: Adapted from Tidd Joe, Bessant John and Pavitt Keith K., *op. cit.*, 2005

Disruptive innovation is usually carried out by companies that, given their small size, have fewer resources; nevertheless, they compete with established companies on market segments that the latter tend not to see. Indeed, companies established on their markets focus on satisfying the needs of their most profitable core clientele and in so doing, they develop a sort of short-sightedness regarding clients. This pushes them into over-offering on certain segments while neglecting the needs of other clients whose expectations are seen as less important or different. Disrupters address precisely these clients, designing products and services whose use value is better suited to this segment that established companies leave by the wayside. Furthermore, suitable functionalities often go hand in hand with attractive pricing.

According to Christensen, disruptive innovations originate in the needs of the least demanding clients or in segments that established companies have left aside. Indeed, these players have a natural tendency to neglect less demanding clients in favour of satisfying the demands of the most profitable ones. This generates a double problem: first, these companies deliver an offer that is often over-evaluated in terms of functionality for a target clientele that is not always ready to pay the corresponding price (some characteristics are considered super-fluous). Second, this positioning leaves the field open to any disruptor proposing a "good enough" offer to clients that established companies do not target.

Disrupters can also try to transform non-clients into clients, thereby creating a *de facto* new market. For example, in the late 1970s, by offering an affordable solution suited to SMEs or individual use, manufacturers of home printers managed to compete with Xerox, which at the time was firmly centred on a full offer of services for large companies. Similarly, snowboard manufacturers came up with a simple and easy-to-learn riding experience for the 1980s generation, thereby totally disrupting the traditional manufacturers of ski equipment. In so doing, they opened up winter sports to adolescent urban skateboarders who would then feel the same sensations on snow.

Christensen's research shows that existing companies' inability to take advantage of disruptions in their environment is not due to a lack of resources, managerial incompetence or the speed of industry cycles. It is more a question of their basic inability to question a business model whose efficiency relies on a specific configuration. Indeed, according to Christensen, the business model is the characteristic signature of a company's strategic posture, *i.e.*, the way the company decides to implement its strategic entrepreneurial choice, first by addressing a value proposition for a client segment that perceives that value; second, by generating profit according to a specific logic related to that proposition; and third, by mobilising and organising its resources in terms of pre-defined strategic objectives. In other words, a company's capacity to transform an opportunity into a new sustaining or disruptive value proposition depends on how far taking this opportunity would disturb the company's business model and on its willingness and aptitude to absorb this disturbance. From this viewpoint, the configurations required to develop disruptive innovations are characterised by specific strategic postures; these differ from the configurations needed for sustaining innovation. Companies facing disruptive innovations resulting from a new approach to "client demand" generally react by acquiring the new entrant or deciding to break with their existing model and create an autonomous unit specifically devoted to exploring these innovations. They hope in this way to benefit when the innovations are more widely distributed in the industry by integrating the new technology or processes into their core business. But on the ground, companies have not always succeeded, for it often requires a complete transformation of their existing business model, highlighting the need for internal disruption emphasising the new offer's modes of delivery. In this perspective, Joshua Gans[11] notes that companies encouraging integrated organisation, whose internal management of strategic capabilities is strongly valued by their final clients, and whose reputation goes beyond their offer's functional aspects, are more efficient when confronted with disruption. Indeed, these companies are structurally configured to manage disruptive innovation systemically, thus maintaining their organisational consistency.

Many studies have followed on from Christensen, making the link between the company's organisational configuration and the nature of innovation undertaken. Nizar Becheikh, Réjean Landry and Nabil Amara[12] listed these studies and showed that they converged in terms of the negative impact of cost leadership strategies on the probability of innovating outside the value network for manufacturing SMEs, thus in fact favouring sustaining innovation. On the contrary, differentiation strategies have a determinant effect on the propensity to innovate inside as well as outside the company's value network and on the degree of innovation novelty (radicalness).

The Source of Innovation

The question of the source of innovation is also strongly related to the company's business model. In the 1970s, experts hotly debated the value proposition and performance associated with a technological innovation, known as technology-push, or to a market innovation, known as market-pull. In technology-push innovation, the company appropriates technological advances to launch new products or set up new processes. In market-pull, innovation results from an in-depth analysis of users' needs for the innovation; this in turn leads to seeking the right technologies to satisfy those needs. These discussions resulted in a convergence of positions regarding innovation sources, showing that radical innovations, *i.e.*, those generating a change of paradigm, are mainly technology-push, whereas incremental innovations, *i.e.*, those that improve the existing paradigm, are essentially market-pull.[13]

Starting with the above-mentioned assumption that strategy conditions innovation and that certain strategy/innovation fits are preferable to others, the relation between a company's strategic orientation, the source of its innovations and its innovation performance, have been the subject of much research. While it appears that the company's technological orientation facilitates technology-push innovations but has little influence on market-pull innovations, the results concerning companies' market orientation are less clear cut. Some studies have underlined that a market orientation stimulates market-pull innovation, while others finds that, on the contrary, focusing excessively on clients who by nature demand an immediate response to their expectations, translates into innovations with little value and this in turn results in a weakening of the company's innovation competences.[14] On the other hand, recent studies on typologies of innovation users have shown that a market orientation is not simply guided by the market: this orientation can generate technology-push innovation when it generates innovation by relying on *avant-garde* users known as lead users. Indeed, these are users who express needs far in advance of others, and seek or even contribute to the emergence of technological solutions to those needs. The whole challenge for the company is then to identify these lead users.[15]

In recent years, innovation that was centred on users, known as user-driven innovation, has been the subject of many studies aiming to identify lead-users in order to benefit from their capacities to innovate. These studies have furthered the method initially developed by Glen L. Urban and Eric Von Hippel[16] to identify opportunities for radical innovation and developing user-driven innovations that would use these for maximum benefit. Today this method is divided into four phases:

- Phase 1: the company defines the objectives of innovation (for example, find an innovative solution to problem X or develop an innovative concept to access market Y) and constitutes a multidisciplinary team (R&D, marketing, sales, production…) to design these solutions. This multidisciplinarity is essential to ensure that the solutions proposed are consistent in terms of the company's strategic posture and resources;

- Phase 2: the team identifies the main needs and trends for attention. The term "trends" implies the aspects on which lead users are particularly advanced compared with the core clients in the market. Trends are generally chosen on the basis of experts' reports, information from online forums or think tanks but also—though less often—using research literature.
- Phase 3: this is the phase of identifying lead users. Here, individuals who are at the forefront of the trends and who also have a strong personal interest in benefiting from the innovation to be developed are identified. The most recent techniques for selecting these users employ the pyramid method. First, among a small number of users, this means identifying those who, in their opinion, have real needs that existing solutions do not cover and who are at the forefront of the trend. These users are then contacted and the same process is applied until the identified users appear to be sufficiently *avant-garde* (this usually happens after two or three rounds).
- Phase 4: the company organises two- or three-day work sessions with the retained lead users. The company's multidisciplinary teams attend these sessions where techniques such as brainstorming, focus groups, etc. are applied to capitalise on participants' creative potential. Prior to these sessions, it is important to define the rules of intellectual property so that the company can benefit from forthcoming ideas and concepts, commercialising them with no risk of legal proceedings. In most cases, lead users give their ideas freely, hoping to benefit themselves from the innovations that result.

Innovation Activities

As mentioned previously, when companies adopt innovations they embark on a process that influences all other parts of the organisation and all aspects of operations. Such innovations aim to generate competitive advantage or contribute to the efficiency of the existing organisation in response to changes in the internal or external environment or as a preventive measure to influence that environment. This approach to a company's innovation behaviour, innovation activities and their associated objectives are covered by the definition of innovation provided by the Oslo Manual[17] (OECD, p. 49–53).

According to the Oslo Manual, a product innovation "*is the introduction of a good or service that is new or significantly improved with respect to its characteristics or intended uses. This includes significant improvements in technical specifications, components and materials, incorporated software, user friendliness or other functional characteristics.*" Product innovations aim to maintain the loyalty of existing clients on existing markets thanks to novelty and differentiation, or to benefit from market opportunities offering access to new clients. "*A process innovation is the implementation of a new or significantly improved production or delivery method. This includes significant changes in techniques, equipment and/or software. Process innovations can be intended to decrease unit costs of production or delivery, to increase quality, or to produce or deliver new or significantly improved products.*"

Many studies have long underlined that the business objectives of the company's strategic posture and the associated organisational characteristics influence the performance of product or process innovations. Danny Miller and Peter H. Friesen[18] showed that a prospector profile naturally develops product innovation, unless the company is organised vertically, undertakes strict analytical strategic planning and works according to a process of centralized information and decision making. The situation of defender companies is the opposite, with a tendency to process innovation.

The Oslo Manual defines marketing innovation as "*the implementation of a new marketing method involving significant changes in product design or packaging, product placement, product promotion or pricing. Marketing innovations are aimed at better addressing customer needs, opening up new markets, or newly positioning a company's product on the market.*" The question of whether different strategic profiles are associated with different marketing innovation behaviours has been studied by Eric M. Olson, Stanley F. Slater and G. Tomas M. Hult.[19] Based on Miles and Snow's strategic profiles, they have shown that a prospector profile had a stronger tendency to take market opportunities and introduce a strong degree of novelty in their marketing innovation responses to these opportunities. Analysers focus on sustaining incremental marketing innovations aiming to improve existing offers developed internally or captured from prospectors. Analysers also seek profitability from the solutions they adopt. As for defenders, they favour sustaining incremental marketing innovation activities as a response to needs expressed by existing clients.

According to the Oslo Manual, an "*organizational innovation is the implementation of a new organizational method in the company's business practices, workplace organization or external relations. Organizational innovations can be intended to increase a company's performance by reducing administrative costs or transaction costs, improving workplace satisfaction (and thus labour productivity), gaining access to non-tradable assets (such as non-codified external knowledge) or reducing costs of supplies.*" Organisational innovation is distinct from other organisational changes in that it is the implementation of a new organisational method that has not yet been used in the company, or that results from a significant strategic choice. Innovations in business practices involve implementing new methods of organisation and new processes for running the company's operations (new CRM, new policy of quality management…).

As for innovations in workplace organisation, these concern implementing new methods of sharing responsibility and decision-making among employees and the company's different units, or reorganising the company's value chain. Innovations in external relations involve new ways of organising relations with other companies or institutions such as new types of subcontracting or new forms of cooperation with external actors (clients, research centres, suppliers…). Among examples of organisational innovations, we can mention ERP systems, distance work, lean management, communities of practice, cooperation between companies and universities, etc.

The distinction between technological (product or process), organisational and marketing innovations is important, because the three stem from potentially different strategic choices. However, much research has shown that these different innovation activities interact and seem to be mutually complementary. Cécile Ayerbe,[20] for example, underlines the process of coactivation and/or inter-innovation induced by technological innovation and resulting in organisational adaptation, so that in return, the right organisational configuration facilitates decision-making about new product and/or new market development that may well call on new technological choices. The results of this research support the adaptive cycle approach proposed by Miles and Snow (see Chap. 3). This is seen as a general physiology of the company's organisational behaviour to maintain or generate a competitive advantage through internal change where choices of entrepreneurial adaptation (choosing new strategic segments and the offers to adapt to these segments), technological adaptation (choosing new technological processes to produce this offer) and organisational evolution (new management and business practices).

The keystone of diagnostic missions for innovation is the continuous fit between adaptive strategic choices and innovation choices. Indeed, the purpose of such missions is to assess the fit between the innovation practices the company adopts to take advantage of technological or market opportunities and the entrepreneurial, technological and organisational choices of its strategic positioning. Such a diagnostic only makes sense and is only legitimate if the different generic strategic postures give rise to distinct innovation behaviours characteristic of the company that adopts them. According to Miles and Snow,[21] defenders, prospectors and analysers innovate in different ways throughout the adaptive cycle. They all seek a continuous fit between their product/market choices, technological choices, and organisational choices. Miles and Snow show that each strategic posture is reinforced through the company's adaptive choices and characterises its strategy and innovation behaviour over the long term.

If many studies show that strategy "predicts" innovation, and that innovation allows the company to reach its strategic objectives, other studies, including those carried out by Dean M. Schroeder,[22] have come to the opposite conclusion. Schroeder sees innovation as the source that pushes companies to respond to a changing competitive environment. In the same vein, Gary Hamel[23] pleads for *"strategic innovation"* that leads companies to continuously rethink their business model in the face of changes in their external environment. This systemic approach to strategic management of innovation is illustrated by the adaptive innovation cycle that Louis Raymond and Josée Saint-Pierre,[24] professors of management at the University of Quebec at Trois-Rivières, developed from Miles and Snow's adaptive cycle. Figure 6.4 shows this adaptive innovation cycle.

The logic of self-reinforcement of the strategy/innovation relationship during the adaptive cycle therefore generates a dominant strategic trajectory that portrays the coherence between the company's strategic posture and its innovation behaviour. Prospectors systematically seek to innovate by anticipating market changes or even influencing these changes through their R&D efforts to develop new products or services, new technologies or even new markets.

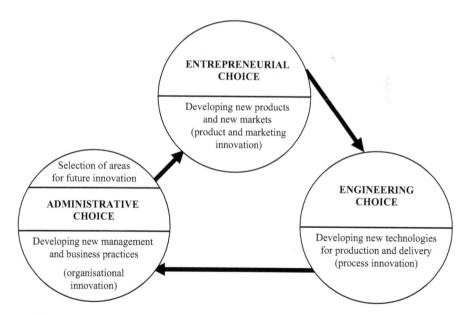

Fig. 6.4 The adaptive innovation cycle
Source: Raymond Louis and Saint-Pierre Josée, *op. cit.*, 2010. Adapted from Miles Raymond E. and Snow Charles C., *op. cit.*, 1978

Defenders are more "conservative" in their innovation behaviour, tending to increase the quality/price ratio of their products or services while at the same time favouring operational efficiency. As for analysers, they innovate by associating the improvement of an existing, well-established offer with innovation in terms of products or services recently introduced by prospectors; they improve these and distribute them more effectively.

However, this dominant logic can also lead the company to adopt innovation behaviours that are unsuited to hypercompetitive contexts. In her article *Transient Advantage*, published in the *Harvard Business Review* in 2013, Rita Gunther McGrath highlights certain traps that company CEOs often fall into:

- "*The trap of the pioneer*": indeed, few industries confer a lasting competitive advantage on being first. Pioneers who explore new horizons are obliged to exploit their innovations as fast as possible or risk being caught up by follower companies that will not have to bear exploration costs. Prospectors regularly face this challenge.
- "*The trap of the established position*": innovations raise the question of a more or less rapid "return on innovation." Indeed, companies tend to exploit existing processes, products or technologies for as long they can without really improving them significantly. This innovation behaviour pays off until competing innovations have made their mark, rendering existing offers obsolete. This is a frequent problem for defenders.
- "*The trap of excess-quality*": in the "exploitation" mode mentioned above, companies tend to propose a level of quality that their clients are not ready to pay for. When a new product that focuses on their real needs comes out, clients tend to abandon the established company's offer. The competition between defenders and analysers is an illustration of this transfer of clientele towards analysers.
- "*The trap of established resources*": it is often difficult for companies to reallocate resources devoted to exploiting a profitable activity towards exploring a new one. This is the defenders' dilemma, for they naturally focus on the efficient long-term exploitation of their strategic domain of activity.
- "*The trap of sporadic innovation*": in many companies, innovation is a sporadic process. Instead of benefiting from a continuous dynamic that generates new ideas likely to create new competitive advantages, the company functions in "reactive" mode, unable to exploit its innovations long term, unlike their competitors who have incorporated innovation into their business model.

6.2.1.3 Strategy, Innovation and Performance: The Importance of Context for Capturing Innovation Revenues

Above we mentioned the need for fit among the attributes of the company's strategic posture and those of its innovation behaviour in the interests of innovation efficiency. However, this fit only makes sense if it also induces increased performance. The question of performance resulting from the strategy/innovation fit has been the subject of much research that shows this fit to be a significant predictor of organisational efficiency. Shaker A. Zahra and Jeffrey G. Covin focused precisely on this predictability. In their article *The Financial Implications of Fit Between Competitive Strategy and Innovation Types and Sources,* published in 1994, they showed that when companies stray from the predictive models of strategy/innovation fit, there is a significant reduction in associated performance for defender, prospector and analyser strategic profiles. Similarly, Zahra and Covin[25] also showed that from a performance point of view, choices of technological product or process innovation should be assessed according to their overall consistency with the company's competitive strategy rather than independently. Other recent studies, such as that undertaken by Abraham Carmeli, Roy Gelbard and David Gefen,[26] highlighted the influence of the companies' innovation behaviour and the characteristics of this behaviour on the relationship between companies' strategic posture and performance. These authors suggest that a wish for innovation strongly directed towards change and adaptation improve companies' performance both directly and indirectly by a lever effect on the consistency of their strategic posture. Maria J. R. Ortega[27] has shown that technological innovations are a fundamental element of the amplifying effect of competitive strategy on companies' profitability for as long as the innovation attributes agree with the strategic attributes.

From a performance point of view, the strategy/innovation fit should also take account of the company's external and internal contingences. Surveillance of the company's external environment is key for identifying signals from the market and developing the strategic capabilities that will support the right strategic posture and the deployment of appropriate innovation behaviours. This dual internal and external adjustment is essential if companies, especially SMEs whose resources are limited, are to reap the benefits they expect from their innovation behaviour.

Internal/external adjustment is delicate and in a consulting mission, the consultant must assess the company's capacity to carry out this dual adjustment. Indeed, if companies innovate to respond to changes in their external or internal environment, internal organisational factors have different influences on innovation depending on the company's strategic posture, and external contingencies related to the company's different markets influence its capacity to innovate differently. Stefano Breschi, Franco Malerba and Luigi Orsenigo[28] observed that industries differ in the amount of resources that companies devote to innovation, in the degree of innovation generated and in the source of innovation. Furthermore, the uncertainty and complexity of the environment seem to have a significant influence on the organisational management of innovation. Many studies agree that radical innovation occurs during periods of disruption in an industry's environment while incremental innovation occurs during periods of adaptation. Moreover, periods of technological change seem to strengthen efforts towards radical innovation based on technology whereas situations of intense competition stimulate market-based innovation.

The question of how the company appropriates the benefits of its innovation activities is a major challenge involving arbitrage between exploration and exploitation. Indeed, in the majority of industries, the hypercompetitive situation strengthens the "*transient*" nature of a competitive advantage and the company needs to continuously explore new ideas and innovate to renew its portfolio of competitive advantages, while at the same time exploiting existing advantages to the maximum. The resources and competences likely to generate and renew this portfolio of transitory advantages are different from those required for making the most of these advantages and appropriating the revenue from the company's innovation activities. So, in its exploration process the company identifies an opportunity and uses resources to create an innovative value proposition by testing the new ideas iteratively. In the exploitation process, the company focuses on capturing the profits of innovation and winning or consolidating market shares. By so doing, it forces competitors to react, and they must be able to mobilise resources capable of

Best Consulting Practices in Brief

How can companies be helped to capture the revenues from innovation? This is the main objective of a consultancy mission in innovation management. To answer this question, consultants must first try to identify which phase of the "wave" of innovation revenues the company is currently "surfing" and secondly, know the relative importance to give each phase, given the company's strategic posture. In other words, the good surfer is the company that possesses the right resources for its posture and that can make optimal use in terms of innovation nature, source and activity, to reach its strategic objectives. There again, the "one size fits all" attitude is not suitable. Knowing the strategy/innovation fit is a prerequisite not only for innovation efficiency, but also for capturing the revenues from the innovation.

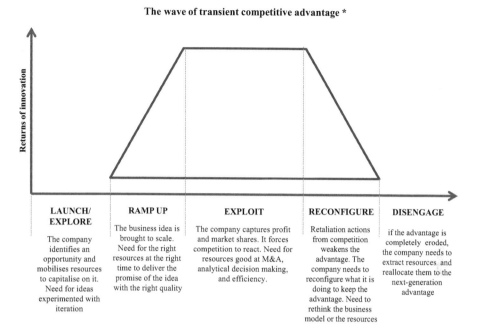

Fig. 6.5 The wave of revenues from innovation
Source: Adapted from Gunther McGrath Rita, *op. cit.*, 2013

analysing and reacting efficiently to this competitive intensity and to market forces, which are likely to influence the exploitation of the innovation. Finally, when the competition's reactions weaken the advantage gained by the innovation, the company must rethink the mode of exploitation of the innovation itself by reconfiguring its use of resources or mobilising them in a new process of exploitation. Figure 6.5 illustrates the different phases of creation and capture of competitive advantages and revenues from innovation activities.

6.2.2 Methodology and Tools for the Mission

A consulting mission in strategic innovation management takes place in three stages. In the first stage, the consultant assesses the company's capability to manage the innovation process efficiently both internally and with different external stakeholders. Gaps should be identified to serve as references for possible corrective action. This diagnostic gives a first analysis of the company's type of innovation management depending on its innovation capabilities and its behaviour, in terms of its perception of the need to innovate and of the way to do this. This first step, known as the "diagnostic of innovation management" relies on two tools: the diagnostic of the management of innovation itself and profiling the company's capabilities in innovation management. In the second stage, the consultant assesses the company's strategic innovator profile in view of its strategic posture. He/she measures the orientation to highlight and the company's subsequent organisation, on exploration and/or exploitation of innovation opportunities. Next, the consultant assesses strategy/innovation fit by looking at the alignment between the characteristics of the company's strategic posture and its innovation behaviour. This second stage, known as a strategy/innovation fit analysis, is based on two tools: The strategic innovator profile and the strategy/innovation fit test. Finally, with recommendations based on the conclusions of the first two stages, the consultant guides the company in its choice of innovation portfolio according to its strategic posture. In all, this consulting mission in innovation management is divided into five main steps, which are summarised in Fig. 6.6.

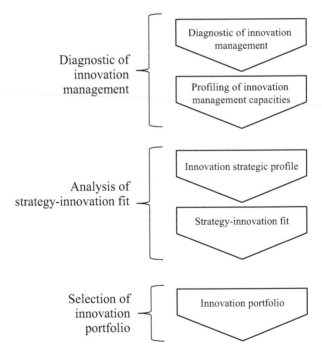

Fig. 6.6 The stages in a mission of strategic innovation management
Source: Authors

6.2.2.1 The Diagnostic of Innovation Management

The question of innovation management is complex. When all is said and done, what is it about? To answer this question, we use the definition given by Joe Tidd, John Bessant and Keith K. Pavitt in their book *Managing Innovation* (p. 40): "*innovation is a core process concerned with renewing what the organisation offers (its products and/or services) and the ways in which it generates and deliver these.*" Whatever the industry or type of organisation, the challenge is to know how the company can obtain a competitive advantage using innovation, and then how it can use this advantage to survive and grow. In general, innovation management involves different successive phases to implement the innovation process, launch the innovation itself and manage its exploitation (see Fig. 6.5):

1. Continuous surveillance of the company's external and internal environment to seek opportunities (latent or expressed needs, results of research, changes in regulations, behaviour of competitors…) that could be potential sources of innovation.
2. Selecting the opportunities where the company will mobilise its resources. At this stage, it is important look at the chosen opportunities in relation to the company's strategic posture and capabilities to know how to use them to develop a competitive advantage.
3. Allocating the resources (either available resources mobilised internally or external resources) for exploring the retained opportunities.
4. Initiating the innovation process—from the first idea to launching a new product and/or service, a new internal process, a new marketing method or a new organisational method to generate competitive advantage.
5. Exploiting all efforts to the greatest extent by optimising the capture of revenues from the innovation.
6. Then, when the competitive advantage weakens, reconfiguring the company to follow up the exploitation of the innovation and identify new opportunities to explore.

Assessing the company's capability to manage innovation means making a list of the criteria conditioning its innovation performance. To make this innovation management diagnostic, Tidd, Bessant and Pavitt propose categorising the criteria elements into the dimensions of strategy, organisation, process, external relations and learning. This assessment shows the consultant the main gaps or areas where the company needs to be accompanied. Table 6.1 and Fig. 6.7 illustrate this diagnostic process.

Table 6.1 Diagnostic of innovation management checklist

Innovation management behaviour: description of practices	Score 1: Not true at all 7: Very true
1 Employees have a clear vision of how innovation can help us compete	
2 Processes exist to help the effective development of new products from idea to launch	
3 The structure of the organisation stimulates innovation more than it prevents it	
4 The company is heavily involved in employee training and skills development	
5 The company has win-win relationships with its suppliers	
6 The innovation strategy is clearly communicated and everyone knows the targets for improvement	
7 Innovation projects are generally completed on time and on budget	
8 Employees work well together transversally (inter-departments)	
9 There is a systematic project review to draw lessons for improvement	
10 The needs of customers and end-users are well understood	
11 Employees are well aware of the company's distinctive competence—What confers a competitive edge	
12 The understanding of customer needs is shared by everyone (not just marketing)	
13 All business units are involved in suggesting ideas for improvements to products or processes	
14 The company regularly works with universities or research centres to develop knowledge	
15 The company learns from its mistakes	
16 The company is structured to explore and exploit opportunities as well as respond to threats (forecasting tools, key indicators)	
17 There are effective mechanisms to drive and manage innovation from idea through successful implementation	
18 The company's structure facilitates quick decision-making	
19 The company works closely with its customers to explore and develop new concepts	
20 The company systematically benchmarks its products and processes with competitors	
21 Top management has a shared vision of how the company will develop through innovation	
22 The company is constantly looking for product opportunities	
23 Communication is effective and is both downward, upward and transverse	

(continued)

Table 6.1 (continued)

Innovation management behaviour: description of practices	Score 1: Not true at all 7: Very true
24 The company regularly collaborates with other firms to develop new products or processes	
25 The company regularly confronts and shares its ideas with those of other firms to learn	
26 Management is particularly involved and supports innovation	
27 There are mechanisms to ensure early involvement of all departments in developing new products/processes	
28 The system of reward and recognition supports innovation	
29 The company develops external networks to access specialist knowledge	
30 The company knows how to capture and disseminate internally new knowledge so that everyone benefits	
31 There are processes of monitoring of technology and market developments, and analysis of their impact for the firm's strategy	
32 There is a clear process for selecting innovative projects	
33 The company facilitates and supports intrapreneurship	
34 The company has close links with the local or national education system to communicate its needs for skills	
35 The company is good at learning from other organisations	
36 The company's innovative projects are closely linked to the strategy	
37 The flexibility of processes allows the rapid conduct of small projects of new product development	
38 Teamwork is effective	
39 The company works closely with lead users to develop new products or services	
40 The management of innovation is driven by key performance indicators	

Control of the dimensions of innovation management	Score 1: Not true at all 7: Very true
Strategy (items 1; 6; 11; 16; 21; 26; 31; 36)	
Process (items 2; 7; 12; 17; 22; 27; 32; 37)	
Organisation (items 3; 8; 13; 18; 23; 28; 33; 38)	
External relations (items 5; 10; 14; 19; 24; 29; 34; 39)	
Learning (items 4; 9; 15; 20; 25; 30; 35; 40)	

Source: Adapted from Tidd Joe, Bessant John and Pavitt Keith K., *op. cit.*, 2005

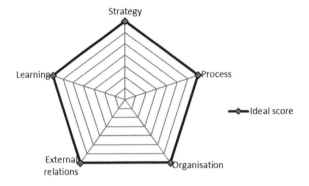

Fig. 6.7 Diagnostic radar of innovation management

From Theory to Practice

The analysis of Hightense's competitive positioning (see Chap. 3, Table 3.6) showed that although the company has significant R&D resources, it has not implemented a systematic process to detect signals from its external environment indicating opportunities the company could take advantage of or threats it should address. Similarly, the company seems to focus on its own mode of functioning and does little benchmarking. Hightense also tends to favour collaboration with lead users in its R&D activities, and customer culture (satisfaction, follow-up, sharing via a CRM tool) does not appear to be distributed among the company's various units. This analysis gives some initial indications regarding innovation management within the company. The diagnostic checklist helps to identify aspects for improvement. Table 6.2 and Fig. 6.8 illustrate the checklist and the resulting diagnostic for Hightense.

These results suggest that the consultant for Hightense can base the mission on the company's fairly high strategic willingness to innovate. The existing organisation serves this strategy well. On the other hand, though the innovation management processes seem fairly appropriate, the practices in place to feed the innovation process (external relations, learning), must be consolidated and expanded.

Table 6.2 Diagnostic of Hightense's innovation management

Innovation management behaviour: description of Hightense practices	Score 1: Not true at all 7: Very true
1 Employees have a clear vision of how innovation can help us compete	5
2 Processes exist to help the effective development of new products from idea to launch	3
3 The structure of the organisation stimulates innovation more than it prevents it	5
4 The company is heavily involved in employee training and skills development	4
5 The company has win-win relationships with its suppliers	4

(continued)

Table 6.2 (continued)

Innovation management behaviour: description of Hightense practices	Score 1: Not true at all 7: Very true
6 The innovation strategy is clearly communicated and everyone knows the targets for improvement	4
7 Innovation projects are generally completed on time and on budget	5
8 Employees work well together transversally (inter-departments)	4
9 There is a systematic project review to draw lessons for improvement	4
10 The needs of customers and end-users are well understood	4
11 Employees are well aware of the company's distinctive competence—What confers a competitive edge	6
12 The understanding of customer needs is shared by everyone (not just marketing)	4
13 All business units are involved in suggesting ideas for improvements to products or processes	6
14 The company regularly works with universities or research centres to develop knowledge	3
15 The company learns from its mistakes	6
16 The company is structured to explore and exploit opportunities as well as respond to threats (forecasting tools, key indicators)	4
17 There are effective mechanisms to drive and manage innovation from idea through successful implementation	4
18 The company's structure facilitates quick decision-making	7
19 The company works closely with its customers to explore and develop new concepts	7
20 The company systematically benchmarks its products and processes with competitors	2
21 Top management has a shared vision of how the company will develop through innovation	3
22 The company is constantly looking for product opportunities	4
23 Communication is effective and is both downward, upward and transverse	4
24 The company regularly collaborates with other firms to develop new products or processes	3
25 The company regularly confronts and shares its ideas with those of other firms to learn	3
26 Management is particularly involved and supports innovation	7
27 There are mechanisms to ensure early involvement of all departments in developing new products/processes	4
28 The system of reward and recognition supports innovation	5

(continued)

Table 6.2 (continued)

Innovation management behaviour: description of Hightense practices	Score 1: Not true at all 7: Very true
29 The company develops external networks to access specialist knowledge	3
30 The company knows how to capture and disseminate internally new knowledge so that everyone benefits	5
31 There are processes of monitoring of technology and market developments, and analysis of their impact for the firm's strategy	3
32 There is a clear process for selecting innovative projects	3
33 The company facilitates and supports intrapreneurship	4
34 The company has close links with the local or national education system to communicate its needs for skills	1
35 The company is good at learning from other organsiations	5
36 The company's innovative projects are closely linked to the strategy	6
37 The flexibility of processes allows the rapid conduct of small projects of new product development	6
38 Teamwork is effective	7
39 The company works closely with lead users to develop new products or services	7
40 The management of innovation is driven by key performance indicators	3

Control of the dimensions of innovation management	Score 1: Not true at all 7: Very true
Strategy	4.75
Process	4.13
Organisation	5.25
External relations	4.00
Learning	4.00

Source: Authors

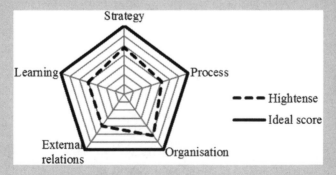

Fig. 6.8 Diagnostic radar of Hightense's innovation management
Source: Authors

6.2.2.2 Profiling the Capabilities of Innovation Management

As mentioned above, doing a diagnostic of innovation management is completed by profiling the company's capabilities for innovation management. From the scores on the dimensions of strategy, organisation, processes, external relations and learning, this profiling highlights various archetypes of capability for innovation management. The resulting profile gives an initial indication of the company's propensity to include innovation processes in its strategic orientations, and secondly, its ability to be organised for mobilising the internal and external resources needed to generate innovation. The type of profile is less vital here than the indication as to the real importance of innovation for the company. In this sense, profiling closes the diagnostic phase of innovation management by responding to the question: *How far does the company consider that innovation is key for reaching its strategic objectives?* Figure 6.9 shows the profiling matrix.

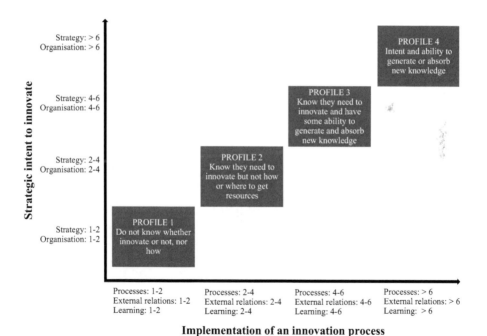

Fig. 6.9 The profiles of innovation management
Source: Adapted from Tidd Joe, Bessant John and Pavitt Keith K., *op. cit.*, 2005

From Theory to Practice

Hightenses diagnostic of innovation management and the scores on the strategy and organisation dimensions show that the company is aware of the need to innovate and seeks to support this orientation through its organisational configuration, which tends to facilitate it. The scores also show that the existing processes are fairly well adapted to this orientation. However, the company's capacity to feed the innovation process through cooperating with external stakeholders (clients, suppliers, experts) and develop new knowledge must be improved. Hightense's type 3 innovation management profile (as illustrated in Fig. 6.10) shows that the consultant should focus on the fit between the company's strategic posture and the innovation behaviour pertaining to this type of posture (where to look for opportunities, which resources to mobilise or obtain and how to combine these?).

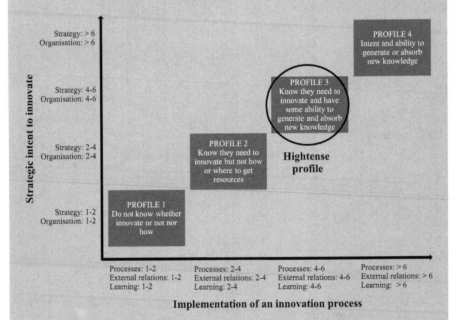

Fig. 6.10 Hightense's innovation management profile
Source: Authors

Best Consulting Practices in Brief

In the initial phase of the diagnostic mission of innovation management, the consultant should assess how the company manages innovation, measuring its propensity to include innovation into its strategic orientation and configure its organisation and resources to serve innovation. To do this, the consultant has two tools available: the diagnostic checklist on innovation management and the profiling matrix of innovation management. These tools serve as a basis to further

(continued)

(continued)

understand the company's posture towards innovation—at which point is it important to innovate? They could also be used later in different contexts such as: a specific diagnostic of innovation behaviour depending on the company's strategic posture, a benchmark to compare with the competition, an initial snapshot for a specific strategic posture that will be updated as part of good innovation practices, etc. At this stage, the question for the consultant is not so much to know whether the company has a high score in the various dimensions assessed, but rather to use the information to make the company's innovation practices coherent *vis a vis* its chosen strategic posture and strategic development options.

6.2.2.3   The Analysis of the Strategic Innovator Profile

How strategic is innovation to the company? The question is essential for a consulting mission and to articulate strategic posture with innovation. Indeed, if the fit between strategic posture and innovation behaviour is a powerful determinant of company performance, the question must also be asked as to whether innovating companies surpass those that have no systematic wish to innovate. This question leads to another: Should the companies favour the exploration of future innovations, or rather focus on exploiting innovations that are already on the market? Here again, the intensity of exploration or exploitation is strongly conditioned by how far innovation plays a role in reaching the company's strategic objectives.

These questions have been much studied. Research suggests that strategic posture influences innovation management decisions as well as the type of performance to be expected from these decisions. Furthermore, studies seem to show that the role of innovation as a means to reach strategic objectives depends on the economic context, the industry and the company's strategic capabilities. On this subject, Helena Forsman and Serdal Temel,[29] working with small companies with fewer than fifty employees, explain that the occurrence of innovation (does the company innovate continuously or sporadically?), its intensity (does the company innovate in different directions?) and its degree of novelty are not always associated with increased performance.

Indeed, these studies suggest that companies should see their innovation policy in terms of performance objectives related to their strategic posture and the external context (market forces that influence their strategic business units, macroeconomic environment). To generate the performance expected, innovation management therefore means adjusting the company's innovation behaviour to its strategic behaviour.

We suggest relating strategic behaviour and innovation behaviour by using Miles and Snow's generic framework of strategic configurations. Indeed, their adaptive cycle of strategic choices is initiated by the company's entrepreneurial choice either towards a process favouring the exploration of opportunities to create new competitive advantages, or the exploitation of existing competitive advantages. Our approach combines Miles and Snow's referential framework with the transient competitive advantage approach proposed by Rita Gunther McGrath.[30] Table 6.3 illustrates this analysis of the company's innovator strategic profile.

Table 6.3 Analysis of the innovator strategic profile

The company is focused on extending existing competitive advantages	Exploitation *vs.* exploration							The company is capable of exploring new competitive advantages
	1	2	3	4	5	6	7	
Budgets, staff and other resources are controlled by heads of established businesses								Critical resources are controlled by a separate group that does not run businesses
Tendency to extend the scope of established advantages whenever possible								Tendency to move away from an established advantage early to explore new opportunities
No process for disengaging from a business								Pre-established process to exit businesses
Disengagements from existing businesses are painful and difficult								Disengagements are part of the normal business cycle
Willingness to avoid failures even in situations of uncertainty and complexity								Failures are inevitable and an integral part of the learning process
Annual budget planning, even multi-annual								Short-term, quarterly or even rolling budget planning
Compliance with established plans, once formalised								Adaptation of established plans, depending on contingences
Optimisation in utilisation of assets								Flexibility in utilisation of assets

(continued)

Table 6.3 (continued)

The company is focused on extending existing competitive advantages	Exploitation *vs.* exploration							The company is capable of exploring new competitive advantages
	1	2	3	4	5	6	7	
Innovation is an on-again, off-again process								Innovation is an ongoing, systematic core process
Difficulty in pulling resources from a successful business to fund more uncertain opportunities								Pulling resources from a successful business to fund more uncertain opportunities is a normal practice
The most skilled employees spend a lot of time managing problems and solving crises								The most skilled employees often work on new opportunities for the company
Stability of organisational structure and processes and integration of new ideas into the existing structure								Adaptation of organisational structure to potential opportunities
Emphasis on analysis over experimentation								Emphasis on experimentation over analysis
Request from top management to justify any situation								Understanding from top management that there may be no justification for certain situations
Mean score								*Exploitation – exploration orientation*
	1	2	3	4	5	6	7	
		Defender		*Analyser*		*Prospector*		
Strategic posture of innovation								*Check the fit of innovation practices with the associated strategic profile in terms of nature, source and innovation activity*

Source: Adapted from Gunther McGrath Rita, *op. cit.*, 2013

From Theory to Practice

The analysis of Hightense's strategic innovator profile confirms the analysis of its strategic posture undertaken during the mission of assessment of the company's strategic positioning (see Chap. 3) and the diagnostic of innovation management. Indeed, though Hightense's strategic entrepreneurial orientation is that of a prospector seeking to take advantage of product or market opportunities, the company limits its wish to explore new opportunities through behaviours that are more favourable to exploiting existing competitive advantages. The results therefore show a strategic innovator profile closer to the analyser, meaning that the company capitalises at once on its advantages in its SBU1 core business of high power energy engineering and seizes opportunities to generate new competitive advantages on strategic business units close to this core business, such as SBU2.1 of medium and low power energy engineering. Table 6.4 details this analysis.

Table 6.4 Analysis of Hightense's strategic innovator profile

The company is focused on extending existing competitive advantages	Exploitation vs. exploration							The company is capable of exploring new competitive advantages
	1	2	3	4	5	6	7	
Budgets, staff and other resources are controlled by heads of established businesses	7							Critical resources are controlled by a separate group that does not run businesses
Tendency to extend the scope of established advantages whenever possible					5			Tendency to move away from an established advantage early to explore new opportunities
No process for disengaging from a business	1							Pre-established process to exit businesses
Disengagements from existing businesses are painful and difficult				4				Disengagements are part of the normal business cycle
Willingness to avoid failures even in situations of uncertainty and complexity				4				Failures are inevitable and an integral part of the learning process
Annual budget planning, even multi-annual							7	Short-term, quarterly or even rolling budget planning

(continued)

Table 6.4 (continued)

The company is focused on extending existing competitive advantages	Exploitation vs. exploration							The company is capable of exploring new competitive advantages
	1	2	3	4	5	6	7	
Compliance with established plans, once formalised	7							Adaptation of established plans, depending on contingences
Optimisation in utilisation of assets	6							Flexibility in utilisation of assets
Innovation is an on-again, off-again process	7							Innovation is an ongoing, systematic core process
Difficulty in pulling resources from a successful business to fund more uncertain opportunities	7							Pulling resources from a successful business to fund more uncertain opportunities is a normal practice
The most skilled employees spend a lot of time managing problems and solving crises	6							The most skilled employees often work on new opportunities for the company
Stability of organisational structure and processes and integration of new ideas into the existing structure				4				Adaptation of organisational structure to potential opportunities
Emphasis on analysis over experimentation	6							Emphasis on experimentation over analysis
Request from top management to justify any situation			3					Understanding from top management that there may be no justification for certain situations
Mean score	5.3							*Exploitation—exploration orientation*
	1	2	3	4	5	6	7	
Strategic posture of innovation	*Defender*		*Analyser*		*Prospector*			*Check the fit of innovation practices with the associated strategic profile in terms of nature, source and innovation activity*

Source: Authors

Best Consulting Practices in Brief

After this analysis, the consultant should question any gap between the resulting innovator profile and the company's desired strategic posture. Here it is recommended to work at two levels with the company's CEO and top managers.

- *Check the fit between the company's strategic posture and innovation behaviour* to realign first, the dimensions of its innovation behaviours (natures, sources, activities) and, second, if necessary, to restore the fit among the dimensions of its strategic posture. Indeed, non-alignment of the strategic dimensions would also result in a poor strategy/innovation fit.
- *Possibly rethink the company's chosen entrepreneurial orientation* according to its strategic capabilities and align the technological and organisational choices accordingly. The resulting strategic posture will *de facto* imply a new innovation behaviour.

6.2.2.4 The Test of Strategy/Innovation Fit

Since the development of generic strategic configurations, many studies have shown that although various configurations allow companies to expand on a specific market, their number is in fact limited.[31] These configurations are therefore described as ideals in the sense that any company that approaches them will improve its capability to create a competitive advantage. These generic configurations therefore give the consultant a solid and reliable analytic framework. Starting from the postulate above, that innovation is a way for the company to reach its strategic objectives, several studies[32] have shown the predictive nature of these generic strategic postures in terms of innovation behaviour.

The typology of Porter's generic strategies just like Miles and Snow's generic configurations' approach to the adaptive cycle (see Chap. 3), provide frames of reference that are very suitable—and tried and tested—to a predictive approach between strategic choice and innovation choice for generating competitive advantage. Moreover, these models are complementary. Porter proposes an approach to strategy that is directed more towards the external environment; it is based on the company's choice of positioning *vis a vis* clients (through an advantage of differentiation or price) compared to the competition. Miles and Snow suggest an approach that focuses more on the company and its entrepreneurial, technological and organisational choices. According to this view, the entrepreneurial choice consists of innovating by adopting the right products or services to enter markets where the company wishes to expand; technological choices refer to innovating in suitable processes for producing and distributing these products or services, and organisational choices imply innovating in the design and implementation of organisational solutions with a view to both optimising the internal business management and adapting to changes in the environment. Since the proposed profiles are ideals, each strategic profile is associated with an ideal predictive profile of innovation behaviour in terms of innovation nature, source and activity.

As mentioned previously, in assessing the level of strategy/innovation fit, the consultant embarks upon a key stage of the mission of strategic management of innovation. First, this means having a precise view of the company's strategic posture to compare with the closest "ideal" strategic posture. Second, it means identifying precisely the dimensions of the company's innovation behaviour to also determine whether this behaviour is in line with what is expected given the strategic posture.

Table 6.5 and Fig. 6.11a–d guide the consultant in this approach. The first lists the predictive associations of strategy/innovation fit using strategic profiles that combine Miles and Snow's and Porter's typologies. The figures show the ideal innovator profiles of a low-cost defender, a differentiated defender, a prospector and an analyser.

6.2.2.5   The Choice of Innovation Portfolio

The real aim of a consulting mission in strategic management of innovation is to help the company to generate competitive advantages along with the associated revenues and profits through efficient management of a balanced portfolio of innovation activities. Advising a company in innovation portfolio management implies, above all, an awareness that the content of this portfolio is strongly related to the company's strategic posture. Indeed, given its entrepreneurial, technological and organisational choices, the company will deploy its innovation efforts according to very disparate choices in terms of risk and expected return on investment. In other words, the company's first objective in terms of distributing its innovation efforts is to construct the portfolio that will produce the best return compared to the chosen risk.

Bansi Nagji and Geoff Tuff[33] developed a tool to help in the choice of innovation portfolio inspired from Ansoff's growth matrix (see Chap. 4). Their matrix, known as the innovation ambition matrix, substitutes Ansoff's choices of products and markets (existing or new) by choices of innovations and target markets in terms of their closeness to the company's existing situation. According to this classification, companies pursue three levels of ambition in terms of innovation: expanding their core business activities, taking opportunities that are adjacent to their core business and creating new "transformational"

Table 6.5 Strategy and innovation combinations

Strategy-innovation fit			Strategic profiles			
			Low-cost defender	Differentiated defender	Prospector	Analyser
Innovation types	Sources of innovation	Technology-based	XXX	XX	X	XX
		Market-based	X		XXX	XXX
	Nature of innovation	Incremental	XXX	XXX		XXX
		Radical	X		XXX	XX
		Sustaining	XXX	XXX	X	XXX
		Disruptive			XXX	X
	Activities of innovation	Process	XXX	XX	X	XX
		Product	X	XX	XXX	XX
		Marketing	X	X	XX	XXX
		Organisational			XX	XXX
	Objective of innovation	Price Competitiveness	XXX	X		X
		Superior Quality or Service		XXX	XX	XXX
		Entering New Markets			XXX	XX

Source: Authors

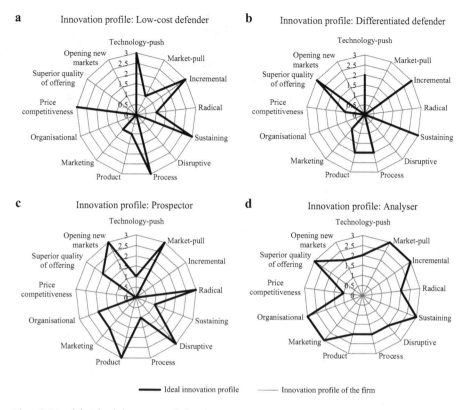

Fig. 6.11 (a) Ideal low-cost defender innovation profile. (b) Ideal differentiated defender innovation profile. (c) Ideal prospector innovation profile. (d) Ideal analyser innovation profile
Source: Authors

From Theory to Practice

The analysis of the fit between Hightense's innovation profile and the ideal innovation profile of a prospector points to areas of convergence but also of distance between the company's innovation practices and the expected predictive profile. The results of Table 6.6 and Fig. 6.12 show that Hightense's innovation behaviour is in line with some key dimensions of its entrepreneurial and technological choice as prospector (see Chap. 3). It is true that Hightense favours developing an innovating offer and diversifying into new markets by relying on a highly R&D intensive technological orientation and solid competences in product design. These choices translate into the radical and disruptive dimensions of its innovation activities for product innovation.

Table 6.6 Analysis of Hightense's strategy/innovation fit

Strategy-innovation fit		Strategic profiles							
		Low-cost defender		Differentiated defender		Prospector		Analyser	
Innovation profile 0: not favoured; 3: favoured		Ideal	Hightense	Ideal	Hightense	Ideal	Hightense	Ideal	Hightense
Source of innovation	Technology-push	3		2		1	3	2	
	Market-pull	1		2		3	1	3	
Nature of innovation	Incremental	3		3		0	2	3	
	Radical	1		0		3	3	2	
	Sustaining	3		3		1	3	3	
	Disruptive	0		0		3	2	2	
Activity of innovation	Process	3		2		1	3	2	
	Product	1		2		3	3	2	
	Marketing	1		1		2	0	3	
	Organisational	0		0		2	0	3	
Objective of innovation	Price competitiveness	3		1		0	0	1	
	Superior quality of offering	0		3		2	3	3	
	Opening new markets	0		0		3	2	2	

Source: Authors

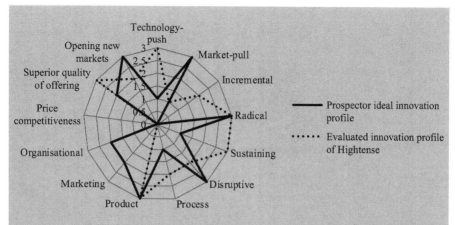

Fig. 6.12 Hightense's innovation profile and closeness to the ideal prospector innovation profile
Source: Authors

On the other hand, the incremental and sustaining dimensions favour Hightense's core energy engineering competences, and the importance the company gives to innovations in processes associated to these previous dimensions are closer to an analyser innovation profile. Similarly, Hightense does not favour marketing innovation since it has no competences in the matter; nor does the company wish to innovate in its organisation to better capture market opportunities. This gap is reinforced by its weak tendency to market-pull innovation and strong tendency to technology-push innovation.

Best Consulting Practices in Brief

The gap in the analysis of Hightense's strategy/innovation fit compared to the predictive model of an innovation prospector highlights once again the double question the consultant faces when analysing the company's strategic innovator profile. Is it better to guide the company towards innovation behaviour suited to a prospector profile, or, starting from an analyser's innovation behaviour, help it to rethink its strategic posture to adopt the entrepreneurial, technological and organisational choices of an analyser?

The first option would probably oblige the consultant to work with Hightense's senior management on the company's strategic posture to increase the level of fit with the ideal prospector's strategic posture. The second option would involve focusing on the fit among the different characteristics of the adaptive strategic choices of the analyser's posture, before optimising the strategy/innovation fit.

The consultant should look at this approach, bearing in mind the construction of the company's innovation management choices, especially in terms of innovation portfolio distribution.

THE INNOVATION AMBITION MATRIX

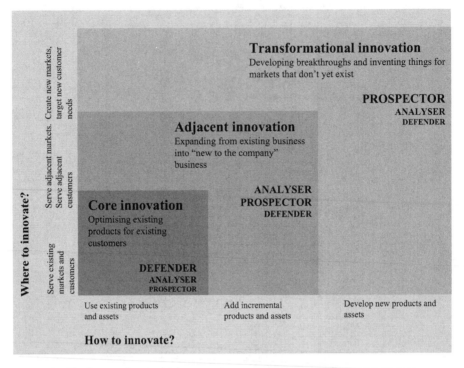

Fig. 6.13 The innovation ambition matrix
Source: Adapted from Nagji Bansi and Tuff Geoff, *op. cit.*, 2012

competitive spaces from scratch. The entrepreneurial choices and objectives of the Nagji and Tuff matrix reflect the different types of entrepreneurial choices of Miles and Snow's adaptive cycle and combine innovation ambition with strategic posture. Figure 6.13 illustrates this combination.

The innovation portfolio profile is strongly related to the company's capabilities to explore, retain and exploit internal but also external knowledge. Ulrich and Eckhard Lichtenthaler[34] propose a classification of these capabilities, essential for effective knowledge management to develop the company's innovation portfolio. They consider that exploring the company's internal knowledge refers to the capability of generating new knowledge through R&D activities, communities of practice, brainstorming etc. External exploration refers to efforts devoted to acquiring knowledge from external sources such as scientific conferences, purchase of licenses and industry and competitive intelligence. The retention of internal knowledge aims to retain competences and good practices inside the company. The retention of external knowledge depends on the capacity to maintain relations with external stakeholders that possess know-how and information the company needs but that it has deliberately chosen not to develop internally. The exploitation of internal knowledge refers to internal innovation, *i.e.*, the capability of using internally generated or externally acquired knowledge, to develop a new value proposition within the company's offer. External exploitation consists of identifying opportunities for the use of the company's knowledge by partners who wish to value and exploit that knowledge for themselves.

These capabilities of exploration, retention and exploitation of internal and external knowledge rely, respectively, on inventive or absorptive capacities, transformative or connective capacities or innovative or desorptive capacities. Table 6.7 describes this classification.

The propensity to encourage the development of exploration, retention or exploitation capabilities underlies the constitution of an innovation portfolio. From then on, these capabilities must be developed according to the company's innovation ambitions and are specific to each strategic posture. Figure 6.14 illustrates this alignment.

The question then is to know how to distribute the innovation portfolio among core, adjacent and transformational innovation. From a strictly stock market value viewpoint, studies show that a distribution of 70% core, 20% adjacent and 10% transformational corresponds to an optimisation of the innovation portfolio. This is only an indication and must be taken with caution. Indeed, this distribution depends on various factors:

- First of all, the company's strategic posture, its strategic entrepreneurial, technological and organisational choices.
- Then, the industry and market forces influencing this industry towards increased or limited competition, low or high entry costs, clients' receptiveness to substitutes or the dynamism of the company's upstream value network.
- Finally, the company's development stage: early (with no core business basis) and favourable to exploration and risk-taking to attract investors; or more mature and more focused on exploiting the existing situation.

Taking the company's strategic posture as a basis, the consultant can use the innovation portfolio distribution in Fig. 6.15 as a starting point.

Table 6.7 Classification of knowledge management capabilities

	Knowledge exploration	Knowledge retention	Knowledge exploitation
Internal level (intracompany)	**Inventive capacity:** *The company's ability to internally explore new knowledge.* Starting from the perception of particular opportunities requiring new knowledge to be properly explored, the company creates this new knowledge and connects it with its existing knowledge **Key point:** The higher the level of prior knowledge, the higher the company's Inventive capacity	**Transformative capacity:** *The company's ability to retain knowledge inside the organisation.* The company sets up processes to maintain knowledge internally and subsequently reactivate it **Key point:** The higher the level of prior knowledge in a given field, the easier to maintain and reactivate it **Key issue:** Path-dependency (focused knowledge) of knowledge retention may hamper disruptive innovation	**Innovative capacity:** *The company's ability to internally exploit knowledge.* The company sets up processes to match inventions with the context of their final market (market scanning to sell inventions!) **Key point:** The higher the level of prior knowledge in a given technology or market, the easier to identify valuable commercialisation opportunities
External level (intercompany)	**Absorptive capacity:** *The company's ability to explore external knowledge* Starting from the perception of particular opportunities requiring new knowledge to be properly explored, the company sets up processes to acquire external knowledge and incorporate this knowledge new to the company into its existing knowledge base **Key point:** The company needs prior related knowledge to understand the absorbed knowledge	**Connective capacity:** *The company's ability to retain knowledge outside the organisation boundaries* (alliances, relational and networking capabilities, ….) The company sets up processes to maintain knowledge accessible via inter organisational relationships and subsequently reactivate it **Key point:** The higher the level of prior knowledge in a given field, the easier to manage intercompany relationships and retain knowledge externally	**Desorptive capacity:** *The company's ability to externally exploit knowledge* The company sets up processes to identify opportunities with external recipients (partners, licensees, …) to exploit company's knowledge and subsequently transfer the knowledge to these recipients. **Key point:** Large scope of sufficient prior knowledge **Key issue:** Identifying opportunities with external recipients is difficult

Source: Adapted from Lichtenthaler Ulrich and Lichtenthaler Eckhard, *op. cit.,* 2009

The innovation ambition / knowledge capacity matrix

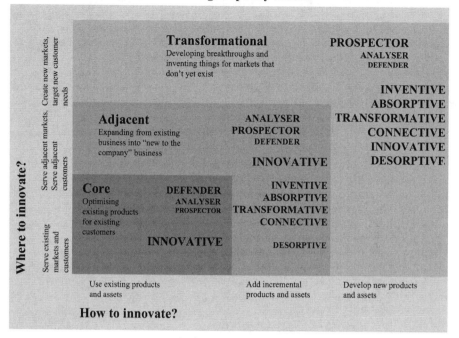

Fig. 6.14 The innovation ambition/knowledge management capabilities matrix
Source: Adapted from Nagji Bansi and Tuff Geoff, *op. cit.*, 2012; and Lichtenthaler Ulrich and Lichtenthaler Eckhard, *op. cit.*, 2009

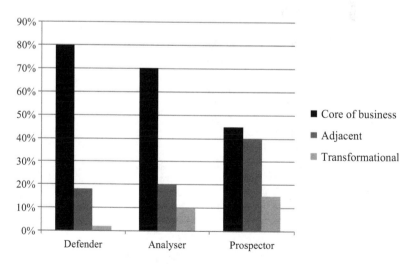

Fig. 6.15 Innovation distribution portfolio according to strategic posture
Source: Adapted from Nagji Bansi and Tuff Geoff, *op. cit.*, 2012

From Theory to Practice

The analysis undertaken as part of the mission on Hightense's strategic positioning (see Chap. 3) and the use of the attractiveness/assets matrix of directional policy resulted in the decision to develop its core business of high power energy and diversify by developing new competences in the business of medium and low power energy. By deploying this strategy, the company identified a particularly interesting opportunity in the electronics industry. Indeed, its conductive foam, initially designed to avoid energy loss, turned out to be highly resistant to rises in interconnection temperatures and could be useful in optimising electronic equipment, thereby obtaining a substantial reduction in the amount of material (plastics, composites) contained in these devices. The company therefore considers that it could generate a real disruption in this industry in terms of equipment conception and design. As a result, it decided to intensify the exploration of this new competitive space known as SBU3.

The analysis of the resources (R&D, personnel, time) allocated to Hightense's innovation portfolio results in the distribution shown in Fig. 6.16. The result shows a portfolio distribution closer to that of analyser.

At this stage, the consultant has all the elements related to the company's innovator profile, to the closeness of its innovation behaviour *vis a vis* the ideal predictive behaviour of its strategic posture and the distribution of its innovation portfolio. He/she can now use all these elements to finalise the mission and accompany the company in its choice of optimal strategic posture and most pertinent innovation behaviour to optimise its chances of reaching its strategic objectives.

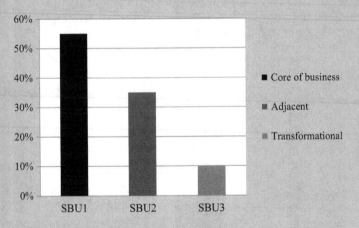

Fig. 6.16 Hightense's innovation portfolio distribution
Source: Authors

Notes

1. Damanpour Fariborz and Evan William M., "Organizational Innovation and Performance: The Problem of Organizational Lag", *Administrative Science Quarterly*, vol. 29, no 3, 1984, p. 392–409.
2. King Andrew A. and Baatarrtogtokh Baljir, "How Useful Is the Theory of Disruptive Innovation?", *MIT Sloan Management Review*, vol. 57, no 1, 2015, p. 76–90.
3. Hamel Gary and Prahalad Coimbatore K., "Strategic Intent", *Harvard Business Review*, vol. 67, no 3, 1989, p. 148–161.
4. Zahra Shaker A. and Covin Jeffrey G., "The Financial Implications of Fit between Competitive Strategy and Innovation Types and Sources", *The Journal of High Technology Management Research*, vol. 5, no 2, 1994, p. 183–211.
5. Vaona Andrea and Pianta Mario, "Firm Size and Innovation in European Manufacturing", *Small Business Economics*, vol. 30, no 3, 2008, p. 283–299.
6. Pavitt Keith K., "Sectoral Patterns of Technical Change: Toward a Taxonomy and a Theory", *Research Policy*, vol. 13, 1984, p. 343–373.
7. European commission (2009–2012), *ERMIS: Effective Reproducible Model of Innovation System*, Programme Interreg IVC.
8. Damanpour Fariborz, "Organizational Innovation: A Meta-Analysis of Effects of Determinants and Moderators", *Academy of Management Journal*, vol. 34, no 3, 1991, p. 555–590.
9. Tidd Joe, Bessant John and Pavitt Keith K. , *Managing Innovation,* John Wiley & Sons, New York, 3rd ed., 2005.
10. Henderson Rebecca M. and Clark Kim B., "Architectural Innovation: The Reconfiguration of Existing Product Technologies and the Failure of Established Firms", *Administrative Science Quarterly*, vol. 35, no 1, 1990, p. 9–30.
11. Gans Joshua, "The Other Disruption. When Innovations Threaten the Organizational Model", *Harvard Business Review*, vol. 94, no 3, 2016, p. 78–84.
12. Becheikh Nizar, Landry Réjean and Amara Nabil, "Lessons from Innovation Empirical Studies in the Manufacturing Sector: A Systematic Review of the Literature from 1993–2003", *Technovation*, vol. 26, no 5–6, 2006, p. 644–664.
13. Dosi Giovanni, "Technological Paradigms and Technological Trajectories: A Suggested Interpretation of the Determinants and Directions of Technical Change", *Research Policy*, vol. 11, no 3, 1982, p. 147–162.
14. Christensen Clayton M. and Bower Joseph L., "Customer Power, Strategic Investment and the Failure of Leading Firms", *Strategic Management Journal*, vol. 17, no 3, 1996, p. 197–218.

15. Lettl Christopher, "User Involvement Competence for Radical Innovation", *Journal of Engineering and Technology Management,* vol. 24, no 1–2, 2007, p. 53–75.

16. Urban Glen L. and Von Hippel Eric, "Lead User Analyses for the Development of New Industrial Products", *Management Science,* vol. 34, no 5, 1988, p. 569–582.

17. OECD, *Oslo Manual – Guidelines for collecting and interpreting innovation data,* OECD Publishing, 2005.

18. Miller Danny and Friesen Peter H., "Innovation in Conservative and Entrepreneurial Firms: Two Models of Strategic Momentum", *Strategic Management Journal,* vol. 3, no 1, 1982, p. 1–25.

19. Olson Eric M., Slater Stanley F. and Hult G. Tomas M., "The Performance Implications of Fit among Business Strategy, Marketing Organization Structure and Strategic Behavior", *Journal of Marketing,* vol. 69, no 3, 2005, p. 49–65.

20. Ayerbe Cécile, "Innovations technologique et organisationnelle au sein de PME innovantes: complémentarité des processus, analyse comparative des mécanismes de diffusion", *Revue internationale PME,* vol. 19, no 1, 2006, p. 9–34.

21. Miles Raymond E. and Snow Charles C., *Fit, Failure and the Hall of Fame,* Free Press, New York, 1994.

22. Schroeder Dean M., "A Dynamic Perspective on the Impact of Process Innovation upon Competitive Strategies", *Strategic Management Journal,* vol. 11, no 1, 1990, p. 25–41.

23. Hamel Gary, *Leading the Revolution,* Harvard Business School Press, Cambridge, 2000.

24. Raymond Louis and Saint-Pierre Josée, "R&D as a Determinant of Innovation in Manufacturing SMEs: An Attempt at Empirical Clarification", *Technovation,* vol. 30, 2010, p. 48–56.

25. Zahra Shaker A. and Covin Jeffrey G., "Business Strategy, Technology Policy and Firm Performance", *Strategic Management Journal,* vol. 14, no 6, 1993, p. 451–478.

26. Carmeli Abraham, Gelbard Roy and Gefen David, "The Importance of Innovation Leadership in Cultivating Strategic Fit and Enhancing Firm Performance", *The Leadership Quarterly,* vol. 21, no 3, 2010, p. 339–349.

27. Ortega Maria J. R., "Competitive Strategies and Firm Performance: Technological Capabilities' Moderating Roles", *Journal of Business Research,* vol. 63, no 12, 2010, p. 1273–1281.

28. Breschi Stefano, Malerba Franco and Orsenigo Luigi, "Technological Regimes and Schumpeterian Patterns of Innovation", *The Economic Journal,* vol. 110, no 463, 2000, p. 388–410.

29. Forsman Helena and Temel Serdal, "Innovation and Business Performance in Small Enterprises: An Enterprise-Level Analysis", *International Journal of Innovation Management*, vol. 15, no 3, 2011, p. 641–665.

30. Gunther McGrath Rita, "Transient Advantage", *Harvard Business Review*, vol. 91, no 6, 2013, p. 62–70.

31. Hambrick Donald C., "On the Staying Power of Defenders, Analyzers, and Prospectors", *Academy of Management Executive*, vol. 17, no 4, 2003, p. 115–118.

32. Chereau Philippe, "Strategic Management of Innovation in Manufacturing SMEs: Exploring the Predictive Validity of Strategy-Innovation Relationship", *International Journal of Innovation Management*, vol. 19, no 1, 2015, p. 1–37. Zahra Shaker A. and Covin Jeffrey G., "Business Strategy, Technology Policy and Firm Performance", *Strategic Management Journal*, vol. 14, no 6, 1993, p. 451–478. *Id.*, "The Financial Implications of Fit Between Competitive Strategy and Innovation Types and Sources", *The Journal of High Technology Management Research*, vol. 5, no 2, 1994, p. 183–211.

33. Nagji Bansi and Tuff Geoff, "Managing Your Innovation Portfolio", *Harvard Business Review*, vol. 90, no 5, 2012, p. 67–74.

34. Lichtenthaler Ulrich and Lichtenthaler Eckhard, "A Capability-Based Framework for Open Innovation: Complementing Absorptive Capacity", *Journal of Management Studies*, vol. 46, no 8, 2009, p. 1315–1338.

Further Reading

On the Relationship Between Strategy and Innovation

Chereau Philippe, "Strategic Management of Innovation in Manufacturing SMEs: Exploring the Predictive Validity of Strategy-Innovation Relationship", *International Journal of Innovation Management*, vol. 19, no 1, 2015, p. 1–37.

King Andrew A. and Baatartogokh Baljir, "How Useful Is the Theory of Disruptive Innovation?", *MIT Sloan Management Review*, vol. 57, no 1, 2015, p. 76–90.

Vaona Andrea and Pianta Mario, "Firm Size and Innovation in European Manufacturing", *Small Business Economics*, vol. 30, no 3, 2008, p. 283–299.

Zahra Shaker A. and Covin Jeffrey G., "The Financial Implications of Fit Between Competitive Strategy and Innovation Types And Sources", *The Journal of High Technology Management Research*, vol. 5, no 2, 1994, p. 183–211.

On Innovation Management

Dodgson Mark, Gann David M. and Phillips Nelson, *The Oxford Handbook of Innovation Management*, Oxford University Press, Oxford, 2014.

Lichtenthaler Ulrich and Lichtenthaler Eckhard, "A Capability-Based Framework for Open Innovation: Complementing Absorptive Capacity", *Journal of Management Studies*, vol. 46, no 8, 2009, p. 1315–1338.

Tidd Joe, Bessant John and Pavitt Keith K., *Managing Innovation*, John Wiley & Sons, New York, 3rd ed., 2005.

Vian Dominique, *ISMA 360° – La Boussole de l'entrepreneur innovateur*, De Boeck, Bruxelles, 2013.

7

(Re)Designing the Business Model

7.1 The Consulting Mission

Most consulting missions focus on the answers companies need to the key questions they ask (or should ask) regularly: who are my clients? What do they consider valuable? How can we generate revenue by offering what they really want? What is the best profit formula to create value for clients at an appropriate cost for the company? By answering these questions, the consultant helps the company design a business model to implement its strategy. It is a delicate task intended to allow the company to generate a competitive advantage through having its own model that will be better than existing alternatives. The process should either deliver more value to a specific clientele, or rethink the way the company could create value more effectively by implementing a new set of best practices that put it ahead of the competition.

For Joan Magretta,[1] building a business model most often means writing a new version of the story of the company's value chain. This new story revisits both parts of the value chain, first reviewing the way the company organises its activities to produce value (design, materials purchase, manufacturing…); second, examining the activities associated with selling this value (identifying clients, prospecting, sales, distribution, delivery…). Just like the different chapters of a story, the components of each part as well as the two parts themselves must fit together coherently if they are to generate a viable model. Indeed, it is from this very fit that the company will obtain its competitive advantage. According to Michael E. Porter,[2] when the

© The Author(s) 2018
P. Chereau, P.-X. Meschi, *Strategic Consulting*, DOI 10.1007/978-3-319-64422-6_7

company's different activities are aligned, it is very difficult for competitors to obtain the same competitive advantage without reconstructing the very same system of alignment and interactions among activities.

The fit of a business model is rarely achieved immediately. Indeed, after his/her initial premise, the CEO must continuously adjust and adapt the model. Each decision and initiative must be analysed regarding the current model's economic performance. If the expected performance is lacking, the CEO should re-examine the various components of the company's business model and their internal fit. In this sense, Magretta considers that "*business modelling is the managerial equivalent of the scientific method – you start with a hypothesis, which you then test in action and revise when necessary*" (Magretta 2002, p. 88).

In recent years, the hypercompetitive situation and the need to continuously rethink the way companies continue to create value for their clients have conflated the terms business model and strategy. However, the two notions are very different and this confusion partly explains the failure of many business models designed by companies that seem biased in the process, being more interested in seeking problems to a solution than a solid basis for the strategic management of their development. Indeed, although any viable company relies on an efficient business model, this is only a systemic organisation that creates coherence—or fit—among the company's activities and constructs a value proposition for clients that generates lasting profits. The business model is not the company's strategy, for it takes no account of an essential dimension of performance: competition. Competition is a matter for strategy.

In working out its strategy, the company chooses how it intends to do better, differently from its competitors. The company then aims to use competences and resources that it alone possesses and/or that it combines in a unique way to make a value proposition that clients recognise as better, on a market chosen according to specific characteristics favourable to the company (see Chap. 3). If companies in the same industry propose the same offer to the same clients in the same way, there is little likelihood that these companies will develop, let alone survive. Clients would have negotiating power and the harshness of the competition would force the least resistant companies to disappear.

In this sense, business model and strategy are closely linked. The effectiveness of one depends on the pertinence of the other. A company cannot develop using exactly the same business model as the competition, unless it is distinguished by a more pertinent strategy in terms of target clients and markets and in terms of offer and type of value proposition. Similarly, a company cannot apply the same strategy as a competitor and be profitable in the long term unless it deploys this strategy more efficiently on the basis of a differentiated business model.

In a business model mission, the consultant needs to help the company's CEO and top managers to design a model that will result in a more effective deployment of competitive strategy. This means responding to the following questions:

Who are the company's clients? What problems do these clients have that the company wants to solve? What solution to the problem can the company offer that clients will value? How can we organise the company's activities to develop and deliver this offer? Will this offer and the underlying organisation generate lasting profit?

From these questions, various missions or parts of missions arise in terms of (re)designing or adapting the company's business model. A first type of mission could be to assess the current business model in the company's existing strategic business unit, or to construct a new business model in a new strategic business unit by looking at the business model in relation to the company's internal and external environments. This approach, based on the mission of strategic positioning (see Chap. 3) is intended to optimise or design a business model that takes into account the economic contingences, trends, market and industry forces as well as the company's strategic capabilities.

As a continuation of the previous mission, the consultant can first assess the new business model's strengths and weaknesses and then assess the opportunities it creates and threats it guards against. This type of mission has a dynamic view of implementing strategy. The consultant focuses on assessing the pertinence of the business model in terms of the fit among the different activities of the company's value chain and its capacity to generate a new competitive advantage rather than maintain the existing one.

Finally, another mission directly related to the strategic management of innovation missions (see Chap. 6), could be to disrupt the business model by constructing an innovative model that would change the company's value network—and therefore its competitive space. The new business model would then constitute a sustainable competitive advantage in itself, by changing the rules of the game between the company and its competitors.[3]

7.2   Theory, Methodology and the Tools for the Mission

7.2.1   Theoretical Background

7.2.1.1   Business Model: What Exactly Does This Mean?

If ever there were a contest for the greatest management buzzwords in recent years, the concept of business model would come somewhere near the top. However, few of those who use the term are comfortable when they try to give concrete expression to the different notions and dimensions it covers. This is a shame, because a good business model is essential for any company wishing to expand, whether it is starting up or already well established.

The term business model has flourished in the literature of management and strategy since the 1990s, mainly with the advent of the Internet and e-business. These new media obliged companies to question the way they proposed their offers and gave rise to numerous opportunities for accessing new customers. From this viewpoint, as Magretta says, a business model is the story that explains how a company works and responds to the three main questions:

- Who are my clients?
- What do they value?
- How can we generate revenue by offering what they expect at an appropriate cost for the company?

Another approach is to define a business model by the main characteristics that make it efficient. This is how Mark W. Johnson, Clayton M. Christensen and Henning Kagermann[4] see it. They suggest that a business model is a blueprint comprising four interacting elements: a customer value proposition, a profit formula, key resources and key processes. Johnson, Christensen and Kagermann's configuration is the architecture underlying the various articulations of all the business model components proposed to date.

For Johnson, Christensen and Kagermann, the *"customer value proposition"* (*"CVP"*) is the *"job to be done"* by the company to solve specific customers' problems by creating a specific offer. A prerequisite to designing this offer—solving the problem—is understanding all aspects of the problem and ways of solving it. The bigger the problem, the less satisfied customers are with existing solutions; the better the company's solution compared to the existing alternatives, the higher the CVP. Today, the notion of customer must be seen in a wider perspective; the customer is the user beneficiary of the value proposition, especially in the context of platform business models (see further).

The *"profit formula"* is the model the company chooses to create value for itself while also offering value to the client. The profit formula is made up of the following:

- *"Revenue model"*: price × volume.
- *"Cost structure"*: variable costs, fixed costs, economies of scale. The cost structure is mainly determined by the cost of key resources required for the business model.
- *"Margin model"*: the contribution of each transaction needed to make profit depending on expected sales volume and cost structure.
- *"Resource velocity"*: the speed of stock rotation, use of fixed and current assets. According to Johnson, Christensen and Kagerman, this parameter should be determined by the price required to deliver the CVP and the resulting variable costs and gross margin. This then defines what the velocity and scale of using resources need to be.
- *"Key resources"* are assets such as people, technology, products, facilities, equipment, points of sale and brands required to design and deliver the CVP. Here, the company focuses on the key assets that create value for both the customer and the company as well as looking at how these assets interact. These are the strategic competences and resources—strategic capabilities—on which the company builds up its competitive advantage regarding customers (see Chap. 3).
- *"Key processes"* are the operational and managerial processes the company sets up to create continuous growing value. They comprise recurrent activities, operations and tasks such as training, R&D, production, budgeting, communication, sales, controlling etc. Key processes also include rules, performance metrics and good practices.

Johnson, Christensen and Kagermann see these four components as the main blocks of each business model. CVP and the profit formula correspond to value for both the customer and the company. Key resources and processes describe how this value is delivered to the customer and the company. From this point on, the efficiency of a business model depends on the fit among these components. Any significant modification of one component will impact the others and thereby affect the coherence of the whole. Figure 7.1 illustrates this blueprint and the interactions among the blocks.

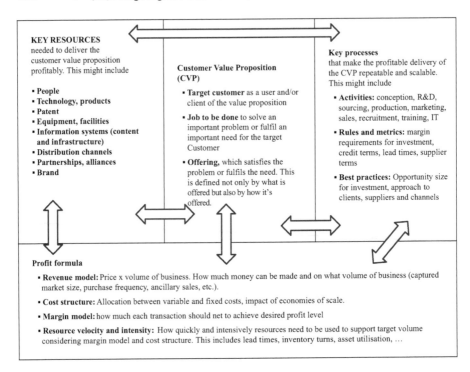

Fig. 7.1 Business model blocks
Source: Adapted from Johnson Mark W., Christensen Clayton M. and Kagermann Henning, *op. cit.*, 2008

Ramon Casadesus-Masanell and Joan E. Ricart[5] provide the most uncluttered version of the business model. These authors consider the business model as a set of managerial choices and their consequences. For them, companies make three types of choices when building a business model:

- *"Policy choices"* that determine actions taken by the company across all its operations (subcontracting to return-to-work organisations, compensation policy, setting up in tax-free zones, incentives for car-sharing etc.);
- *"Assets choices"* or choices about the tangible resources the company decides to deploy to carry out its activities (equipment, technology, video-conference systems…);
- *"Governance choices"* or choices concerning the decision-making processes in terms of deciding between policies and assets (how do you decide whether to subcontract or produce internally, whether to go from laser cutting to waterjet cutting, whether to invest in interactive whiteboards for students…).

The consequences of these choices are either flexible or rigid. Flexible consequences appear rapidly, for example, reduced sales after choosing to significantly increase prices, or increased customer numbers in a bar after choosing to set up free WiFi. A rigid consequence has lasting results in the company's business model. Therefore, co-operation between departments induced by allocating a percentage of the annual individual bonus to "contributing to the group's success" would tend to have a lasting effect, even if the percentage were reduced or even stopped. Rigid consequences allow companies to build up sustainable competitive advantages because they take longer and are more complicated for competitors to imitate.

According to Casadesus-Masanell and Ricart, by making selecting a business model and taking account of their consequences, companies enter a virtuous cycle of aligning on strategic objectives and strengthening competitive advantages. Therefore, the consequences of these initial choices lead to others that will in turn influence the business model and so on. In this sense, Casadesus-Masanell and Ricart's approach to the business model shows many similarities to the adaptive cycle of strategic configurations that Miles and Snow put forward in 1978. Figure 7.2 illustrates the business model alignment cycle.

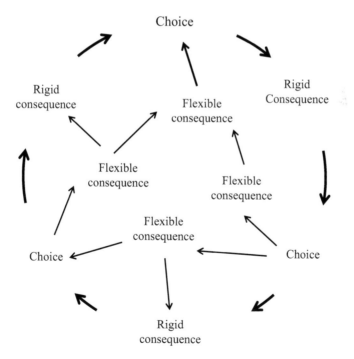

Fig. 7.2 The virtuous cycle of the business model alignment
Source: Adapted from Casadesus-Masanell Ramon and Ricart Joan E., *op. cit.,* 2011

After reviewing the set of developments and research related to the concept of the business model, Christoph Zott, Raphael Amit and Lorenzo Massa[6] conclude that it is a system centred in an organisation's activities whose objective is to create value. A business model is, therefore, a systemic and holistic approach that helps to understand how an organisation articulates its activities with each other to create value. These authors also note that the phenomenon of value creation is part of a value network that can include suppliers, partners, distribution networks or associations that allow the organisation's field of competences and resources to be extended.

All these approaches agree that the different perspectives of the business model concept converge to define it as a system by which an organisation (a company or any other structure) creates, delivers and captures value (economic value, social value…) in relation to a network of partners.

Nevertheless, if companies show so much interest for the business model concept, it is because they see it (intuitively or not) as a dynamic way of aligning competitive strategy and operational strategy. Indeed, the business model is an integral part of the strategic planning process (see Chap. 3). As mentioned above, it is the blueprint for implementing the company's strategic choice of competitive positioning towards target customers and its choices of allocating and organising the means to support this positioning.

7.2.1.2   Business Model and Strategy

As we have already underlined, there is often a great deal of confusion between the concepts of business model and strategy. This confusion is harmful because it can lead to inappropriate decision-making in terms of strategic management. It is also understandable, for although business model and strategy are two distinct concepts, they are also strongly related. In the following paragraphs, we clarify the differences between business model and strategy while showing the reader why their alignment is necessary and how they are correlated.

The business model as we have defined it refers to the logic of how the company organises its activities, and creates and captures value in each of its strategic business units. Strategy is the plan the company defines to create a sustainable, unique and profitable position by deciding to implement a set of distinctive activities. It therefore implies that the company has previously chosen how it intends to position itself in the market to obtain an advantage over the competition, in the eyes of its customers. Strategy is reflected in the choices about the types of customers sensitive to this positioning, the problem these customers need the company to solve, the solution offered to solve it, and the means implemented to obtain the desired level of profitability. However, the above only reflects the company's strategy: it is not the strategy itself.

According to Casadesus-Masanell and Ricart, strategy is the *"contingent plan"* of the type of business model to use for the company to implement its competitive positioning. The notion of contingency belongs to strategy, not to the business model. Strategy is determined according to contingences—variable conditions—that come from the market (customers' and suppliers' negotiation power, new entrants, substitutes, the intensity of competition…) or from the macro-economic and industrial environment (crises, trends, laws, technological breakthroughs…). These contingences can vary in intensity. Contingences should only influence the business model indirectly, if the company changes its strategy because of them. Indeed, even if by definition every company has a business model, not every company has a deliberate strategy that results in optimising the business model according to the external environment. This is notably the case with companies that Miles and Snow[7] describe as *"reactors."* These companies show no coherence between strategy and business model and are thus unable to develop a sustainable competitive advantage.

We can therefore conclude that strategy induces the business model that is best suited to its implementation. Just as there are advantageous alignments between a company's strategy and its innovation behaviour, there are also strategy/business model combinations whose fit is better than others. In general, this fit is not to be found immediately. Indeed, the aim of strategy is to build a competitive advantage by defending a unique positioning or by exploiting an idiosyncratic combination of resources; but this positioning and these resources only very gradually build up throughout cycles of choices that will tend towards the effective implementation of the strategy. The company must therefore develop the business model that allows it to speed up these cycles.

If strategy predicts the business model, the business model will in turn influence strategy. Indeed, the business model's virtuous cycle will automatically show up the dysfunctions that prevent it from supporting the strategy. These dysfunctions result either from a faulty construction of the blocks comprising the business model, or from the impact of the above-mentioned contingences on the relevance of the strategy itself—and therefore on the business model supposed to support that strategy. In the first case, the company should redesign its business model. In the second, it should re-examine its strategy and possibly adapt its business model to the new strategy. In this sense, the business model acts as a dynamic barometer of the consistency of the company's strategic choices.

This contribution of the business model to a more dynamic view of strategy in a context of hypercompetition and transient competitive advantages (see Chaps. 3 and 6), is put forward by Benoît Demil and Xavier Lecocq.[8] These authors argue in favour of a dynamic consistency not only between strategy and business model, but also between and even within the different blocks that constitute the business model. Demil and Lecocq consider that a business model is permanently in a state of disequilibrium because, since resources are never used optimally, dysfunctions persist, thereby offering opportunities to design new processes to develop new knowledge and thus be better able exploit the said resources. Here a virtuous circle also occurs among the main components of the business model: resources (R), competences (C), and the organisation (O) of activities within the company's internal value chain and with the actors of its external value network and finally, the customer value proposition (V). Through their interactions, these "RCOV" blocks determine the company's structure and volume of costs and revenues, and therefore, its margin. Consequently, the longevity of the competitive advantage depends on the company's capability to continuously revisit, develop and align each of these RCOV blocks. Figure 7.3 illustrates the relationships among the different components of the business model according to Demil and Lecocq.

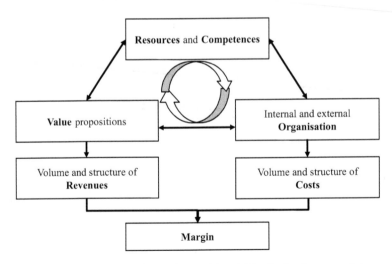

Fig. 7.3 The RCOV blocks and their relationship within the business model
Source: Adapted from Demil Benoît and Lecocq Xavier, op. cit., 2010

7.2.1.3 The Specific Case of Platform Business Models

Platforms have existed for a long time as structures that link businesses and consumers. Food courts link customers and restaurants, shopping malls link customers and shops, pay TV channels link advertisers and subscribers. However, the Internet has made it easier and less expensive to build and deploy a platform business model. Internet platforms, now generally known as digital platforms, have also modified the nature of companies' strategic choices and consequently the nature of the relationships among business model components. There are three main changes[9]:

1. From resource control to resource orchestration: traditionally, companies' resources are considered strategic when they are intrinsically valuable, rare, and ideally, inimitable and non-transferable (see Chap. 3). Unlike digital platform companies, in conventional pipeline type companies, these resources are mostly tangible assets. In digital platform business models, it is difficult to imitate the relationships among all the stakeholders and their respective contributions to the community; in other words, it is hard to imitate the interactions and organisation among the company's resources, clients and partners.
2. From internal optimisation to external interaction: in pipeline-type business models, companies concentrate on optimising their internal value chain. In digital platform business models, companies focus on optimising the management of their external value chain that connects producers and consumers.
3. From focusing on customer value proposition to ecosystem value proposition: in conventional business models, companies design offers to respond to customers' unsatisfied needs or unresolved problems. In digital platform business models, offers must be valued by the whole of the ecosystem of producers and consumers. If these are satisfied, the ecosystem will develop in the form of an iterative virtuous circle.

Digital platform business models can be divided into four basic categories[10]: content, commerce, context and connection. These categories are characterised by differentiated value propositions for the ecosystem in question and specific revenue streams. Table 7.1 shows the mission, the value proposition and the revenue model of each digital business model category. Digital platform business models also vary according to four main key success factors—social networking, interaction between companies and clients, personalisation/customisation, and added value for users. Table 7.2 shows the relevance of each of these factors for each business model.

Table 7.1 Digital platform BM: missions, value propositions and revenue models

Type of BM	Mission	Value proposition	Revenue model
BM of content	Companies collecting, selecting, compiling, distributing, and/or presenting online content. Ex.: Online journals, Wikipedia	Providing convenient and user-friendly access to various types of user-specific content	Mostly online advertising, but increasingly subscription and pay-per-use (freemium model)
BM of commerce	Companies initiating, negotiating, and/or fulfilling online transactions. Ex.: Amazon, Ventes Privées, PriceMinister, Dell	Providing a cost-efficient exchange place for buyers and sellers of goods and services, thus substituting or supporting transaction functions	Direct sales revenues or indirect revenues from commissions
BM of context	Companies sorting and/or aggregating available online information. Ex.: Google, Yahoo!, Bing, Qwant	Providing structuration of information already existing on internet and facilitating navigation for internet users to reduce intransparency and complexity	Mostly online advertising
BM of connection	Companies providing physical and/or virtual network infrastructure. Ex.: EarthLink, Outlook	Providing the prerequisites for exchange of information over the internet	Online advertising, subscription, time-based billing, volume-based billing

Source: Adapted from Wirtz Bernd W., Schilke Oliver, and Ullrich Sebastian, *op. cit.*, 2010

Table 7.2 Digital platform BM: relevance of key success factor per business model type

Business model	Social networking	Company-client interaction	User-added value	Customisation/personalisation
	Social identity: sense of belonging; Social trust: confidence that people from the same network will reciprocate; Virtual word of mouth in the community; Increased consumer power: importance of user's influence of the company's choices	Customer centricity: put customer at the center of company's BM; Interaction configuration: structure the process of interactions with clients; Customer response: dialogue with each client and aggregate information; Cooperative value generation: include clients in improvement of offering (Stata, Linux....)	User-generated content (individual profiles, videos, websites....); User-generated creativity: include clients in the design of offering; User-generated innovation: (open-software, lead users); Shared sources of revenues (innocentive, Quirky...)	Personal customisation: give possibility to users to reconfigure the website; Group customisation; Social customisation: customising offering according to social layers
Content BM	++	+	++	+
Commerce BM	–	++	0	+
Context BM	+	–	0	+
Connection BM	++	+	0	+

Source: Adapted from Wirtz Bernd W., Schilke Oliver, and Ullrich Sebastian, *op. cit.*, 2010
++ very high relevance, + high relevance, 0 medium relevance, – low relevance

Best Consulting Practices in Brief

When consultants accompany companies in building their business model, they embark on a delicate mission where they must distinguish between two complementary but distinct domains of analysis. The first, strategy, focuses on the question "Are we doing the right things?" The second, the domain of the business model, focuses on the question "Are we doing things right?"

Building a business model means creating coherence between the answers to both these questions. The consultant's first task is therefore to see that the different components of the business model correspond to the company's strategic objectives. Then he/she should optimise the complementarity between these elements to stabilise the business model and exploit the competitive advantage created by the customer value proposition as fast as possible, as profitably as possible and for as long as possible.

7.2.1.4 Why, When and How to Reinvent the Business Model?

The hypercompetition that reigns in most industries obliges companies to adapt their business model regularly or even to design a new one in order to deploy their strategy. A study published by PwC in 2015 revealed that 54% of CEOs and top managers in the world envisaged diversifying outside of their traditional markets.[11] This finding is confirmed by a 2014 study by the Boston Consulting Group of 1500 executive managers, which showed that 94% had already or envisaged redesigning their business model.[12] However, the success of such a process is very hit and miss. Many companies struggle to reinvent themselves, not because they cannot manage to change what has to be changed, but because they wait too long to do it. The job of realigning the strategic objectives with the business model components requires too much disruption in terms of the new customer value proposition, the resources needed and their mobilisation, key processes that must be reconstructed at the same time that the profit formula is redefined.

Too many companies also appear to lose sight of the very nature of the components of their business model and the interdependence of those components. Does the customer value proposition still give sufficient value? Are the key processes suitable or do they generate a certain inertia in delivering the offer? Are the resources still fit for purpose or should they be renewed? Are the revenue model and cost structure still appropriate for generating the expected margin? This loss of contact with the reality of their business prevents companies from knowing whether they can continue to exploit the existing business model or whether they need to change it.

A new strategic orientation does not always require the company to rethink the content of its business model's components. The existing business model often still fulfils its functions and only needs to be slightly adapted. This is the case when the new customer value proposition can be delivered by:

- using the same profit formula;
- mobilising most of the current key resources;
- following existing key processes;
- applying the same rules, the same good practices and the same performance metrics as those currently in use.

In a recent plea[13] against the "obsession" of business model innovation at all costs, Clayton Christensen, Thomas Bartman and Derek van Bever even declared that the vocation of any business model is to increase coherence and interdependence among the value proposition, profit formula and resources and processes. So, by nature, a business model should not be changed radically, but rather evolve in line with the effectiveness of its answers to external and internal contingences and consequently, towards stability. These authors describe this evolution as a journey where the business model passes from being at a creation stage, through sustaining innovation, until it finally reaches the desired level of efficiency. The first "creation stage" focuses on developing a meaningful value proposition that is attractive enough to respond to the needs of early adopter customers. It is key in this first stage, centred on information seeking (market, uses, competitors, value network) to collect information on the customer needs as yet not covered and the best practices that will result in an innovative proposition that is significantly more suitable to attract the targeted clients. At this stage, the company must seek to align its resources with the value proposition, but the business model remains informal and exploratory. If the company reaches the second stage, sustaining innovation, there is no longer any need to prove the interest of the value proposition for the target clients or for the ecosystem related to the business model. This second stage is no longer one for questioning clients, but rather of listening carefully to their preferences. This means defining the processes and organisation that will allow the company to integrate their demands and deploy the offer on a larger scale, to satisfy a growing demand with increased profitability. In other words: better products can be sold at higher prices to the existing market. The company then adopts a "know-thyself" attitude towards its business model where it is important to measure the effectiveness of the articulation and alignment among the business model's different components.

The key indicators focus on the constituents of the income statement to maximise products and reduce costs. In the third stage, known as business model efficiency, innovation efforts centred on the value proposition must be backed up by more systemic efforts for innovation that run throughout the entire business model. Companies always tend to modularise the structure of their business model by optimising the content and scope of their key internal and external activities towards standardisation, re-evaluating key resources and practices, even in rethinking the profit formula. In the efficiency stage of innovation, the indicators of the strategic model for profitability (see Chap. 4), such as return on sales, the asset turnover coefficient and the return on investment are tracked with special care. Nevertheless, it is also during this systematic effort to standardise the interdependencies among the business model components that companies run the risk of listening to shareholders rather than heeding market signals and the decline of the customer value proposition, which may lead to clientele atrophy. Figure 7.4 illustrates the three stages of the business model's "journey."

Nevertheless, it may happen that the company reinvents its entire business model. This is when implementing the company's strategy requires the significant reconfiguration of all the existing business model components. This reconfiguration does not happen overnight and can be anticipated through a process of "planned opportunism." Planned opportunism is an

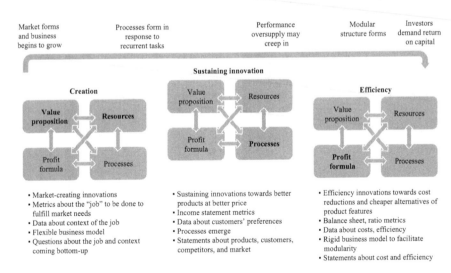

Fig. 7.4 The three stages of the business model's "journey"
Source: Adapted from Christensen Clayton M., Bartman Thomas, and Van Bever Derek, *op. cit.*, 2016

organised process through which companies in hypercompetitive contexts consider that although the future is less and less predictable and harder and harder to shape, the environment can give out weak signals that indicate political, societal, technological, environmental and regulatory trends and changes, not to mention customer needs and behaviours.

According to Vijay Govindarajan,[14] planned opportunism allows companies to stop thinking in linear mode while enriching their business model and preparing for strategic innovation. This implies considering change as an organisational routine. In other words, planned opportunism: (1) creates a virtuous circle of new idea generation and enrichment, (2) develops the company's capacity to prioritise, investigate and act on these ideas, and (3) builds up an adaptive culture of continuous change.

A culture of planned opportunism involves the company's business model in a permanent mode of questioning: who will be our future clients? What will they value? Which technologies are likely to generate new opportunities while disrupting our activities? Who will our future competitors be? What aspects of our value proposition will they provide alternatives for? Should we change our go-to-market strategy? Which regulatory changes might impact our activities?

Johnson, Christensen and Kagermann identified five strategic circumstances in which the responses to the above questions should result in a new business model:

1. A large number of clients do not have access to a market because existing solutions are too expensive or too complicated to acquire or use. An example of this might be an opportunity for creating a disruption in the business model to make an offer available to emerging economies.
2. An innovating technology might need a new business model in order to exploit all its potential or to take advantage of new opportunities (*i.e.*, Apple and MP3 technology). An established technology might benefit from a new life cycle by supporting a new value proposition for new customers. In this case, the transformation of the business model is based on the combination of six business model characteristics that link technological innovation and the new market needs[15]: (1) a more personalised CVP, (2) products recycled in a closed loop model, (3) content shared between the producer, the provider and the consumer that reduces costs, (4) a revenue model based on use, (5) a collaborative ecosystem that spreads the risks and (6) an adaptable agile structure. These characteristics are often found together in companies that transformed their industry's business model, such as Airbnb, Amazon, Dell, Google Adwords, Ikea, Lego, or Uber.

3. Refocusing on the specific *"job to be done"* to propose a currently non-existent customer value proposition can mean fundamentally redesigning the business model. Notably, it is an option when competing companies focus on continuously improving their offer aimed at the same client segment; these companies seem to be affected by a sort of "client myopia" that pushes them into standardising their offers towards the dead-end of a dominant design. This was the option taken by FedEx, which decided to access the market of package delivery by targeting high-speed long-haul reliable deliveries rather than launching a front-end price and marketing war to surpass UPS.
4. The need to fend off low-end disrupters. The new business model initiated by Massive Open Online Courses (MOOCs) allowed business schools and universities to stand up to low-price competition from institutes of continuing education.
5. The imperative to react against intensifying competition from new entrants by changing the rules of the game, using a new business model and redefining the CVP. This is the case of tool manufacturer Hilti that, when faced with stiff competition from bottom-of-the-range products, went from selling high quality reliable tools to hiring tools based on *"reliability and performance."*

Embarking on reworking a business model is an important strategic decision and a delicate process that should not be undertaken unless the company goes beyond simply changing the intrinsic components of its business model; it must also modify its CVP, its profit formula model, its key resources and the processes to be implemented at the level of the target industry or market. Before deciding to change the business model, an affirmative answer to the following four questions give a reasonable indication of the chances of success:

1. Does the new CVP create real customer loyalty?
2. Are the business model components (CVP, profit formula, resources and key processes) aligned optimally in the new business model?
3. Does the new business model work independently of the model of the company's core business?
4. Does the new business model create disruption relative to competitors?

Looking at these questions will undoubtedly lead to the conclusion that rethinking the business model for an incumbent company can never be a process carried out in fits and starts, because the above-mentioned conditions for success underline the iterative emergence of a new efficient model.

Again, we remind consultants of the reality principle that they should hold dear, highlighted by Chris Zook and James Allen[16] in their research: efficient companies do not reinvent themselves. They continuously reinforce the differentiating nature of their business model components to constantly optimise the competitive advantage thereby obtained. These companies constantly adapt each component to changes in their market. This allows them to exploit their business model on existing products or markets and explore innovating versions of the model on new products or markets without ever losing sight of the basis of their differentiation. The key challenges are indeed coherence and perpetual realignment. Here Zook and Allen confirm the principle of dynamic consistency of the business model proposed by Demil and Lecocq.

> **Best Consulting Practices in Brief**
>
> Work on the company's business model requires the consultant to step back from "fashionable trends." The siren song of disruption and new competitive spaces that are, so far, competitor-free, may well draw the unprepared company towards uncharted waters. If the disruption succeeds, it is mainly because, in a continuous process of differentiation of its business model components, the company manages to outrun its competitors and see them disappear behind the horizon. The consultant should then concentrate on the company's capacity to work in a mode of dynamic consistency between strategy and business model. He/she should notably check its capacity to perceive the first signs of needing to change the CVP before the others, adjust its profit formula accordingly and constantly adapt its resources and key processes to deliver the new CVP profitably. The consultant should then assess the company's aptitude to generate new opportunities through these "adaptive" components of the business model and take advantage of them to outdistance its competitors.

7.2.2 Methodology and Tools for the Mission

A consulting mission on the company's business model is done in three main stages. First, the consultant should thoroughly examine the business model components to construct the blueprint and highlight the interactions among these components. Next, he/she must position the business model within the company's environment to examine it in context. This first stage, known as the "contextual formalisation of the business model" is based on two tools: the business model's blueprint and its strategic positioning. In the second stage, the consultant assesses the business model's potential to generate a sustainable competitive advantage for the company. This second stage, known as the "diagnostic of the business model" starts by a diagnostic of the business model's effectiveness, *i.e.*, its alignment with the company's strategy, the coherence among its components and its soundness over time. The consultant follows this with the diagnostic of the business model's competitive positioning, identifying the opportunities and threats it addresses and the strengths and weaknesses generated by each component. Finally, if necessary, in a final stage known as "optimisation of the business model," the consultant may extend the mission by optimising the company's differentiation vis a vis the competition in a business model innovation approach. In all, the business model consulting mission is organised into five main stages, as illustrated in Fig. 7.5.

7.2.2.1   The Business Model Blueprint

The formalisation of the business model is an essential prerequisite to the mission. Indeed, it is vital that the consultant and the company share the same representation of the blueprint for implementing the company's strategy. As mentioned earlier, strategy refers to the choice the company has previously

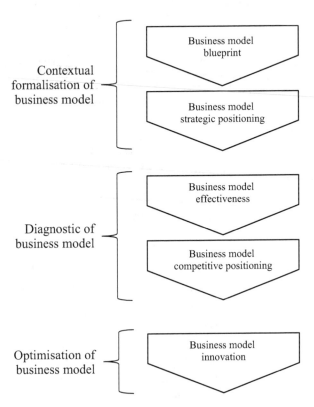

Fig. 7.5 The stages of a business model mission
Source: Authors

Table 7.3 The business model canvas

8 Key partners	6 Key activities & practices	2 Value proposition	4 Customer relationships	1 Customer segments
Company-provider and company-producer partnerships to secure the upstream value chain	*That help provide the VP profitably, reproducibly, and at a large-scale*	**Solution**	*Means used by the company to conquer, hold and retain consumers and partners of the business ecosystem*	*Distinct consumer (user or buyer) groups and partners of the ecosystem targeted by the company that:*
Strategic alliances between non-competitors	**Activities:** *design, R&D, procurement, production, marketing, sales, recruitment, training, SI*	*The bundle of products and / or services developed by the company for each specific targeted consumer segment and partner of the ecosystem …*		*Have needs that require different handling*
Partnerships between competitors: Coopetition	**Rules and key indicators:** *margin requirements, rules on accounts receivables & payables, quotes conversion rate, …*	**To the Problem**	**3 Channels**	*Are addressed via different distribution channels*
Joint venture to develop a new VP		*… to solve the problem (or satisfy the need) specific to each targeted consumer segment and partner*	*How to raise awareness about the VP, make it available and provide it to consumer segments and partners of the ecosystem*	*Require relationship management specific to each group*
Support from local authorities	**7 Key resources**		*Make known the existence of the offer*	*Have distinct levels of profitability*
…	*Required to provide the VP to consumers and partners through selected distribution channels, by establishing appropriate relationships, and according to the revenue model decided.*		*Allow consumers to evaluate the VP*	*Are interested in different aspects of VP*
	Physical assets (equipment, facilities, IS…)		*Allow consumers to purchase the offer*	*Who will be early adopters?*
	Human Resources		*Deliver the offer*	
	Intellectual assets (patents, trademarks, reputation		*Maintain the VP after the purchase*	
	Financial assets			

9 Cost structure			5 Revenue model	
Distribution of expenses into variable and fixed costs, impact of economies of scale according to:			**Turnover model:** *price x volume of sales. How much can the company expect to earn and how to achieve this level of sales (market size captured, purchase frequency, additional sales…)*	
Key activities			**Margin model:** *how much margin each transaction must generate to achieve the expected profitability*	
Key resources				
Key partnerships				

Source: Adapted from Osterwalder Alexander and Pigneur Yves, op. cit., 2010

made about how it intends to position itself in the market to gain a competitive advantage in the eyes of its clients. The choices about the types of customers sensitive to this positioning, the problem they need solving, the offer that solves it and the means implemented to obtain the required level of profitability, reflect this strategy and are formalised in the business model.

Johnson, Christensen and Kagermann's configuration of the business model, arranged around a customer value proposition, a profit formula, key resources and processes, has served as a generic architecture for multiple versions to date of how the business model components can be articulated. Among these versions, the business model canvas proposed by Alexander Osterwalder and Yves Pigneur[17] provides a pragmatic approach as to how the company creates, produces and captures value. This canvas of the business model comprises nine blocks covering the dimensions of customers, offer, infrastructure and financial viability. It is presented as the blueprint for a systemic implementation of the company's strategy through an organisational configuration that uses key resources and processes to come up with a profitable customer value proposition. In the case of a platform business model, it is important to consider each block as a component of the ecosystem incorporating the company, its clientele of users or buyers and the different stakeholders targeted by the value proposition. Table 7.3 illustrates the Osterwalder and Pigneur's canvas.

From Theory to Practice

The analysis of Hightense's strategic positioning (see Chap. 3), led to the decision to continue the company's development in its SBU1 (high power energy engineering) and to diversify by mobilising new competences in SBU2 (medium and low power). In the framework of this analysis, the consultant was able to identify the company's key resources in its strategic business units by establishing Hightense's competitive positioning (see Table 3.6). He/she can now draw up the company's business model canvas according to its strategic posture. This was initially defined as that of a prospector, solving the problem of interconnection energy losses that had become particularly relevant in electro-intensive industrial companies since the deregulation of electricity prices and in a context of the decreased competitiveness of the European industry. Table 7.4 describes the business model of Hightense.

The business model canvas points out the building of the competitive advantage in each block regarding the opportunities Hightense wishes to take advantage of (the problems to be dealt with) and the company's strategic capabilities. This canvas highlights the interrelationships among the blocks.

(continued)

(continued)

Table 7.4 Hightense's business model canvas

8 Key partners	7 Key activities	2 Value proposition	4 Customer relationships	1 Customer segments
Referencing with domestic electricity suppliers	**Activities:** *Electro-technical R&D*	**Solution** *Energy optimisation audits (preventive process)*	*Network of alumni from engineer schools*	*Electro-intensive industries: chemicals, steel, glass*
Network of available free lance engineers	*Energy audit + technical report*	*Energy engineering (tailored solutions)*	*Cost of energy audit deducted if contract signed*	*Countries where the price of electricity is free and increasing*
Network of specialised retailers of electro-technical equipment	*Engineering of unique solutions* *Production of conductive foam device*	*Patented conductive foam device*	*Referred as technical partner of energy suppliers*	*Countries with incentives to reduce energy consumption*
"Energy" competitive clusters	*Installation, maintenance* *Energy consumption monitoring*	*Guaranteed energy savings (95%)*	*Shared platform with the client for tele-monitoring of energy consumption*	*Who will be early adopters?*
ADEME (French agency for environment and energy management) and its European counterparts	*Patenting* *Scanning of calls for tender + application file*	*Easy and quick installation of device* *No overheating (easier maintenance)*	*Yearly audit of energy optimisation*	*Factories of chlorine-soda electrolysis under construction or shifting to the membrane technology in Europe*
	Scanning of new plant construction/renovation + electrolysis technology shift	*Permanent device* *Monitoring of energy savings*	**3 Channels** *Referencing with electricity suppliers as bid specifiers (cf. energy savings tax incentives)*	
	Bid preparation **Rules and metrics:**	**To the Problem** *Major interconnections energy losses (up to 30%)*	*Direct prospection (e-mailing) with key accounts in Europe (heads of maintenance) via technical file of energy savings simulation*	
	Control of commercial margin *Request for down payment* *Follow-up of conversion rate*	*Repeated maintenance operations requiring interruption production interruptions*	*Answers to technical calls for tender*	
	6 Key resources *R&D unit with industrial tool for "real situation" tests*	*Risks during maintenance due to high temperature*		
	Portfolio of electrotechnical patents with world coverage			
	Electrotechnical engineers			
	High self-financing capacity			
	ISO 14001 certification			
	Technical intelligence specialist			

9 Cost structure: directed towards production of value
Variable costs: *raw materials (conductive metals, chemicals), equipment; fees of freelance experts, sales costs (audit and prospecting campaigns)*
Fixed costs: *HR, production tool, patent costs, certification tests, renewal certification…*

5 Revenue model: fixed + dynamic
Turnover model: *fixed on audit charged at day price (offered if engineering contract signed) + sale of electrotechnical equipment + dynamic on % of energy savings realized*
Margin model: *calculation of break-even point on the basis of a variable cost margin rate of xx% and an average contract value of xxx K€*

Source: Authors

Table 7.5 Strategic positioning of the business model—contextualisation of each component with external contingences

		Business model components: influences of external contingences on the component of the BM									
Contingences		Customer segments	Value proposition	Channels	Customer relationships	Revenue model	Key resources	Key activities	Key partners	Cost structure
Macro-environment	Political									
	Global economy									
	Social/cultural trends									
	Technological trends									
	Legal/regulation trends									
	Availability of resources and raw materials									
Industry forces	Intensity of competition rivalry									
	Barriers to entry									
	Risks of substitute products									
	Relationships with stakeholders of the value network									
	Relationships with other facilitating stakeholders									
Market forces	Importance of the problem/need									
	Market trends									
	Clients loyalty									
	Interest and viability of revenue model									
	Interest of priority segments									

Source: Authors

7.2.2.2   The Business Model Strategic Positioning

The business model is an integral part of the strategic planning process and constitutes the blueprint for implementing the strategic competitive choices *vis a vis* the target clients and how to allocate and organise the means to support this positioning. For this reason, all the business model components are meant to allow the company to deploy its strategy efficiently according to the contingences of the external environment. It is therefore important to know if these components actually support the strategy by being appropriate to these contingences.

The consultant must therefore examine each component through the lens of the macro-environment influences, the industry forces and the specific target markets. This approach also serves as a basis for the diagnostic of the business model's effectiveness and competitive positioning. Here it is a matter of identifying the determinants of the solidity of the competitive advantage attached to each component. Table 7.5 illustrates the different points arising between each component and each contingency.

From Theory to Practice

Table 7.6 illustrates the analysis of the strategic positioning of Hightense's business model with a focus on the value proposition component. The analysis of the different contingences shows that the value proposition established according to the *"job to be done"* to solve high power customers' problem deals efficiently with most of the contingences. A first assessment of the solidity of the competitive advantage shows that the company is strongly differentiated and limits the risk *vis a vis* substitute offers. Furthermore, the value proposition not only responds to clients' needs but also considers the contingences related to the actors of the industry value chain.

(continued)

Table 7.6 Strategic positioning of Hightense's business model—contextualisation of the value proposition

Contingences		Influences of external contingences on the component: value proposition
Macro-environment	Political	European governments have established incentives for effective energy management.
	Global economy	Inderdependence and competition between countries disadvantage the competitiveness of European industry.
	Social/cultural trends	Energy management is a societal issue. The most costly energy is "lost" energy.
	Technological trends	Many high-power facilities shift technology and favour solutions for lower energy consumption technologies.
	Legal/regulation trends	EU member states impose constraining regulations that foster energy management.
	Availability of resources and raw materials	Access to electrical energy is significantly different among European countries. There is an inflation of the market price of conductive metals (Cu, Arg...).
Industry forces	Intensity of competition rivalry	Major players of high-power plants maintenance leave the European market (desindustrialisation of Europe).
	Barriers to entry	Electro-technical competences are less and less taught in Europe. Feasability tests and prototyping require significant investments in R&D and equipment.
	Risks of substitute products	Substitute solutions are not appropriate, are costly (frequent maintenance operations).
	Relationships with stakeholders of the value network	Energy suppliers look for complementary technical solutions to remain competitive (cost of energy). Suppliers of conductive metals have a high bargaining power.
	Relationships with other facilitating stakeholders	National energy agencies promote solutions for energy management. Energy clusters contribute to raise awareness of industrials for energy management.
Market forces	Importance of the problem/need	Cost of electrical energy is constantly increasing, thus hampering productivity of high-power plants. CSR issues are more and more taken into account (durable solutions, safety of staff...).
	Market trends	High-power installations are seldom changed in Europe. Upgrading and optimising existing installations is favoured over heavy investments. Efficient energy management is a key issue.
	Clients loyalty	Electro-technical expertise is mandatory for optimising existing installations. Knowledge of industrial processes and equipments is a KSF of client's loyalty.
	Interest and viability of revenue model	Industrial clients favour "paying for performance" and transparency of pricing.
	Interest of prioritary segments	European high-power manufacturing industries fight for survival against emerging economies.

Source: Authors

Solidity of competitive advantage	Content of the value proposition
(1) (4)	***Solution***
	1. Audit of energy optimisation (preventive)
(4) (7) (5)	2. Industrial engineering (customised solutions)
	3. Patented foam device
	4. Reduction of energy losses (95%)
(1) (4) (8)	5. Easy and quick installation of foam device
	6. Anti-warming device (facilitated
(1) (2) (5)	maintenance)
	7. Durable device
(4) (8)	8. Monitoring of energy savings
(1) (2) (3) (7)	To the Problem
	Significant energy losses (up to 30%) in
	electrical connections
(1) (2)	Repeated maintenance operations requiring
	production interruption
	Critical maintenance operations due to high
(1) (2) (3)	temperature in connections
(1) (2) (3) (4) (5) (6) (7) (8)	
(2) (3) (4) (7)	
(3) (4)	
(4) (5) (6) (7)	
(1) (2) (4)	
(1) (2) (3)	
(4) (8)	
(4) (5) (7)	

> **Best Consulting Practices in Brief**
>
> After formalising and contextualising the business model, the consultant now knows the different components for implementing the company's strategy and has made a first assessment of their fit with the contingences of the external environment. The next step is to continue the mission with a diagnostic of the business model's effectiveness—first, by measuring the coherence of each component with the company's strategic posture and second, by measuring the robustness of the whole of the business model, its internal fit through the strength of the interactions among its different components. The effectiveness diagnostic is followed by the diagnostic of competitive positioning of the strengths and weaknesses and the opportunities and threats that emerge from the business model.

7.2.2.3   The Diagnostic of the Business Model Effectiveness

As we have already seen, the company's strategy induces the business model best suited to its implementation, and it is important that the company deploys the strategy that will be the most coherent in terms of fit, with the strategic posture chosen. Miles and Snow's typology of strategic postures (see Chap. 3) is particularly suitable for investigating the strategy/business model fit. Indeed, this typology is rooted in the principle of the adaptive cycle that is highly compatible with the dynamic consistency dimension of a business model. This strategy/business model fit must occur for the entrepreneurial, technological and organisational choices of the adaptive cycle and for each of the business model components.

However, beyond this, the differentiating nature of the business model is part of the solidity of the interactions among its various components. This inter-component fit aims to build a particularly differentiated competitive advantage that is hard for competitors to imitate. Indeed, the business model's systemic and holistic aspect gives a VRIST dimension (see Chap. 3) that becomes a strategic capability in its own right. The business model effectiveness diagnostic highlights the components that we describe as the "core of business model," *i.e.*, those components that support the business model framework and the competitive advantage. This also leads to the emergence of components known as "core of strategy," *i.e.*, those showing the greatest fit on the entrepreneurial, technological and organisational dimensions of the strategic posture. Finally, the business model effectiveness diagnostic highlights the different levels of fit among the entrepreneurial, technological and organisational choices and all the business model components. This last assessment clarifies possible gaps between the choices making up the strategic posture. In this sense, as mentioned in Sect. 7.2.1, the business model that itself is predicted by the strategy, in return influences the internal fit of the strategic posture. Table 7.7 shows how to undertake a diagnostic of business model effectiveness.

Table 7.7 Diagnostic of business model effectiveness

Components	N°	Intercomponent fit (1: very weak; 5: very strong)									Fit with strategic posture (1: very weak; 5: very strong)			"Core of strategy" components →
		1	2	3	4	5	6	7	8	9	Entrepreneurial	Technology	Organisational	
Segments of clientele	1	▓												
Value proposition	2		▓											
Channels	3			▓										
Customer relationship	4				▓									
Revenue model	5					▓								
Key resources	6						▓							
Key activities	7							▓						
Key partners	8								▓					
Cost structure	9									▓				
"Core of business model" components ↑														↓ Fit strategic choices/ business model
Overall BM fit														Overall strategy/ BM coherence

Source: Authors

From Theory to Practice

Hightense is characterised by a strategic posture with prospector tendencies (see Chap. 3). However, the analysis of the company's innovation behaviour (see Chap. 6) showed up practices that were sometimes far from the prospector profile. The diagnostic of Hightense's business model effectiveness guides the consultant in identifying the strategy implementation choices that made the company deviate from its ideal prospector profile, which could hinder the business model's effectiveness.

Indeed, Table 7.8 shows that the "core of business model" components, which guarantee the robustness of the model's architecture, are well distributed among the value proposition, revenue model, key resources, partnerships and the cost structure. On the other hand, the components linked to business development channels and customer relationships as well as the key activities related to these components weaken the business model. This arrangement complements the diagnostic of Hightense's competitive positioning and strategic capabilities (see Chap. 3 Table 3.6). In terms of the strategic choices/business model fit, the analysis shows that, in general, the business model components support the technological choices of Hightense's prospector profile.

However, the prospector's entrepreneurial posture towards a changing product portfolio to seize new market opportunities is weakened by Hightense's focus on a clientele that is little inclined towards disruptive innovation. It is also weakened by a go-to-market model and a customer relationship approach little focused on market-pull innovation and little supported by market intelligence activities, benchmarking or consolidating primary and secondary data in a CRM tool. Furthermore, even if the organisational choice of prospector favouring internal flexibility, open innovation and management by project are in line with the typology of the target clientele, value proposition, revenue model, key partnerships and cost structure, this choice is not supported by the other components.

Finally, the results of the diagnostic of business model effectiveness show that the competitive advantage of Hightense's prospector profile is mainly based on its business model components of value proposition, revenue model, key partnerships and cost structure.

(continued)

(continued)

Table 7.8 Diagnostic of effectiveness of Hightense's business model

Components	N°	Intercomponent fit (1: very weak; 5: very strong)									Fit with strategic posture of prospector (1: very weak; 5: very strong)			"Core of strategy" components
		1	2	3	4	5	6	7	8	9	Entrepreneurial	Technology	Organisational	
Segments of clientele	1		5	3	3	5	4	4	5	5	2	4	4	3.3
Value proposition	2	5		3	3	5	5	5	5	5	5	4	5	4.7
Channels	3	3	3		2	4	2	3	4	5	2	3	3	2.7
Customer relationship	4	3	3	2		5	4	3	5	5	3	4	3	3.3
Revenue model	5	5	5	4	5		5	3	5	5	5	5	5	5.0
Key resources	6	4	5	2	4	5		5	5	5	3	4	3	3.3
Key activities	7	3	5	3	3	3	5		4	5	3	5	3	3.7
Key partners	8	5	5	4	5	5	5	4		5	4	4	4	4.0
Cost structure	9	5	5	5	5	5	5	5	5		5	5	5	5.0
"Core of business model" components		4.13	4.5	3.25	3.75	4.63	4.38	4	4.75	5	3.6	4.2	3.9	Fit strategic choices/ business model
Overall BM fit		4.3									3.9			Overall strategy/BM coherence 3.9

Source: Authors

7.2.2.4   The Diagnostic of the Business Model Competitive Positioning

The analysis of the interactions among the business model components and with the strategic posture choices shows the dysfunctions obstructing the strategy as well as the strengths underpinning the competitive advantage. Similarly, this analysis points out opportunities that the business model should allow companies to seize and highlights the risks and threats from which they should be shielded. In this sense, the diagnostic of effectiveness prepares the diagnostic of the business model competitive positioning.

The analysis of the business model strategic positioning in its environment (see Tables 7.5 and 7.6) helped to assess the coherence of the business model with regard to external contingences in an external/internal logic. The diagnostic of competitive positioning starts from the business model in an internal/external logic and completes this first approach and the diagnostic of effectiveness by proposing a dynamic assessment that takes account of the company's capability to create or defend a competitive advantage with regard to the opportunities and threats inherent to the business model and its constituent components.

Osterwalder and Pigneur recommend carrying out this diagnostic of competitive positioning by doing an analysis of the strengths and weaknesses, opportunities and threats (SWOT) of each component of the company's business model, while keeping a systemic view of the process. Indeed, a weakness identified in a certain component may have consequences on other components or even on the whole of the business model.

Using a SWOT analysis addresses two types of question *vis a vis* each component of the business model and the model as a whole. The first type consists of questioning the company's strengths and weaknesses in its capability to implement its strategy based on its business model. The second is directed towards the opportunities that the business model allows the company to take and that it could benefit from by relying on its internal value chain. This line of enquiry also points to threats related to external forces that weigh down the business model.

In this way, Osterwalder and Pigneur propose a pragmatic approach that shows up internal or external zones that support the business model—strengths and opportunities—and constraining zones—weaknesses and threats for deploying the strategy. Figure 7.6 illustrates the approach to the diagnostic of competitive positioning.

8 Key partners	7 Key Activities	2 Value proposition	4 Customer relationships	1 Customer segments

• Referencing with domestic electricity suppliers
• Network of available free lance engineers
• Network of specialised retailers of electro-technical equipment
• "Energy" competitic clusters
• ADEME (French agency for environment and energy management) and its European counterparts
	Activities:
	• Electro-technical R&D
	• Energy audit + technical report
	• Engineering of unique solutions
	• Production of conductive foam
	• Installation, maintenance
	• Energy consumption monitoring
	• Patenting
	• Scanning of new plant construction/renovation + electrolysis technology shift
	• Bid preparation
	
	Rules and metrics :
	• Control of commercial margin
	• Request for down payment
	• Follow-up of conversion rate
		Solution
		• Energy optimisation audits (preventive process)
		• Energy engineering (tailored solutions)
		• Patented conductive foam device
		• Guaranteed energy savings (95%)
		• Easy and quick installation of device
		• No overheating (easier maintenance)
		• Permanent device
		• Monitoring of energy savings
			• Network of alumni from engineer schools
			• Cost of energy audit deducted if contract signed
			• Referred as technical partner of energy suppliers
			• Shared platform with the client
			  monitoring of energy
			• Yearly audit of electricity optimisation
				• Electro-intensive industries: chemicals, steel, glass
				• Countries where the price of electricity is free and increasing
				• Countries with incentives to reduce energy consumption
				
				Who will be early adopters?
				  of chlorine-soda electrolysis under construction or shifting to the membrane technology in Europe

		To the **Problem** • Major inter-connections energy losses (up to 30%) • Repeated maintenance operations requiring interruption production interruptions • Risks during maintenance due to high temperature	**3 Channels** • Referencing with electricity suppliers (cf. energy savings tax incentives) • Direct prospection (e-mailing) with key accounts in Europe (heads of maintenance) via technical file of energy savings simulation • Answers to technical calls for tender	
	6 Key resources • R&D unit with industrial tool for « real situation » tests • Portfolio of electrotechnical patents with world • High self-financing capacity • ISO 14001 certification • Technical intelligence specialist			
9 Cost structure : Directed towards production of value • Variable costs: raw materials (conductive metals, chemicals), equipment, fees of free lance experts, sales costs (audit and prospecting campaigns) • Fixed costs: HR, production tool, patent costs, certification tests, renewal certification, …			**5 Revenue model: fixed + dynamic** • Turnover model: Fixed on audit charged at day price (offered if engineering contract signed) + sale of electrotechnical equipment + dynamic on % of energy savings realized • Margin model: Calculation of break-even point on the basis of a variable cost margin rate of xx% and an average contract value of xxx K €	

Strengths   Weaknesses

Opportunities   Threats

Internal / External

Supportive   Constraining

Fig. 7.6 The diagnostic of the business model competitive positioning
Source: Adapted from Osterwalder Alexander and Pigneur Yves, *op. cit.*, 2010

From Theory to Practice

The diagnostic of Hightense's business model competitive positioning highlights the emergence of numerous opportunities generated by the company's strengths. Its possession of many particularly innovating world patents on products and processes means the company can envisage diversifying its markets towards more competitive fields such as tenders for communities on high power installations, low power domestic electricity or even the electronics sector for which problems of miniaturisation and reducing the consumption of plastic materials are hampered by problems of overheating in connections. Similarly, the logic of sharing revenues from energy savings (savings for clients, percentage of economies for Hightense) involves not only regular on-site follow up, but also via tele-monitoring. This type of relationship with the client and this model of revenue opens perspectives for diversifying the offer towards tele-optimisation of energy consumption. In another register, the model of variable costs based on external electro-technical expertise opens perspectives of "delegation of skills" services with no risk of "inter-contracts" management.

On the other hand, the diagnostic confirms the company's weaknesses in terms of business development efforts and opportunity identification. Indeed, Hightense focuses mostly on its mainstream clientele of high power installations whose perimeter is severely threatened. The whole question is knowing whether

(continued)

(continued)

Hightense will know how to take advantage of the opportunities mentioned above. Figure 7.7 summarises the field of possibilities that emerge from the diagnostic of the Hightense's business model competitive positioning.

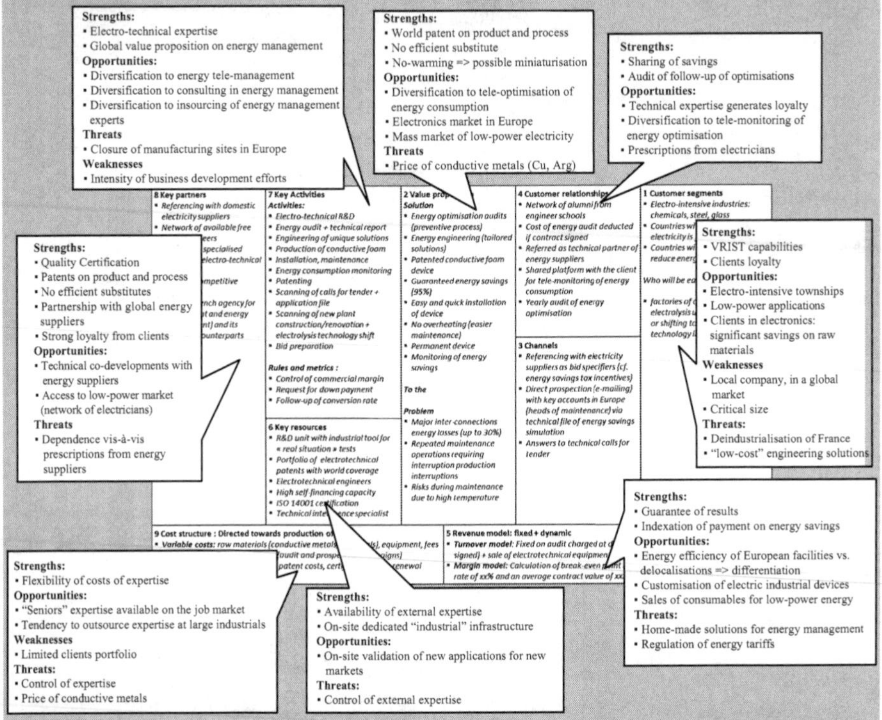

Fig. 7.7 The diagnostic of the competitive positioning of Hightense's business model
Source: Authors

Best Consulting Practices in Brief

The diagnostic of the business model has allowed the consultant to assess the effectiveness of the business model, *i.e.*, the coherence between the company's strategic posture and the means deployed to implement it. The more the fit among the entrepreneurial, technological and organisational choices is supported by the components of the business model, the more the company can develop and maintain its competitive advantage. But the consultant must also assess the intrinsic robustness of the business model itself by assessing its intercomponent fit. This first level of diagnostic of effectiveness will give a systemic view of the company's potential to apply its strategy. This allows the consultant to relate the response to the question "Is the company doing the right things"? (*i.e.*, referring to strategy), to the answer to the question "Is the company doing things right"? (*i.e.*, referring to the business model).

By highlighting the company's strengths and weaknesses with the diagnostic of the business model competitive positioning, the consultant identifies the opportunities that could generate new sources of competitive advantage, as well as the threats that could alter the existing competitive advantages. This is a particularly important, yet delicate, step that maps the perspectives for the company's development and growth on the basis of its strategic capabilities.

7.2.2.5 The Innovation of the Business Model

The conclusion of a consulting mission on the business model consists of using the results of the previous steps to assess the pertinence of redesigning the company's business model by increasing the value of the existing proposition to customers or submitting a new value proposition to new customers, while increasing the value captured by the company itself. This process implies, on one side, making the most of the components related to the design, delivery and valuation of the offer for the target segments of clientele. On the other hand, carrying out the most pertinent activities effectively by using the most appropriate resources to maintain maximum value for the company needs to be undertaken.

This valuation/optimisation duality is particularly compatible with the *Blue Ocean Strategy* developed by W. Chan Kim and Renée Mauborgne[18] (see Chap. 2). The "*blue ocean*" approach is methodical and systemic. It questions the pertinence of a company's value proposition and business model in a competitive context, and proposes to address a new value proposition in a different way to new clients so that the company can free itself from the competitive game. Among the contributions of Kim and Mauborgne's approach, we can mention that it questions the generally accepted mutual exclusion between high differentiation and low costs.

For Kim and Mauborgne, the company cannot really innovate by offering customers high value while keeping a large share of this value for itself, unless it systematically applies four questions to the dominant business models:

1. Which dimensions of the business model components are considered indispensable, but should in fact be abandoned?
2. Which dimensions of the business model components should we focus on less, compared to our usual practices?
3. Conversely, which dimensions of the business model components should we focus on more, compared to our usual practices?
4. Which new dimensions that we have never developed should appear?

When these questions of business model innovation are applied to each component of the business model, the interactions between components are clear and result in refining the blueprint of strategy implementation. The innovation of the business model also makes it necessary to check that the virtuous cycle mentioned by Casadesus-Masanell and Ricart works well and strengthens the inter-component fit. If this is not strengthened, certain dimensions of the components concerned should be reduced or abandoned and others increased or created.

The logic of innovation of the virtuous cycle, or dynamic consistency mentioned by Demil and Lecocq, is generally the approach retained in a mission of business model innovation, compared to a logic of business model disruption. This logic helps to combine exploiting the business model on existing products or markets and exploring innovative versions of the model on new products or markets in "*blue ocean*" mode. This may lead to the emergence of new competitive spaces, in Kim and Mauborgne's sense, which will in turn lead to designing a new business model. If this happens the company should apply steps 1 to 3 described in Fig. 7.5 to the new business model to thoroughly check its strategic coherence and inter-component robustness.

However, a radical modification of the business model can only create a transient competitive advantage. Indeed, being essentially the reflection of the company's new strategic posture, the new business model will soon be taken as a reference by competitors to implement the new strategic choices they consider pertinent. In view of this, the company will have to continue optimising its strategy/business model fit to build a new competitive advantage over competition.

From Theory to Practice

Kim and Mauborgne's questions can be applied to both categories of components of the business model canvas presented by Osterwalder and Pigneur:

- First, the components of customer value creation: the segments of clients with the greatest demand, the value proposition, distribution channels, customer relationships and revenue model.
- Second, the components of value capture for the company: key resources, key activities, key partners and cost structure.

As described previously, we apply these questions to optimise the business model so that the company can distance itself from competition rather than to disrupt the existing business model. Figure 7.8 illustrates the responses to the questions for each component for Hightense's business model. The results show that the valuation/optimisation approach induces real innovation choices for the business model.

1. In terms of clientele in its SBU 1 (high power), the company should refocus on countries where energy management is encouraged through government policy, especially regarding renewable energies, those whose energy costs decrease companies' profitability, and on the most electro-intensive sectors having a significant number of prospects. Furthermore, the power of big electricity suppliers pushes the company into reconsidering prospecting directly on its national territory and consolidating partnerships with these players.
2. The price of electricity remains relatively low in France and the gap with other EU countries is about 20% lower for industries and 21% lower for households. However, the price of electricity is still high compared to other energies. This suggests creating an offer for the low power market and domestic electricity (SBU 2) and implies launching a mass-market activity targeting the network of electricians as end users.
3. The company only gets very little value from its electro-technical expertise. Enabling big manufacturers of electro-technical material to exploit Hightense patents under license would generate new revenues without increasing the company's cost structure. This implies creating a licensing-out activity to get value from these patents.
4. Hightense's strong customer loyalty derives from a results-based revenue model that is a big incentive. Checking these results requires tele-monitoring by Hightense. Setting up such a process could result in a new service of energy tele-optimisation, in the form of a subscription that would generate recurring revenues while increasing the perceived value of the company's offer.
5. Finally, the electro-technical expertise of Hightense's network of external experts could result in an offer of energy-management under "delegation of skills." This type of offer is not yet widespread and responds particularly well to the objectives of externalising the costs of industrial installations in Europe.

(continued)

(continued)

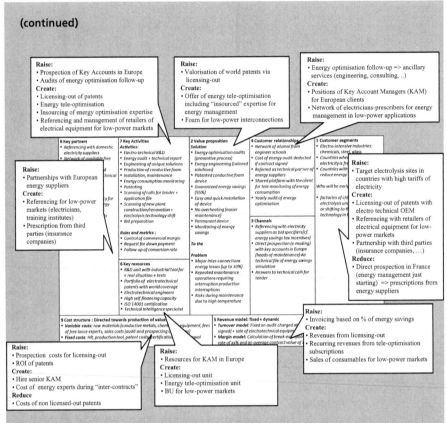

Fig. 7.8 Optimisation of Hightense's business model
Source: Authors

Notes

1. Magretta Joan, "Why Business Models Matter", *Harvard Business Review*, vol. 80, no 5, 2002, p. 86–92.
2. Porter Michael E., "What Is Strategy?", *Harvard Business Review*, vol. 74, no 6, 1996, p. 61–78.
3. Kim W. Chan and Mauborgne Renée, "Creating New Market Space", *Harvard Business Review*, vol. 77, no 1, 1999, p. 83–93.
4. Johnson Mark W., Christensen Clayton M. and Kagermann Henning, "Reinventing Your Business Model", *Harvard Business Review*, vol. 86, no 12, 2008, p. 57–68.
5. Casadesus-Masanell Ramon and Ricart Joan E., "How to Design a Winning Business Model", *Harvard Business Review*, vol. 89, no 1–2, 2011, p. 100–107.
6. Zott Christoph, Amit Raphael and Massa Lorenzo, "The Business Model: Recent Developments and Future Research", *Journal of Management*, vol. 37, no 4, 2011, p. 1019–1042.
7. Miles Raymond E. and Snow Charles C., *Organizational Strategy, Structure and Process*, Stanford University Press, Stanford, 2003.
8. Demil Benoît and Lecocq Xavier, "Business Model Evolution: In Search of Dynamic Consistency", *Long Range Planning*, vol. 43, no 1, 2010, p. 227–246.
9. Van Alstyne Marshall W., Parker Geoffrey G. and Choudary Krishna, "Pipelines, Platforms, and the New Rules of Strategy", *Harvard Business Review*, vol. 94, no 4, 2016, p. 54–62.
10. Wirtz Bernd W., Schilke Oliver, and Ullrich Sebastian, "Strategic Development of Business Models – Implications of the Web 2.0 for Creating Value on the Internet", *Long Range Planning*, vol. 43, 2010, p. 272–290.
11. PwC, "2015 US CEO Survey: Top Findings—Grow and Create Competitive Advantage", n.d., www.pwc.com
12. Lindgardt Z. and Ayers M., "Driving Growth with Business Model Innovation", October 8, 2014, www.bcg.perspectives.com
13. Christensen Clayton M., Bartman Thomas, and Van Bever Derek, "The Hard Truth About Business Model Innovation", *MIT Sloan Management Review*, vol. 58, no 1, 2016, p. 30–40.
14. Govindarajan Vijay, "Planned opportunism", *Harvard Business Review*, vol.94, no 5, 2016, p. 54–61.
15. Kavadias Stelios, Ladas Kostas and Loch Christoph, "The transformative business model", *Harvard Business Review*, vol. 94, no 10, 2016, p. 91–98.
16. Zook Chris and Allen James, "The Great Repeatable Business Model", *Harvard Business Review*, vol. 89, no 11, 2011, p. 107–114.
17. Osterwalder Alexander and Pigneur Yves, *Business Model Generation*, John Wiley & Sons, New York, 2010.
18. Kim W. Chan and Mauborgne Renée, *Blue Ocean Strategy*, Harvard Business School Press, Cambridge, 2005.

Further Reading

On the Different Types of Business Models and Their Construction

Osterwalder Alexander and Pigneur Yves, *Business Model Generation*, John Wiley & Sons, New York, 2010.

Van Alstyne Marshall W., Parker Geoffrey G, and Choudary Sangeet Paul, "Pipelines, Platforms, and the New Rules of Strategy", *Harvard Business Review*, vol. 94, no 4, 2016, p. 54–62.

Wirtz Bernd W., Schilke Oliver and Ullrich Sebastian, "Strategic Development of Business Models – Implications of the Web 2.0 for Creating Value on the Internet", *Long Range Planning*, vol. 43, 2010, p. 272–290.

On the Strategy/Business Model Relationship

Casadesus-Masanell Ramon and Ricart Joan E., "How to Design a Winning Business Model", *Harvard Business Review*, vol. 89, no 1–2, 2011, p. 100–107.

Magretta Joan, "Why Business Models Matter", *Harvard Business Review*, vol. 80, no 5, 2002, p. 86–92.

Zook Chris and Allen James, "The Great Repeatable Business Model", *Harvard Business Review*, vol. 89, no 11, 2011, p. 107–114.

On Business Model Innovation

Christensen Clayton M., Bartman Thomas, and Van Bever Derek, "The hard truth about business model innovation", *MIT Sloan Management Review*, vol. 58, no 1, 2016, p. 30–40.

Johnson Mark W., Christensen Clayton M. and Kagermann Henning, "Reinventing Your Business Model", *Harvard Business Review*, vol. 86, no 12, 2008, p. 57–68.

Kim W. Chan and Mauborgne Renée, *Blue Ocean Strategy*, Harvard Business School Press, Cambridge, 2005.

Nunes Paul and Breene Tim, "Reinvent Your Business Model Before It's Too Late", *Harvard Business Review*, vol. 89, no 1–2, 2011, p. 80–87.

8

Conclusion

8.1 The Conditions for a Successful Strategic Consulting Mission

In 1983, Larry E. Greiner and Robert O. Metzger[1] wrote "*management consulting is an advisory service contracted for and provided to organizations by specially trained and qualified persons who assist, in an objective and independent manner, the client organization to identify management problems, analyse such problems, recommend solutions to these problems, and help, when requested, in the implementation of solutions.*"

The notion of "*advisory*" suggests that although consultants are responsible for the quality of their recommendations, they are certainly not there to replace the client company's management and they have no formal authority. "*Objectivity and independence*" require that they have no financial, administrative, political or affective relationship with the client. "*Trained and qualified*" means that, beyond their individual competences and experience, consultants rely on methodologies, tools and knowledge specific to the business of strategic consulting.

This description is still true today and highlights all the complexity of a mission in strategy consulting. It is complex for companies that will likely face resistance to change from members of their organisations. It is also complex for consultants, who must put the interests of the client company before all other considerations, without losing sight of their own objectives—or those of their employer. The consultant's objective is, therefore, to carry out the mission efficiently (providing the client with detailed and tangible deliverables) and effectively (respecting or optimising the workload schedule). Given the cost of acquiring clients, generating repeat business is also particularly important.

© The Author(s) 2018   **233**
P. Chereau, P.-X. Meschi, *Strategic Consulting*, DOI 10.1007/978-3-319-64422-6_8

The client company resorts to strategy consulting because of explicit or implicit needs. Explicit needs have to do with the problems directly encountered by the company in terms of its strategy *vis a vis* interactions with its external environment (its choices of market, positioning…) and towards managing and developing its resources so that it can implement this strategy (growth options, business model, SBU portfolio…). In this situation, the company calls on a consultant because it considers its internal resources to be insufficient or thinks the challenges and their solutions cannot be viewed objectively from inside the organisation.

Quite apart from such explicit needs, a company may decide to resort to the services of a consulting agency for more indirect reasons. These may relate to the need to justify a decision that has already been taken—here an expert opinion from outside can help to counter possible internal conflicts. In this case, the CEO can add weight to his/her decision by rationally spelling out the state of play, providing objective scenarios of development or using coherent arguments for taking new opportunities.

Managing the client/consultant relationship is of major importance in conducting a mission. For Anthony C. Griffin,[2] this relationship is subject to numerous dilemmas linked to the authenticity of the facts (the facts are clear and expressed by both the consultant and the client) and the consultant's credibility (technical and interpersonal expertise). Griffin lists different dilemmas that are regularly encountered in strategy consulting missions and suggests various solutions, as shown below.

Dilemmas	Responses
The client is not one, but several people, all of whom may have slightly differing objectives	Convince the main actor (the one who will make the final decision) of the advantage of setting out the objectives of all the stakeholders involved
	Get the client to create a steering committee for the mission project, involving the main stakeholders
The client is either passive or wants to run everything, preventing the smooth running of mission	Explain clearly that the objectives cannot be reached if the client does not cooperate. Try a different approach
	Refocus the objectives (and possibly the mission budget) according to the client's behaviour and agree on these new objectives
The company personnel are uncooperative, putting obstacles in the mission's way	Identify those who are blocking the project and ask for their opinions on key points to help them contribute
	Ask the client to change these people for more cooperative members, who have equal legitimacy

(continued)

(continued)

Dilemmas	Responses
The client has hidden agendas and does not act upfront towards the mission	Model authentic behaviour to the client explaining the problems and letting him/her know that hidden agendas will be damaging for the mission
	Remind the client of the mission's objectives and ask for explicit confirmation that the client shares these
Expectations for results are too high, given the means allocated by the client company (personnel, budget)	Before beginning the project, adjust either the objectives or the budget
	Have regular reviews of the mission's progress and make sure commitments are respected
The company's everyday operational priorities conflict with those of mission	Meet the relevant managers and explain why their contribution and experience as "practitioner" is essential to the mission's quality.
	Fix complementary strategic and operational priorities and make sure of the commitment of actors involved
The consultant does not have control over the way the mission is carried out	Make sure that the respective responsibilities and contributions are clearly set out in the contract with the company
	Explain the risk of being "told what to do" (this type of client/consultant relationship will have an adverse effect on the deliverables)
	(Re)clarify the roles and responsibilities of each party

These dilemmas and their responses are mainly related to the mission's specifications. It is therefore advisable to refer to these whenever necessary. A strategic consulting mission cannot be thought out, formalised, negotiated or conducted efficiently without such specifications. The budget proposal should serve as a contractual and methodological frame of reference that is shared by the consultant and the client company.

8.2 How to Sell a Consulting Mission

8.2.1 Approaching Clients and Building Legitimacy

Whatever triggered the initial contact with the client company (direct prospection, incoming call for a consulting proposal, call for tender, recommendation from a third party), the relationship between the company and the consultant will be set by this first contact if the mission is agreed. Indeed, this will be the first opportunity for the consultant to establish a real relationship with the client, confirm his/her credibility and build legitimacy.

The first rule is to think of this first contact as an integral part of the mission. This is a limited and very useful risk for both the consultant and the client company. Indeed, even if the contract has not been signed, both parties can benefit from this first exchange. Clients gain information about the state of the art of tools and methods of strategic management, while consultants can access information on the industry from the "field" and promote their expertise by relating it to the client company's context.

Starting with the idea that the first contact must be win-win, consultants should try to lead the discussion—a more comfortable position—by respecting the following principles:

- Reiterate the context of the meeting (it is always useful and often relevant to recall what initially triggered the meeting).
- Briefly present the objectives of the meeting and the (generic) value proposition on offer. This could be a long experience (but a short explanation) in the client company's industry, the consulting team's rare capabilities, proprietary tools and methods that have helped other clients, which could also benefit this potential client.
- Rapidly focus the discussion on the company's challenges and put the client "to work": ask about his/her priorities, the contingences of the business, the challenges facing the industry and the company, any previous experience of outside consulting and the outputs from the company's standpoint. The objective of these exchanges is to obtain detailed information from the client's words and use this verbatim as the basis for the budget proposal for the mission.
- Refer to the challenges mentioned by the company point by point and give some possible responses or services that the consulting firm could provide. The objective of this detailed review is to show the client that the consultant knows how to listen and understands the company and its context as a whole. It serves to reassure the client that the consultant can provide some or all of the solutions to the problems mentioned.
- By this point, the consultant should have aroused the client's interest and the client should be asking for a detailed consulting proposal on the specific points discussed. This is also the stage where the consultant should be able to find out the limits of the budget allocated to the mission (or at least how important the subject is for the company).
- Remind the client of the specific items the proposal will cover, let the client know any complementary information he/she will need to provide for the proposal and an approximate date when the consultant will be ready to present it (it is always better to explain the detailed proposal face to face).

This initial meeting is crucial for both parties. It allows the client company to set out all the challenges it faces and might also point to the need for outside resources to deal with some of these. The consultant will have given the client a taste of methodological know-how, "whetting their appetite" for more. Through questioning the client, the consultant will also have measured the client's explicit and implicit needs to adapt the budget proposal to the company's internal context.

8.2.2 Drawing Up the Mission Budget Proposal

The quality of the budget proposal depends on three things. First, to a large extent it depends on the quality of information gathered during the initial meeting described above (this should have allowed the consultant to offer a contextualised response); second, it depends on the description of the methodology, tools and competences that the consultant will use to analyse, assess, diagnose, plan scenarios and potentially implement the company's strategy. Finally, the quality of the proposal also depends on the potential value the client attaches to the mission's deliverables. Depending on the mission's complexity, setting out the budget proposal may require several competences and sometimes take several days of work.

We suggest dividing the proposal into nine parts:

1. The table of contents
2. The context of the mission
3. The client request(s)
4. The consulting firm's value proposition
5. The mission content
6. The mission team
7. The mission budget and timeframe
8. The consulting firm's references
9. The conditions of the contract

1. **The table of contents.** A summary of how the proposal is organised makes it easier for the client to understand and shows, at a glance, the soundness of the approach. This promise of high quality content must of course be demonstrated in the rest of the proposal with each part being contextualised in the document given to the client.

2. **The context of the mission.** Here the consultant can arouse the client's interest in collaborating and sharing the company's resources with those of the consulting firm for the sake of the mission's success. Giving a detailed description of the context, opportunities, threats, strategic orientations and organisational components, and expressing these as often as possible in the CEO's own words, should get the client to think: "this consultant has really understood our company and our objectives. He/she will know how to put him/herself in our shoes because he/she talks our language." Indeed, the first justification the CEO will put forward in accepting the proposal is that the consultant completely understands the company's context.

3. **The client's request(s).** This part of the proposal makes explicit the client company's request and the mission's objectives. Here, the consultant fixes the boundaries of the consultation (which strategic orientations to explore, which markets and strategic business units to study, which divisions of the company are involved…). The consultant asks key questions that the mission will answer and formalises the expected results in terms of deliverables.

4. **The value proposition.** At this stage of the proposal, the consultant describes the *ad hoc* offer that will respond to the client's key demands. He/she formalises the main steps of the mission and how it will answer these, and highlights the competences (business and industry expertise) and resources (databases, partner networks…) that will be used for the mission. Here the consultant shows that although robust tools and methods will be used, the approach is specific and focused on the client company's objectives.

5. **The mission content.** This is the heart of the proposal. It contains the different stages of the mission, describing each one's content, and how it will be implemented, according to the same framework:

   - *the objectives of the stage:* the question to be answered;
   - *the methodology:* the action plan to respond to the question;
   - *the tools used:* the analytic tools on which conclusions are based;
   - *the teams involved:* who does what on the consultant's/client's side;
   - *the deliverables:* the finished product provided at the end of the stage.

   The level of detail is very important. It serves as a set of specifications common to client and consultant teams during the mission.

6. **The mission team.** This describes the members of the consulting team. Here, members' qualifications and experience in the company's industry should be described as well as the type of missions they have undertaken. This lends credibility and legitimises the choice of the individuals involved. The proposal should also detail the roles and responsibilities of each consultant and the team's managerial process (who runs the team and the hierarchy among members).

7. **Mission budget and timeframe.** This part of the proposal must be well prepared and clearly presented. All consultants have seen clients who leaf through a proposal then go straight to the budget to "get an idea." Hours of work can be wasted if the budget does not reflect the quality and quantity of resources involved. The budget must therefore clearly point out the title and objective of each stage of the mission. It must detail the number of days' work involved for each stage, the budget and the timeframe for implementing the recommendations. For this last item, the consultant should take care to mention that keeping to the time frame would also depend on the client's availability.

8. **References.** Referring to similar types of missions with the same challenges allows the client to connect the proposal with real cases. We suggest making these references anonymous. This shows the client that his/her business will also be dealt with confidentially and highlights that the consultant's priority is the mission's success, not the client's potential "calibre."

9. **Contractual conditions.** This final section of the proposal fixes the contractual rules of both parties' mutual engagement. It contains traditional clauses of service provider's contracts such as: types of service, engagements of each party, launching conditions; start date; early exit clauses, *force majeure*, confidentiality, contract termination; disputes and litigation, and terms of payment.

Constructing a consulting proposal requires particular attention. The proposal demonstrates both the consulting firm's expertise and professionalism; it serves to promote the offer and is a sort of prototype of what the mission will consist of and how client and consultant will work together.

The client/consultant relationship is central to the mission's success and the budget proposal must reflect this. Indeed, a consulting mission is an experience of mutual transfer of know-how, cross-fertilisation and good practices. The consultant's explanations as to how he/she works will be evidence of these. In this sense, the budget proposal is an invitation for sincere cooperation based on shared methodologies, tools and knowledge.

Index[1]

---

[1] Note: Page number followed by "n" refers to notes.

© The Author(s) 2018

P. Chereau, P.-X. Meschi, *Strategic Consulting*, DOI 10.1007/978-3-319-64422-6